Class struggle and women's liberation
1640 to today

by Tony Cliff

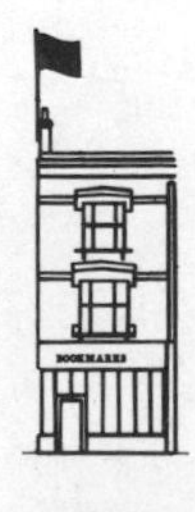

BOOKMARKS

Class struggle and women's liberation
by Tony Cliff

Second printing May 1987
First published April 1984
Bookmarks, 265 Seven Sisters Road, London N4 2DE, England
Bookmarks, PO Box 16085, Chicago, Illinois 60616, USA
Bookmarks, GPO Box 1473N, Melbourne 3001, Australia

ISBN 0 906224 12 8

Printed by A Wheaton and Company, Exeter, England
Typesetting by Kate Macpherson, Bristol
Cover design by Peter Court

Bookmarks is linked to an international grouping of socialist organisations:

AUSTRALIA: **International Socialists**, GPO Box 1473N, Melbourne 3001.
BELGIUM: **Socialisme International**, 9 rue Marexhe, 4400 Herstal, Liege.
BRITAIN: **Socialist Workers Party**, PO Box 82, London E3.
CANADA: **International Socialists**, PO Box 339, Station E, Toronto, Ontario.
DENMARK: **Internationale Socialister**, Morten Borupsgade 18, kld, 8000 Arhus C.
FRANCE: **Socialisme International** (correspondence to Yves Coleman, BP 407, Paris Cedex 05).
IRELAND: **Socialist Workers Movement**, PO Box 1648, Dublin 8.
NORWAY: **Internasjonale Sosialister**, Postboks 5370, Majorstua, 0304 Oslo 3.
UNITED STATES: **International Socialist Organization**, PO Box 16085, Chicago, Illinois 60616.
WEST GERMANY: **Sozialistische Arbeiter Gruppe**, Wolfgangstrasse 81, D–6000 Frankfurt 1.

Contents

This book is published with the aid of the **Bookmarks Publishing Co-operative**. Many socialists have a few savings put aside, probably in a bank or savings bank. While it's there, this money is being loaned by the bank to some business or other to further the aims of capitalism. We believe that it is better loaned to a socialist venture to further the aims of socialism. That's how the Bookmarks Publishing Co-operative works. In return for a loan, repayable at a month's notice, members receive free copies of books published, plus other advantages. There are about 100 members, as far apart as Hackney and Australia.
Like to know more? Write to Bookmarks Publishing Co-operative, 265 Seven Sisters Road, Finsbury Park, London N4 2DE, Britain.

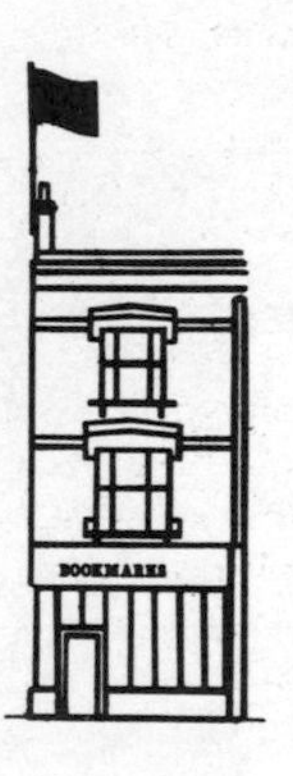

Foreword

My thanks to Mary Phillips for doing a lot of translation from the German, and Donny Gluckstein from the French. Many comrades read the manuscript and helped with their comments: Abbie Bakan, Ian Birchall, Norah Carlin, Lindsey German, Pete Goodwin, Noel Halifax, Sheila MacGregor, Ann Rogers, Ahmed Shawki, Harriet Sherwood, Lionel Sims, Sharon Smith, Lionel Starling and Jane Ure-Smith. Special thanks to Alex Callinicos who put a great amount of work into editing the manuscript, and to Peter Marsden for bringing the book to publication.

Above all I am indebted to Chanie Rosenberg, who radically revised, made readable and typed different versions of the work three times. But my debt to her is far greater than this, and consists of the unfailing moral support and friendship she gave me during the two years it took me to write the work.

TONY CLIFF

Tony Cliff is a leading member of the Socialist Workers Party. His earlier publications include **Rosa Luxemburg** (1959), **Russia: A Marxist Analysis** (1963, republished as **State Capitalism in Russia** (1974)), **Incomes Policy, Legislation and Shop Stewards** (1966) with Colin Barker, **The Employers' Offensive: Productivity deals and how to fight them** (1970), **The Crisis: Social Contract or Socialism** (1975), **Lenin** (four volumes 1975–9) and **Neither Washington nor Moscow** (1982).

Introduction

Two different movements have sought to achieve women's liberation over the past hundred or more years, Marxism and feminism.[1] Both wish to eradicate women's unequal and oppressed position in present-day society, and to replace it with the full and genuine equality of men and women. However, they explain women's oppression in very different ways, and pursue strategies which are quite opposed to one another.

Feminism sees the basic division in the world as that between men and women. The cause of women's oppression is men's urge to dominate and control them. History is the story of the unchanging patriarchal structures through which men have subjugated women. The only way to abolish these structures is for women, of whatever social class, to unite against men, of whatever class.

For Marxism, however, the fundamental antagonism in society is that between classes, not sexes. For thousands of years a minority of men and women have co-operated to live off the labour of the overwhelming majority of working men and women. The class struggle between exploiter and exploited, whatever their sex, is the driving force of historical change. Women's oppression can only be understood in the context of the wider relations of class exploitation.

There can be no compromise between these two views, even though some 'socialist feminists' have in recent years tried to bridge the gap between them. Since the time of the great Utopian thinkers of the early nineteenth century, Saint-Simon, Fourier and Robert Owen, socialists have seen their goal as the *total* liberation of the human race — the abolition of class exploitation *and* sexual oppression and all other forms of oppression.

Marx and Engels were able to show, by developing the materialist concept of history, that only the class struggle can achieve socialism and women's liberation. The exploitation which men and women workers alike experience in their work leads them to organise collectively against capitalism. It is the struggle of this united working class which will sweep away oppression and exploitation alike.

The aim of this book is to show how women's liberation depends on the class struggle. Its background is the feminist movement of the past fifteen years. To grapple with this movement's ideas, which are often hazy, one has to deal with a number of the issues it raises.

First, the movement's concept of women's place in history.

The women's movement rightly complains that women are 'hidden from history'. But it does not connect this invisibility with the class nature of the way history is written and taught in our society. For this concentrates on the activities of ruling elites — kings, generals, prime ministers, Popes, bankers, factory owners, great artists, scientists and philosophers. All — with the exception of a few queens, empresses and Joan of Arc — were men. Hence history is written as a male story. But only a tiny minority of men gained the privilege of being included. So the complaint that *women* are excluded from history, without noticing that practically all men suffer the same fate, accepts the basic elitist tenets of 'official' history. The only consistent opponents of this prevailing set of ideas are Marxists, who declare that 'the history of society is the history of class struggle', and hence that the exploited and oppressed classes — men *and* women — are as much the *subject* of history as the ruling classes.

Of course bourgeois historians do include the mass of the people as *objects* of history, affected by the actions of the rulers. In similar vein the women's movement mostly see women as *objects* of history, as *victims* of male oppression. Feminists tell us what society, or individuals, have done to women. By and large women appear passive, or at best, reacting to male pressures. The foremost advocate in recent years of the 'victim' concept of women's place in history has been Simone de Beauvoir. For her, women were perpetually passive, and the exceptions — the 'great' women such as Joan of Arc or Elizabeth I of England — earned their greatness by somehow managing to appropriate the properties of masculinity.

An added notion to that of women being 'victims' is that they are unchanged by history, that women perpetually embody feminine qualities which are more decisive that anything else. The values advocated by the women's liberation movement are always contrasted with those of the oppressors — 'the way men do things'. Men represent 'hierarchy', 'patriarchy', 'power'; women represent sisterhood, solidarity, community. Political parties and trade union organisations are described as 'masculine structures', 'male type organisations'. Offenders among feminists are often described as being 'like men'.

In this the women's movement mirrors the values and standards established by the most reactionary men in the past. It was people most hostile to women who always invoked women's eternal, unaltering nature: the eternal feminine was used as an excuse to justify various forms of social and legal restrictions on women.

The tendency to regard practically all women as basically alike leads many in the women's movement to present practically all men as the same. See, for instance, one of the most influential books in the women's liberation movement, Kate Millett's **Sexual Politics**:[2] all men are described as callous patriarchs, contemptuous of women, with arrogant strength which they use to oppress women. How untrue the description is when one looks at the male slave of the past, or at today's harrassed, alienated male worker, seen as an individual — even the machismo of many is far more an expression of lack of strength than of its presence.

The traditional view of women, by giving women certain inherent and unchangeable qualities, explains social and cultural patterns as the result, not of outside forces, forces in the society in which we live, but as the result of the very nature of women themselves. This is broadly accepted by the women's movement, if in inverted form. The most extreme wing of the women's liberation movement — the Radical Lesbians — by defining woman-to-woman relationships as a political statement, do nothing but reverse the traditional definition of women in terms of their relationships with men.

Throughout this book we shall try to demonstrate that there is no more a coherent group called 'women' than there is one called 'men', except on the biological level. The gulf between slave-owner and slave, or king and peasant, makes the concept 'men' meaningless — likewise, the gulf between the slave-owner's wife and the female slave makes the concept 'women' also meaningless.

Because of its prevailing views, the women's movement falls into using the terms 'women' and 'women's oppression' in a vague, undifferentiated and a-historical way. For female slaves oppression meant physical cruelty, sexual exploitation, forced separation from their children. For the leisured, financially comfortable plantation mistress it meant social and legal restrictions, and repressive sexuality. For working-class women the industrial revolution meant brutal capitalist exploitation plus the horrors of childbearing in terrible conditions (the vast majority of children dying in infancy). For the capitalist's wife it meant an oppressive leisured life. To lump all women together in one word is to miss the specific historical conditions and to sidestep the role of the rich ladies in the enslavement and exploitation of working women and men.

It is common for people in the women's movement to liken women's position to that of slaves, oppressed racial minorities and economically repressed groups. But the similarities are few. Women are not a separate group; they are dispersed throughout the population. If women are the most exploited of workers, they are also among the exploiters. Women's relations with men in the family are radically different from relations between workers and capitalists, or between black and white people: profound and complex economic, sexual and psychological relationships drive women to participate in the family. Blacks are trapped in ghettoes, away from whites. Affection between wives and husbands, mothers and sons, cuts across relationships of domination and submission. Blacks arouse revulsion in white racists; women are *desired* by men — even though on unequal terms.

Women are part of the society in which they live, and hence their situation cannot be studied in a vacuum. How to relate the concept of women's oppression to class exploitation is a central theme of this work.

When it comes to present-day women's oppression, the many proponents of the women's movement talk of that oppression as a product of 'patriarchy'. Male domination is thus interpreted as a supra-historical factor, existing independently of class society or capitalism. In opposition to this view we take as our theoretical cornerstone Frederick Engels' **The Origin of the Family, Private Property and the State** (1884).[3] Engels argues that it was the rise of private property and the division of society into classes which led to the subjugation of women. Under capitalism the production of the necessities of life is a social process, while reproduction — the rearing of children — is a private process, taking place largely in the enclosed family. The oppression of women is rooted in the dichotomy between the two. Hence the fight for women's liberation cannot be separated from the fight against capitalism.

Oppression in itself does not necessarily lead to a struggle for liberation. The oppression of women, by dividing them and imprisoning them in the four walls of the home, leads most often to powerlessness and submission. Only where women, as workers, have collective power do they gain confidence to fight exploitation, and are then also able to fight their oppression as women. The other side of the coin is that women workers, like other oppressed groups, are in a period of social crisis often more spontaneously revolutionary than men.[4] The struggle of workers against exploitation is the key to their successful struggle against *all* oppression. Hence the first step for working-class women in entering the arena of struggle for their liberation as women is to leave the isolation of the home and enter the social area of production.

But this is not 'liberation through work'. Engels describes graphically in his **The Condition of the Working Class in England**

(1845)[5] how working-class life was brutalised and dehumanised by the drawing of women to work in factories. For bourgeois sociologists, economists and historians, exploitation is mere exploitation; for Marxists it is the axis of class struggle, the springboard for human liberation. The brutalisation described by Engels led to a struggle, by women and men, for social changes to the benefit of the working class as a whole, as we shall see.

Throughout this book the emphasis is on working-class women as the *subjects* of history, as history makers.

The history of working women's struggles is so broad and rich that I found it difficult to select the chapters to include in one volume. I have chosen to deal with the struggles as they reach their peaks. On a mountain peak one can get a much clearer general view of the lie of the land than in the valley. In human history, including women's history, revolutions are the peaks. I have therefore chosen to show the role of women in four revolutions. I start with the English revolution of the seventeenth century, when for the first time modern ideas of women's liberation and a new sexual morality blossomed. The French revolution of the eighteenth century and the Paris Commune of the nineteenth century follow, demonstrating the indomitable struggles of working-class women.

Finally comes the story of the Russian revolution of 1917. This was a milestone in the emancipation of women: the first occasion on which the complete economic, political and sexual equality of women was put on the historical agenda. New political, civic, economic and family codes were promulgated, aiming to wipe away at one stroke centuries-old inequalities. The new government granted women the vote, passed divorce and civil laws which made marriage a voluntary relationship, eliminated the distinction between legitimate and illegitimate children.

However, because of the failure of the revolution to spread into the advanced capitalist countries, above all Germany, the isolated Russian Revolution degenerated and the counter-revolution under Stalin took over. Everything was subordinated to the building up of industry. The regime therefore neglected precisely those economic sectors which might have lightened the burden on working women. The regime under Stalin also meant extreme social stratification: the family structure was found useful by the authorities as a conservative influence on society.

The history of efforts to organise working-class women into socialist organisations, like the general history of the working-class movement, is a long story of ebbs and flows, of great achievement and heart-rending disappointments. Yet the struggles go on, even though time and again they have to start as from the beginning.

In the struggle for liberation, of men and women alike, a crucial role must be played by the revolutionary workers' party. Its task is to lead in the class struggle, to fight the prevailing bourgeois ideas, to strive to overcome the unevenness between sections of the working class — including that between women and men — and finally to lead the class in the revolutionary changing of society. History cruelly shows again and again how difficult it has been to build mass socialist parties. These difficulties could not but affect the efforts to win women workers.

Five chapters of this book are devoted to the successes and failures of organising working women into the socialist movement between 1860 and 1920: in the United States, Germany, Russia, France and Britain.

The growth of these different movements was varied and uneven. Firstly, economic development varied considerably from country to country. The connections between the position of women in economic and social life, which therefore also varied, and the ideas developed by socialist women, from which grew the political and organisational pattern of the socialist women's movement, were tenuous and complicated. Hence there is a striking variety of working women's movements, greater even than the variety between working classes in different countries, and far greater than the variation in economic development between countries.

But after the 1920s the question of women's liberation was swept aside under the hammer blows of economic crisis, Nazism, Stalinism and the resurgence of right-wing Social Democracy. Only half a century later did a new women's movement reappear in the deepening crisis of world capitalism in the late 1960s and early 1970s.

In the later chapters of this book, we look at the contemporary women's liberation movements in the United States and Britain. We consider their social composition and their mode of action. We show how these movements have focussed consistently on areas where men and women are at odds — rape, battered women, wages for housework — while ignoring or playing down the important struggles in which women are more likely to win the support of men: strikes, opposition to welfare cuts, equal pay, unionisation, abortion. The contemporary movements idealise women as *victims* of male supremacy, and not as fighting members of the working class. Instead of concentrating on where women are strongest — in the unions and workplaces — they concentrate on those areas where they are weakest. Hence these women's movements have been pushed to the margins. They have been caught in a process of disintegration, although their ideas still hold a tremdendous sway.

Behind these movements a new middle class has imprinted

special characteristics on the concepts of women's oppression and women's liberation. Both men and women of this class suffer from a sense of alienation — and women feel doubly alienated as they are consistently discriminated against in promotion to higher positions at work. The rebellion of these people leads to what Marx called 'petty-bourgeois socialism': they expose the iniquities of capitalism, but being still individualists, are unable to identify with the working class — the only class able to overcome the source of these iniquities.

Finally we will look directly at women's oppression today. At the family and historical processes that shaped the working-class family: why did the working-class family, which was disintegrating in the period of early capitalism, survive? How and why did *men and women* workers struggle to defend the family, and what price did women have to pay for the partial victory over the harshness of capitalism? Is the family today supportive or oppressive, or both? What is its role as a focus of women's alienation? Can the family be a sanctuary of love and decency in a society that distorts all personal relationships? How does class affect the family? In what way are working-class families different from middle-class families?

The last chapter focusses on the relationship between the exploitation of women workers and their oppression as women. How does oppression affect women, both in society at large and in the family? What is the relationship between the class struggle against exploitation and capitalism on the one hand, and against women's oppression on the other? What organisations are necessary to lead both struggles? We try to place the Marxist concepts of the interrelationships of exploitation, oppression and liberation in their historical context. We argue that women's liberation cannot be achieved without the victory of socialism, and that socialism is impossible without women's liberation.

1
Birth of a dream

The English revolution of the mid-seventeenth century was the dawn of women's liberation. The revolution brought peasant and working women on to the arena of history, and raised many fundamental questions about the structure of society, including women's place in it. The religious and political sects that mushroomed at the time of the revolution and civil war had a special appeal for women. Some sects gave them equal rights. A new morality, including a new sexual morality, blossomed.

Sadly, the blooms withered fairly quickly — when the revolution stopped in its tracks, when a new unity was achieved between the victorious bourgeoisie and the old aristocracy which led to the restoration of the monarchy, the lords and bishops.

The new ideas about women's equality and sexual morality came to life among the radicals of the revolutionary camp. It was among such people that the Levellers, Diggers and Ranters emerged.

The Levellers, who looked upon themselves as 'the middle sort of people', were the representatives of the self-employed peasants and artisans. They resented the concentration of economic power in the hands of the rich. They regarded economic independence — the right to own one's own instruments of production: tools, handlooms, ploughs, and particularly the land itself — as a basic human freedom. They wanted a society of free, independent small producers. They condemned all aspects of exploitative society — the landlords, nobility, monarchy, clergy and lawyers. In their eyes, the key to achieving equality was the equalisation of political power by abolishing property qualifications for voting, establishing equal electoral constituencies and annual elections. The Levellers had considerable influence for a time in the rank and file of Cromwell's army.

The Levellers' crushing defeat by Cromwell in 1649 brought to an end the apocalyptic hopes of the radicals. There was no extension of the franchise, no social reform, no abolition of tithes, no end to the enclosures. Popular dreams were miserably wrecked. But out of this heartbreak there arose the Digger movement. On Sunday 1 April 1649 a small group of poor people collected on St George's Hill in the parish of Walton-on-Thames and began to dig the waste land there, sowing it with corn, parsnips, carrots and beans. It was a symbolic assumption of ownership. They were raided by local landowners and had to move from St George's Hill about August 1649 to Cobham Heath, a mile or two away. Diggers colonies were set up in Northamptonshire (Wellingborough), Kent (Cox Hall), Barnet, Enfield, Dunstable, Bosworth and Nottinghamshire, and possibly in Buckinghamshire and Gloucestershire.[1]

The Diggers went further than the Levellers. They argued that a redistribution of political power was not enough to end exploitation. True freedom demanded the abolition of private property. They were utopian socialists. Gerard Winstanley, their leader, was not the first in this line of socialist thinkers and dreamers, but the breadth of his ideas on wide-ranging issues is fascinating. In the years 1649–50 he published a series of pamphlets which dealt with God and matter, politics and economics, education and science, marriage and the family.[2]

Another product of the Levellers' collapse was the Ranters. They came quite suddenly into prominence in 1649, soon after the final defeat of the Levellers, and for perhaps a year seem to have attracted a mass following, especially among the London poor, though there are reports of their activities from almost every part of England.[3] They 'spoke for and to the most wretched submerged elements of the population, the slum dwellers of London and other cities.' They 'would seem to have attracted a number of embittered and disappointed former Levellers. Where Levelling by sword and by spade had both failed what seemed called for was a Levelling by miracle, in which God himself would confound the mighty by means of the poorest, lowest and most despised of the earth.'[4] 'God the Great Leveller' would come upon the rich and mighty 'as a thief in the night, with my sword drawn in my hand, and like a thief as I am — I say deliver your purse, deliver sirrah! deliver or I'll cut thy throat!' Basically they were confused, mystical anarchists, without any form of organisation.

On questions of family and sex, the Levellers were very attached to private property, and their leader Lilburne made clear the direct relation between monogamy and private property. He strongly advocated both.

Against this, Gerard Winstanley and the Diggers believed in monogamy, but one based on freedom of the partners, freedom from economic or legal shackles, and freedom to choose. As he put it in **The Law of Freedom in a Platform**:

> Every man and woman shall have the free liberty to marry whom they love, if they can obtain the love and liking of that party whom they would marry; and neither birth nor portion shall hinder the match, for we are all of one blood, mankind; and for portion, the common store-houses are every man's and maid's portion, as free to one as to another.
>
> If any man lie with a maid and beget a child, he shall marry her.[5]

Once married they were not to change partners. Winstanley wrote on sexual freedom:

> The mother and child begotten in this manner is like to have the worst of it, for the man will be gone and leave them, and regard them no more than other women . . . after he hath had his pleasure. Therefore you women beware, for this ranting practice is not the restoring but the destroying power of the creation . . . By seeking their own they em-bondage others.[6]

As Christopher Hill observes: 'Sexual freedom, in fact, tended to be freedom for men only, so long as there was no effective birth control. This was the practical basis to the puritan emphasis on monogamy.'[7]

A further practical basis for this emphasis on monogamy, it should be noted, was that stable family life represented a positive improvement for many of the poor in seventeenth-century England. Poor families were constantly broken up as a result of low wages and lack of employment. Women and children were left 'on the parish' as poverty drove husbands and fathers away in search of work; and when these 'parish children' reached the age of seven they were taken from their mothers and apprenticed (not as craft trainees, but as the lowest of servants) to a master or mistress chosen by the parish overseers.

Middle-class puritans castigated the poor for leading 'immoral' lives; Winstanley pointed out that only economic security could provide the conditions for the 'moral stability of the family.'[8]

One group in the English revolution opposed monogamy — the Ranters. One of their leaders, John Robins, 'gave his disciples authority to change wives and husbands — and changed his own "for an example".' Lawrence Clarkson raised this to a theory of complete sexual freedom, then Abiezer Coppe carried the attack even further, into the monogamous family itself. 'Give over thy stinking family duties,' he wrote. For Clarkson the act of adultery was not distinct from prayer: it all depended on one's inner approach. 'To the pure all things, yea all things, are pure,' he emphasised, adultery included.

This was written in 1650: looking back ten years later Clarkson thus described his Ranter principles: 'No man could be freed from sin, till he had acted that so-called sin as no sin . . . Till you can lie with all women as one woman, and not judge it sin, you can do nothing but sin . . . No man could attain to perfection but this way.'[9] Clarkson's position, as reported by a reliable, if not friendly, witness, was summed up in these words: 'They say that for one man to be tied to one woman, or one woman to one man, is a fruit of the curse; but, they say, we are freed from the curse, therefore it is our liberty to make use of whom we please'.[10]

Christopher Hill sums up the Ranters' attitude to sex and work: 'Ranters, I am suggesting, gave ideological form and coherent expression to practices which had long been common among vagabonds, squatter-cottages, and the in-between category of migratory craftsmen.'[11] 'Much of Ranterism was less a new ethic than an expression of of traditional attitudes, some of which derived from the leisured class — dislike of labour, sexual promiscuity, swearing . . .'[12]

Engels observed:

> It is a curious fact that with every great revolutionary movement the question of 'free love' comes into the foreground. With one set of people as a revolutionary progress, as a shaking off of old traditional fetters, no longer necessary, with others as a welcome doctrine, comfortably covering all sorts of free and easy practices between man and woman.[13]

The sexual morality of the Diggers and Ranters related to the social circumstances of the two groups. Morality, like all ideas, habits and customs, is rooted in the economic and social conditions of people, not as a mechanical extension of these, but not isolated from them either.

The sexual revolution, whether in the shape the Diggers gave it, or the Ranters, was a step forward from the old double-standard morality in sexual matters. Both Diggers and Ranters were also very clear about the relation between private property and sex and dreamt of a world in which there would be collective ownership of wealth and freedom for the individual. Their vision was a foretaste of the free society of the future, when men and women would develop as whole human beings. The English revolution gave us something on account.

2

The French Revolution

The French revolution had a dual nature. Throughout the revolution two class struggles took place simultaneously. On the one hand there was the bourgeoisie — the rising class of manufacturers and traders, including even small shop-keepers and workshop-owners, men whose property and wealth depended on developing capitalism — who struggled against the nobility, whose property and wealth were still founded on landed estates. On the other hand there was a class struggle *against* the bourgeoisie by the poor and propertyless, the embryonic working class, the *bras nus* (literally 'those with bare arms' — in other words those who rolled up their sleeves to work). The French revolution was a bourgeois revolution, but it was also the first attempt of the exploited and oppressed to free themselves from all forms of exploitation and oppression.

This was the first modern revolution to involve the broad masses of the people in activity (the English revolution having been overwhelmingly the work of Cromwell's puritan army). Again and again the people pushed the bourgeoisie forward to fight the aristocracy and the monarchy. Repeatedly the poor stormed the prisons, palaces and assemblies, fought reaction, and saved the revolution. It was they who pushed the bourgeoisie beyond the limits it was willing to move: through a constitutional monarchy in 1790–91, to a hesitant republic in 1792–3 headed by the right-wing Girondists, and finally to one headed by the most radical and determined section of the bourgeoisie — the Jacobins headed by Maximilien Robespierre.

The mass of the poor and propertyless sacrificed their lives outside the Bastille and elsewhere, inspired by the hope that their poverty would be ended, that the age-old yoke of oppression by feudal lords, the clergy and monarchy would be overthrown, but they also fought to remove the yoke imposed on them by the bourgeoisie. The political exponents of these aspirations for bread and justice were the *enragés* — literally meaning 'madmen' — a label given by the bourgeoisie to the most extreme party of the revolution. Marx called them 'the principal representatives of the revolutionary movement'. They were the vanguard of the embryo working class, still very weak and lacking homogeneity.

The Jacobins up to a point tolerated the *bras nus* — even used them to overcome the resistance of the royalists and moderate republicans. But once the Jacobins overthrew the Girondists — on 31 May 1793 — they turned on their allies of yesterday. In February–March 1794 they bloodily suppressed the *enragés*. This exposed Robespierre and his friends to a devastating attack from the bourgeois right who thought the revolution had gone far enough. So on 27 July 1794 (in the revolution's own calendar 9 Thermidor) Robespierre and the Jacobins were overthrown. The political power of the *bras nus* having been completely destroyed, the bourgeoisie felt their rule to be stabilised for good.

What was the role of women in the French revolution?

Simone de Beauvoir answers thus:

> The world has always belonged to the males . . . One might expect the French Revolution to have changed women's lot. It did nothing of the kind. That bourgeois revolution was full of respect for bourgeois institutions and bourgeois values; and it was made almost exclusively by men.[1]

This is the opposite of the truth. Women in fact played a crucially important role in the revolution. They may be divided into three separate camps according to their class: women of the nobility, bourgeois feminists, and women of the propertyless classes.

The Bourgeois Feminists

In general the noblewomen were passive throughout the revolution. Inferior to the nobleman, unable effectively to exercise her husband's rights and powers, since her distinct function was to rear the heirs of the family name and fortune, the noblewoman nevertheless shared in the privileges of the aristocracy, hence was a great supporter of the Old Regime.

It was different for the women of the bourgeoisie. The revolution, by breaking down traditional hierarchies of power, stirred them. Bourgeois feminism flourished. Louis XIV's regulations for the election of representatives to the Estates General (or parliament) excluded women from direct participation. But bourgeois women were active in drafting lists of grievances, demands and proposals, the *cahiers* (petitions) of the revolution. Political rights were a central theme of numerous *cahiers*. Thus **The List of Women's Grievances and Demands by Madame b . . . B . . .** stated:

> We believe it only just to allow women, widows or girls, possessing land or other property, to carry their grievances to the King; that it is equally just to count their votes since they are obliged, like men, to pay royal taxes and fulfil business contracts . . . Since representatives must absolutely have the same interests as those they represent, women can only be represented by women.[2]

Another *cahier*, **The Demands of the Ladies on the 1789 National Assembly**, was for the complete abolition of male privileges, including legal authority over wives, and the admission of women without restriction to all political functions. The **Moniteur** of 6 December 1789 carried a review of a *cahier* entitled **Grievances and Complaints of Women in Bad Marriages** which criticised the marriage laws then in force as unjust. It demanded the legalisation of divorce, to do away with marital unions in which 'one is all and the other is nothing . . . one-half commands, the other serves; one oppresses, the other is oppressed and cannot cease being so.' The legal tyranny of husbands was again challenged in 1791 by a group of women in a petition to the National Assembly, protesting against a law which permitted only husbands to appear as plaintiffs in litigation concerning conjugal infidelity and which imposed a two-year sentence on wives found guilty of the offence.

The largest number of feminist proposals appearing in the *cahiers* — thirty-three — concerned improvements in the education of women.[3]

One of the leading bourgeois feminists during the revolution was Olympe de Gouges, a wealthy commoner who pretended to be of noble descent. At the start of the revolution she was a fanatical monarchist. She had no sympathy whatever with the women's protest procession to the king's palace in Versailles on 6 October 1789. The whole system of absolutist monarchy which Louis XIV had brought to completion, seemed to her, in 1789, to be almost sacred. 'Fourteen years' work,' she wrote, 'have improved its excellent constitution . . . It is madness to think of changing it. And yet they do think of doing so. What a time!' In one of her pamphlets de Gouges proposed that women should form themselves into a bodyguard to protect the queen. Only with the king's flight to Varennes did she become a Girondine, a moderate republican.

To the lowest class of her fellow-women she showed no pity

whatsoever. In order to protect honest women and their daughters from the horror of seeing such vileness in the Paris streets, de Gouges wanted to sweep prostitutes off the public thoroughfares and shut them up in separate quarters, belonging to the state and under police protection.[4]

Olympe de Gouges was the author of the most comprehensive expression of bourgeois feminism during the revolution, the **Declaration of the Rights of Women**, which she addressed to the queen. Written in 1790 after the text of the **Declaration of the Rights of Men** had gained wide circulation, this pamphlet focussed attention on equal rights for women by matching it almost article for article. The opening remarks were programmatic: 'This revolution will not be completed until all women are conscious of their deplorable lot and of the rights they have lost in society . . .' She went on to ask: 'Man, are you capable of being just? Tell me, what has given you the sovereign power to oppress my sex? Your strength? Your ability?' She pointed to the harmony and co-operation of the sexes in nature and held up to ridicule man's claim 'to command despotically a sex which has all the intellectual faculties.' The preamble stated that 'the feminine representatives of the nation demand to be constituted in a national Assembly'; and Article 1 proclaimed:

> All women are born free and remain equal to men in rights . . . The aim of all political associations is the preservation of the natural and inalienable rights of women and men . . . The nation is the union of women and men . . . Law is the expression of the general will: all female and male citizens have the right to participate personally, or through their representatives, in its formation.

Subsequent articles prescribed a strict equality of sexes before the law and in every other circumstance of public and private life. Primary rights were defined as 'liberty, prosperity, security and, above all, resistance to oppression'; the political rights to be safeguarded by law and the economic rights to be safeguarded by ending discrimination in all public and private employment. The final paragraph was an appeal for all women to unite in order to reclaim their 'heritage founded on the wise decrees of nature.'

Another prominent bourgeois feminist was the Dutch-born Etta Palm van Aelder, a right-wing Girondine who glamorised her name by adopting an aristocratic title: 'Baronne' d'Aelder. She invited the Princesse de Bourbon to be a patron of one of her charitable organisations. On 1 April 1792 she presented a petition to the Legislative Assembly which spelled out the aims of the bourgeois women. Specifically it demanded education for girls, legal majority for women at the age of 21, political freedom and equal rights for both sexes, and the right to divorce.

Another significant spokeswoman for bourgeois feminism was the Girondine Théroigne de Méricourt, whose real name seems to have been Anne Terwagne. She was perhaps the best known of these three, largely because of the attacks her contemporaries made on her.

Last but not least among the principal advocates of bourgeois feminism was a man, the Girondist Marquis de Condorcet, philosopher and mathematician. His memorandum on the education of women of the élite advanced the principle that 'education must be the same for women as for men.' Both should pursue learning in common, not separately. It was absurd to exclude women from training for professions which were open to both sexes on a competitive basis. They should have equal opportunities to teach at all levels; and, because of their special aptitudes for certain practical arts, theoretical scientific studies would be of particular value to them. Above all, women should be educated in order to rear children intelligently and to guide them in their studies. Condorcet also argued that women property owners, like men, should be granted the vote.

The forward march of the revolution did not treat the bourgeois feminists kindly. The lower classes, particularly its female members, showed no mercy to Olympe de Gouges: when she was put to death by guillotine together with many other Girondist leaders the working women applauded. Théroigne de Méricourt was beaten savagely by a group of working women in the spring of 1793, and this seems to have made her permanently insane. Etta Palm van Aelder had the good sense to leave France before the revolutionary government could arrest her. Condorcet was also guillotined.

The bourgeois feminists did manage to get some reforms as a result of the revolution. Inheritance laws were changed to guarantee male and female children equal rights. New laws gave women a legal majority at the age of twenty-one. Women could contract debts and be witnesses in civil acts. Other legislation changed the laws concerning women's property, giving them some voice in its administration, and acknowledged the mother's part in decisions affecting her children. Revolutionary divorce legislation treated both sexes equally.

Yet some inequalities remained. Women could not serve on juries, and in practice they were excluded from sitting on the Tribunaux de Famille, which attempted to settle family quarrels from 1790 to 1796. Moreover the gains were short-lived. The Napoleonic codes swept away almost every advance the women had made.[5]

Working Women

What was the attitude of the politically active working-class women to the demands of the bourgeois feminists? One historian answered thus: they

> did not oppose divorce laws, educational opportunities or legal and political equality for their sex, but . . . recognised that for women of the propertyless class, the winning of feminine rights was contingent upon the acquisition of workers' rights generally . . . To women of the working class, the problems of inflation, unemployment and hunger were of much greater urgency than the questions of divorce, education and legal status.[6]

The main impetus behind *bras nus* activity was their need to get food at fair prices and in sufficient quantity. According to the historian Labrousse, over the period 1726–91 the average wage-earner spent 50 per cent of his or her wages on bread alone; in the acute years of economic crises, 1788–9, this rose to an average of 58 per cent; in the months of famine and top-level prices of 1789 it soared to an appalling 88 per cent. Hence the constant popular concern over the price and supply of bread.[7] Hence, also, the way the popular masses based their judgement of political organisations on how they related to the need to eat.

Demands for wage rises to compensate for the high price of food were not then an option, even for those who were wage-earners. Large-scale capitalist industry did not exist, nor a trade union movement to take on the struggle. The typical 18th-century unit of production was a small workshop which employed only a few journeymen and apprentices. The journeyman still often ate at his master's table, and slept under his roof. Only among the workers in the new textile manufactories of northern Paris, who may have amounted to a quarter or a fifth of the total working population, were the distinctive characteristics of a modern industrial working class to be found.[8] Not that strikes did not take place, but they were marginal to the popular political movement.[9]

The demand for bread was central to practically all the *journées*, the popular insurrections and demonstrations, which broke out intermittently between 1789 and 1795. Women were the main participants in these demonstrations. As one historian put it:

> The bread riots of the French Revolution . . . whether the march to Versailles on 5–6 October 1789 or, to a less extent, the journées of Germinal and Prairial of Year III were *par excellence* women's days. Where bread was concerned this was their province: a bread riot without women is an inherent contradiction.[10]

Another historian, George Rudé, described the march of the women on Versailles on 5 October 1789 thus:

> On the morning of 5 October the revolt started simultaneously in the central markets and the Faubourg Saint-Antoine; in both cases women

> were the leading spirits; and, from numerous and varying accounts, it appears that in the activities that followed women of every social class took part — both fishwives and stall-holders of the markets, working women of the *faubourg*, smartly dressed *bourgeoises*, and '*des femmes à chapeau*'. In the markets . . . the movement was started by a small girl who set out from the District of Saint-Eustache beating a drum and declaiming against the scarcity of bread; this drew together a large crowd of women, whose numbers rapidly increased . . .
>
> Their first object was bread, the second probably arms and ammunition for their men . . . The [Town Hall] guards were disarmed and their arms handed to the men who followed behind the women and urged them on . . .

Their numbers grew to six or seven thousand.

> Arriving at Versailles in the early evening, the marchers made straight for the meeting of the Assembly, crowded into the benches alongside the startled deputies and, with swords and hunting-knives slung from their skirts, waited for . . . their petition to be presented.[11]
>
> The traditional account of the women's march to Versailles has it that, as they marched, the women chanted, 'Let's find the baker, his wife and apprentice' [meaning Louis XVI, Queen Marie Antoinette, and the Dauphin, the heir to the throne]. It was supposed that the king would, by his very presence among his subjects, ensure a plentiful supply of bread. These hopes were not immediately realised: the bread crisis continued for another month. The day after the royal family's return [to Paris], crowds of women invaded the corn-market and dumped 150 barrels of rotten flour into the river after samples had been shown to the king. On 21 October, during a bread riot in the Hotel de Ville area, the baker Francois was hanged from the notorious lamppost on the Place de Grève . . . The next day in the rue Thibault-au-dé, off the central markets, women caused a riot by insisting on searching a house for hidden grain and flour.[12]

Although economic demands provided the force behind the women's demonstration of October, it merged with the political insurrection launched by the bourgeois parties and supported by the contingents of the Paris National Guard (a body close to the poor and propertyless).

Between November 1789 and September 1791, in sharp contrast, prices were stable or even fell. The standard of living of the workers and peasants improved substantially and there was no public agitation about bread. But this did not mean that the working women of Paris lost interest in the revolution. Indeed, it is clear that many went on acquiring a political education as the movement to abolish the monarchy grew in strength. Women attended the popular clubs and societies, read revolutionary newspapers, and took part in the constant public debate that is part of any revolution.

Look at the remarkable testimony of Constance Evrard, a 23-year-old cook arrested at the big republican demonstration on the Champ de Mars in July 1791. She admitted having been to the Cordeliers Club and mentioned four newspapes that she regularly read. She had gone to the Champ de Mars to sign the republican petition; she described the aim of the petition as 'For a different organisation of the executive power'.[13]

The combination of economic grievances and the advanced political education available in the revolutionary situation was explosive.

From the autumn of 1791 prices rose again, and paper money began depreciating, a movement that was gradual at first, but became more precipitous as the shadow of war lengthened. In 1792 the working woman

> emerges in anger at the interruption of supplies, particularly milk, which the country failed to deliver to the town, and increasingly her voice is heard as the protagonist of price fixation. From mid-1792 local attempts were made to stabilise prices and in Lyons and the large cities of the east, Besançon, Chalons, Vesoul, the impetus came from the local *Club des Femmes* whose recruitment expanded in the course of that year.[14]

On 25 February 1793 the working people took to direct action. To the indignation of the bourgeoisie, who called it looting, they entered shops and forced the shopkeepers to sell their goods at prices they fixed themselves. There were a large number of women among them, especially washerwomen, who were complaining about the high price of soap. That evening at the Jacobin Club, Robespierre voiced his anger: 'When the people rise up, can it not be for a cause worthy of them? Do they have to concern themselves with wretched groceries all the time?'

The following day, 26 February, a delegation of women went to the city hall to ask for price controls on all basic commodities. Jean Pache, just elected mayor of Paris, replied ironically: 'If a fixed price was put on your husbands' work, what would you say? Would you be happy about it?' At the Convention the same day, the Jacobin deputy Barère attacked the demonstrators of the previous day. Another Jacobin deputy, Cambon, declared on the 28th that property was 'under constant threat', and called for a severe law to deal with anyone wanting to interfere with it.

At the beginning of March the Jacobins, offended at being called hoarders and speculators, sent out to affiliated clubs a circular drawn up by Robespierre himself. They denied all responsibility for the women's movement, which they claimed to have opposed with all their power and which they said only their enemies could have provoked. 'The people of Paris can strike down tyrants, but they have nothing to do with grocers. They have better things to do than crush petty hoarders.'

But the *bras nus* were not to be dictated to by the Jacobins. They continued to put pressure on. On 1 May the political temperature rose higher. The spokesman of a deputation from the Faubourg Saint-Antoine, the most advanced working-class area of Paris, who was a tapestry worker called Francois Musine, said at the bar of the Assembly:

> For a long time you have been promising a general maximum on all basic essentials . . . Always promising, never doing anything about it . . . Make sacrifices; forget that most of you are men of property . . . So far, the whole cost of the revolution has fallen on the poor; it's time the rich and the egoists became republicans as well and looked to their courage instead of their property.[15]

As a result of the activities of working women, on 4 May 1793 the Convention succumbed to pressure and took the first step to instituting a system of price controls by enacting the first Law of the Maximum. This fixed a ceiling on the price of essential commodities.

But the law had many loopholes. High prices and severe shortages continued. Women reacted to this by turning again to direct action. On 26, 27 and 28 June they forced tradesmen to sell their goods, particularly soap, at lower prices. Some citizens from the Poissonière section arrived at the General Council of the Commune — the revolutionary city council — on the 28th and suggested that twenty cases of soap that had just been commandeered should be distributed at 20 sous a pound. The Council unanimously rejected the proposal. Jacques Hébert, Deputy Prosecutor of the Commune, took the protestors to task in his paper, **Le Père Duchesne**. 'Damn it! You spend your time catching flies when there are lions to be fought. Great heavens, are we to make war on sugar and soap merchants?'[16]

By the end of August bread queues and bread riots had become daily occurrences in Paris. This was the immediate background to the demonstrations of 4 and 5 September 1793, which led to the Convention under Robespierre finally decreeing the *Maximum Generale*, and setting on foot the revolutionary militia whose task was to ensure the provision of adequate supplies of grain and meat to Paris from the surrounding countryside.

Working women were active not only in the bread riots. They were also very involved in pursuing the revolutionary war against foreign opponents of the revolution who would have restored the French monarchy. They contributed tons of household linen as bandages for the wounded. This linen, the woman's dowry intended to last for life, was often the main asset of a working-class family.

> Women of Pontarlier, a frontier town, contributed their wedding rings — the most pawnable piece of property any woman had — to clothe volunteers; in Besançon street-walkers and women who had toiled all day turned up when they had put their children to bed to knit stockings for the soldiers at the front. In the summer of 1792 when war fever ran high, innumerable addresses were drawn up and sent to the Assembly wherein women stressed their patriotism and swore to feed their children the right sort of milk; the milk of . . . 'good principles, love of the constitution, hatred of tyrants' . . . Moreover and much more significantly, they undertook personally to conduct the internal war while their husbands and sons went to the front: the war against traitors at home and not only actual traitors but potential ones, the children of traitors. On the outbreak of war against Austria the women of Lons le Saulnier, Maçon and the Côte armed themselves with pitchforks and pans and declared they would defend their homes and children in the absence of their men, and if their men were defeated . . . then they would make a last stand. The women of the district of Tarbes in the summer of 1792 armed themselves with kitchen knives and their children with ladles and set out to meet the Spanish. The women of Port en Bessin erected coastal defences lest the English should take them unawares. As early anticipated victory turned into early defeat, antipathy turned more and more against those suspected of internal conspiracy. There is little the equal in hatred and vindictiveness of the venom poured out by women on fleeing priests and the relations of *emigrés* . . . In every outward manifestation in 1793 women were more frenzied, more intense . . . than their men.[17]

The Decline of the Revolution

The demonstrations of 4–5 September 1793 had brought the revolution to its peak. Once the *bras nus* had saved the situation for the Jacobins, the Jacobins turned on them. The revolution started its rightward slide.

Even before Robespierre finally crushed the Girondists on 31 May 1793, he and his friends displayed unequivocal antipathy towards the leadership of the republican women's movement. For example, on 22 February 1793, when a deputation of women had requested the use of the Jacobins' hall to discuss the hoarding of food and rising prices, Robespierre's young brother argued that such a meeting would cause trouble. Another Jacobin went on to declare: 'If we let the women citizens meet here, 30,000 women might assemble and arouse a movement in Paris that would be fatal to liberty.'[18]

The power base of the *bras nus* lay in the *sociétés populaires*, including numbers of women's societies. Of the women's organisations, by far the most important was the *Société des Républicaines*

Révolutionnaires, formally founded on 13 May 1793. Its main leaders were Claire Lacombe, an actress, and Pauline Léon, a chocolate worker. Its membership was entirely from the poor and propertyless classes.

The militancy of the *Société* was best shown by its part in the political strife of the summer and autumn of 1793, in which women played a significant role, participating in the mass demonstrations at the end of May which demanded the arrest of the Girondist leaders, who surrendered on 2 June. Women from the Paris section **Droits de l'homme** [Rights of Man] afterwards rewarded the *Société* for its conspicuous part in the victory with a pennant upon which was inscribed the Rights of Man.

> You have broken one of the links in the chain of prejudice: that one which confined women to the narrow sphere of their households, making one half of the people into passive and isolated beings, no longer exists for you. You want to take your place in the social order; apathy offends and humiliates you.[19]

The *Société des Républicaines Révolutionnaires* grew closer and closer to the most extreme left-wing group in the revolutionary movement, the *enragés*. The newspaper **L'Ami de peuple [Friend of the People**], published by Leclerc, an *enragé* leader, encouraged the women of the *Société* to lead the fight for popular demands. Addressing itself to women, the paper said on 4 August 1793: 'Go forward with your example and your speeches to awaken republican energy and rekindle patriotism in hearts that have grown cool . . . You have earned the right to lead. Glory awaits you!'

However, once the Girondists had been defeated, Robespierre had no need of the working women's support. On 16 September 1793 the Jacobins devoted their evening meeting to a denunciation of the *Société*'s leader, Claire Lacombe, and demanded 'violent measures' against these revolutionary women. Lacombe was arrested. Her release the next day suggests that her accusers had wished merely to frighten her. If so, they did not succeed. Four days later, on the 21st, a delegation from her society proposed, among other demands, that the sections should name a central committee made up of delegates from all the sections. In the past such central committees had presided over the overthrow of the king and the purge of the Girondists.

The Jacobin government had reason for concern. Towards the end of September (as at its beginning) little food was being offered for sale in the public market and little bread at the bakeries, and frequent quarrels were exploding. On 29 September a men's patriotic society identified the *Société des Républicaines Révolutionnaires* with 'the Medicis, an Elizabeth of England, an Antoinette, a Charlotte Corday,' and asked for its dissolution. To these gross charges Claire Lacombe was permitted to reply. 'Our sex,' she told the Convention the next day, 'has produced only one monster, while for four years we have been betrayed, assassinated, by monsters without number of the masculine sex. Our rights are those of the people, and if we are oppressed, we will know how to provide resistance to oppression.'

The Jacobin leaders thereupon proceeded to mobilise the market women, who of course opposed the bread riots and the imposition of price controls, against the *Républicaines*. On 28 October some 6,000 market women invaded the *Société*'s headquarters at Saint-Eustach. On 29 October a deputy of the Convention spoke on the market women's behalf, denounced the members of the *Société*, and accused the women of going after bread 'like pigs at a trough'. These were not good mothers and daughters but — a significant characterisation — a lot 'of emancipated girls, of female troopers'.

A little later one of the women spectators came forward to demand the abolition of all women's clubs. On the following day the revolutionary women were accused by a representative of the Committee of Public Safety of stirring up counter-revolution on behalf of the Girondist leaders who at that moment were on trial for their lives.[20] A few days later deputy Fabre d'Eglantine insinuated that the revolutionary women were composed of prostitutes. Another deputy claimed that women did not have the strength of character needed to govern; political meetings took them away from 'the more important concerns to which nature calls them.' Nature's imperious commands were not to be violated; women could have no political rights.

Forthwith the Convention voted to outlaw all women's clubs. When, on 17 November, a delegation of women came to the General Council of the Paris Commune to protest at the dissolution of the women's clubs, Anaxagoras Chaumette, the Prosecutor of the Commune, told them:

> So! Since when have people been allowed to renounce their sex? Since when has it been acceptable to see women abandon the pious duties of their households, their children's cradles, to appear in public, to take the floor and to make speeches, to come before the Senate? . . . Nature has said to woman, be a woman; the tender cares due to infancy, the details of the household, the sweet inquietudes of maternity, here are your tasks . . . Oh, impudent women who wish to become men . . . what more do you want? . . . Is it right for women to make motions? Is it for women to place themselves at the head of our armies?' (And here Chaumette began to babble, suddenly recalling Joan of Arc.)[21]

The Commune then banned women from attending its sessions. The **Moniteur** published the ban and an article from the Committee of Public Safety entitled 'Advice to Republican Women'. It reminded women of the fate of Marie Antoinette, Olympe de Gouges, and Mme Roland, all of whom were guillotined. The purpose of this reminder was strikingly clear, saying of de Gouges: 'She wished to be a politician and it seems that the law has punished this conspirator for forgetting the virtues appropriate to her sex' — that is, not for the character of her opinions but for having opinions at all.

The Jacobin leaders attacked Claire Lacombe and her associates not only because they were *enragés*, but also because they were women. The Jacobins represented that section of the capitalist class which benefitted enormously from the acquisition of national land during the revolution, from equipping and supplying the army, from manufacturing arms. As bourgeoisie *par excellence* and passionate defenders of private property, they were intensely anti-feminist. For them the bourgeois family was sacred. As the **Communist Manifesto** states: 'On what foundations is the present family, the bourgeois family, based? On capital, on private gain.' For these *nouveaux riches*, women appeared as a significant part of property.

Daniel Guérin's comment is apt: 'The Revolutionary Women were eliminated because they wanted to sow too soon the seeds of a revolution that would liberate women.'[22]

The routing of the *Bras Nus*

The dissolution of the women's clubs was closely linked to the Jacobins' campaign against the *sociétés populaires* in general. These societies, which were not official and did not have high membership fees like the famous Jacobins and Cordeliers, were open to both men and women. The Jacobins feared and hated them because they could not control and manipulate them like they could the official section meetings, and because they provided an audience for those whose views were more sympathetic to the working people's demands. In May 1794 the societies were closed down. The Jacobins were determined to exclude women from public debate and action, whether they were organised separately or participating with men in the popular clubs.

This was accompanied by other defeats of the *bras nus*. The Law of the Maximum, which controlled prices, was relaxed, and soon had no practical significance. On 9 December 1794 the Convention decreed its abolition. The cost of living rose catastrophically.

The Commune of Paris, which had been the power base for the direct democracy of the people, and the revolutionary militia, which had enforced the price controls, were subordinated to control of the central government.

When the revolution had been advancing, religious indoctrination had been rolled back:

> The decision to abolish worship did not come from above but from below . . . One after another, the Paris sections closed churches or used them for other purposes . . . Freed of the weight that had oppressed them for so long, it was as if they had wings. They danced on the overturned tabernacles. The scenes that unfolded throughout France were unlike anything that had ever happened before.

But towards the end of 1793 Robespierre restored the Catholic religion and the Church, and he 'weakened, disorganised and dislocated a mass movement that had impetuously involved itself in the struggle against the priests and the church.'[23]

Throughout the period in which Robespierre had absolute power the material conditions of working people deteriorated drastically. In the same period, especially after March 1794, the Convention imposed wage restraint. This provoked demonstrations of protest at the City Hall on 9 Thermidor itself, the day Robespierre was overthrown by the Right. Robespierre's attack on the Left left him isolated from those who had brought him to power, and had so faithfully supported him just a year earlier.

As we have seen, once the Right had got rid of Robespierre and his supporters, they quickly dismantled the price controls on foodstuffs. The impact on the common people of Paris was devastating. Inflation ran riot. The rising cost of living, the persecution of the Jacobins, the extravagance of rich speculators and war profiteers, the arrogance of the middle class youth, all aroused bitter hostility, and played their part in bringing about the last two bread riots of the revolution in April and May 1795. But above all it was the extreme shortage of bread — at times reduced to a daily ration of 3 or 4 ounces — that caused these riots.

On 25 March women had demonstrated for more bread both inside and outside the Convention and there had been bread riots in the Gravilliers and Temple Sections, involving wage-earners and housewives. On 1 April a crowd invaded the Convention with cries of 'Bread! Bread!' The demonstration was, however, leaderless, and without any clear direction. The demonstrators were warned, and when members of the National Guard appeared, they withdrew without offering any resistance.[24]

On 20 May the demonstrators coming to the Convention were armed and far more bitter than on the previous demonstration. On their hats or pinned to their jackets they wore the seditious slogan: 'Bread and the Constitution of '93!' Another slogan carried was 'Bread or death!' The majority of the demonstrators were women. This demonstration was beaten badly. For the first time since 1789 the government put down a demonstration by force of arms, and thus decisively defeated the people of Paris. They were not to rise again as a social force for thirty-five years — until 1830.

The Convention now voted to exclude women from its meetings; in future they would be allowed to watch only if they were accompanied by a man carrying a citizen's card. Three days later the Convention placed all Parisian women under a kind of house arrest. 'All women are to return to their domiciles unless otherwise ordered. Those found on the streets in groups of more than five one hour after the posting of this order will be dispersed by force and then held under arrest until public tranquility is restored in Paris.'

The defeat of the revolution meant the defeat of working women.

Women turn to Reaction

Now one of the most tragic chapters of the period unfolds. The bourgeois revolution which betrayed working women was now turned upon those same women to transform them into weapons of reaction.

In 1795 the famine, the failure of the bread riots, and the provocation of the rich, who flaunted their wealth, brought working women to complete despair. Famine has always been sexually selective. It is

> perhaps unnecessary to recall the classical manifestations of famine: the death of the weakest, the young and the aged, the increases in the number of miscarriages and the number of still births — but one should bear in mind that the latter are the fate of women, that the whole female body is a grim metering device registering degrees of deprivation. A premature termination of pregnancy or infertility through malnutrition are the best things under these circumstances to be hoped for: better than knowing that one is carrying a dead child, motionless within one or that if one gives birth one will not have the milk to feed it. The mothers of Caen in 1795 were allaying the cries of their new-born children with rags dipped in water — that way they did not take long to die. Then there was watching one's children grow too feeble to cry.

Suicides multiplied. Every day women and children were fished out of the Seine.[25]

During the Jacobin period Parisian women had stayed away from church, and many had been active in the iconoclasm and desecration of places of worship. Now, in 1796, women turned fanatically to Catholicism.

> The Catholicism of 1795 onwards was of the visceral kind: it owed its strength to the rigours of the times, the imminence of death from disease or undernourishment, disillusionment, shame, failure, the sense of contrition which sought . . . the sort of expiatory religion which defies rooting out . . . The women of Coutances fought with each other over whose babies should be baptised first and the priest in

question resolved the problem by a personal estimate of which ones were likely to be dead before he reached the end of the queue; he misjudged in two cases but he sprinkled water notwithstanding on their little corpses. Such a movement had its vicious aspects. It was an essential accompaniment of the White Terror, as in the diocese of Le Puy, where women sought out local Jacobin leaders, clawed them to death or perhaps ripped them limb from limb while the churches of that most clerical of cities were triumphantly reopened.[26]

In Conclusion

The French revolution, by raising class conflicts to their highest pitch, split women into three antagonistic groups: women of the nobility, women of the bourgeoisie, and women of the poor and propertyless classes, the *bras nus*. The specific demands of the women of the *bras nus* were radically different from and antagonistic to the demands of the bourgeois feminists. Their concerns encouraged working-class women to fight bitterly against the bourgeoisie, including its female half. They were spurred on to join forces with the *enragés* in attacking the Jacobins from the left, while bourgeois women were joining the Girondists and making compromises even with the royalists.

The activity and the fate of the working-class women could not be isolated from that of the class to which they belonged. This was demonstrated both in the rise of the revolution and in its decline. Working women rose as their class rose and fell even further than their brothers when their class was routed.

Throughout the revolution the working women of Paris were active participants. However, they had to act in circumstances not of their making. These were the material conditions of the time, the class nature of the revolution, which made it impossible to go beyond bourgeois limits, and the lack of leadership from a more progressive class — the industrial working class, which was only in its embryo at the time. Hence the working women could be active in the demonstrations which from 14 July 1789 to 5 September 1793 pushed the revolution further to the left — from constitutuional monarchy to republicanism, then to democracy. But once the Jacobins, representing the most extreme democratic section of the capitalist class, took power, the working women were to be on the receiving end of their blows. They were *forced* into the embrace of reaction.

3

Women in the Paris Commune

One of the most heroic chapters in the history of working women's struggles is that of the Paris Commune of 1871.

In the summer of 1870 a war broke out between Bismarck's Germany and France under Emperor Napoleon III. For France it was a disaster. On 3 September the entire French army at Sedan was surrounded and the Emperor captured by the Prussians. In the political furore that followed, France was proclaimed a republic. On 28 January 1871 a truce was proclaimed and in February elections were held to a new National Assembly. The result was a massive victory for the monarchist-right throughout the French provinces. At the head of the National Government was Adolphe Thiers, for decades an extreme conservative monarchist. The seat of the National Assembly and the government was Versailles, some ten miles from Paris.

Paris, however, was completely out of step with the central government. From 18 September 1870 until the truce four months later, Paris was under siege by the Prussians. This radicalised the population. It also left the capital in a state of economic collapse. The winter had been the severest in memory. Food and fuel were very scarce. In February there were bread riots. The Parisians also suffered from severe unemployment. For most working men the only source of income was the 1.50 francs daily pay of the National Guard. Practically every working man had taken to arms and the National Guard grew to 300,000.

Thiers, as head of a government which did not rule its own capital, was intent on taking control of Paris. The main obstacle to his plans was the National Guard. On 18 March 1871 his troops tried to seize the National Guard cannons. This assault was repulsed. The representatives of the right fled from the city and the workers elected their own government. The Commune was born.

The Paris Commune of 1871 was a new type of state. As Marx wrote in **The Civil War in France**: 'It was essentially a working-class government, the product of the struggle of the producing against the appropriating class, the political form at last discovered under which to work out the economic emancipation of labour.'[1]

A state without a standing army or bureaucracy was established: all officials, including judges, were elected, were subject to recall, and were paid workmen's wages.

> On March 30 the Commune abolished conscription and the standing army and declared the sole armed force to be the National Guard, in which all citizens capable of bearing arms were to be enrolled. It remitted all payments of rent for dwelling houses from October 1870 until April, the amounts already paid to be booked as future rent payments, and stopped all sales of articles pledged in the municipal loan office. On the same day the foreigners elected to the Commune were confirmed in office, because 'the flag of the Commune is the flag of the World Republic.' . . . On the 6th, the guillotine was brought out by the 137th battalion of the National Guard, and publicly burnt, amid great popular rejoicing. On the 12th, the Commune decided that the Victory Column on the Place Vendôme, which had been cast from captured guns by Napoleon after the war of 1809, should be demolished as a symbol of chauvinism and incitement to national hatred. This was carried out on May 16. On April 16 it ordered a statistical tabulation of factories which had been closed down by the manufacturers, and the working out of plans for the operation of these factories by the workers formerly employed in them, who were to be organised in co-operative societies, and also plans for the organisation of these co-operatives in one great union. On the 20th it abolished night work for bakers, and also the employment offices, which since the Second Empire had been run as a monopoly by creatures appointed by the police — labour exploiters of the first rank; these offices were transferred to the mayoralties of the twenty *arrondissements* of Paris. On April 30 it ordered the closing of the pawnshops, on the ground that they were a private exploitation of the workers, and were in contradiction with the right of the workers to their instruments of labour and to credit.[2]

The heritage of petty bourgeois ideas

Sadly the Commune suffered from the spiritual heritage of generations. France's revolutionary traditions were both an encouragement to revolution and a restrictive mould. As Marx wrote some twenty years before the Commune: 'The tradition of all the dead generations weighs like a nightmare on the brain of the living.'

This tradition can be summed up as petty bourgeois radicalism. It found nourishment in the backwardness of French industry, where small enterprises dominated.

> . . . the Parisian working population of the end of the Empire was still far from being an industrial proletariat. The 1872 census gave 44 per cent of the working population as industrial, but there were probably only about fifteen factories that employed more than a hundred workers apiece, and a further hundred factories each employing between twenty and fifty workers.[3]

The narrow horizons of French workers in small workshops moulded the attitude of many of them towards women. The ideas that dominated here were those of Pierre Joseph Proudhon (1809–1875), the father of French anarchism, which was an ideology *par excellence* of the radical petty bourgeoisie. His views on women, which he expounded in great detail, were reactionary. He pointed to the physical smallness of woman and her supposed passivity in the sexual act as proof of her weaker nature; to her large hips, pelvis, and breasts as proof of her sole function as child-bearer; and to the relative smallness of the female brain (an undeniable, though irrelevant, fact) as proof of her intellectual inferiority. Using a curious system of numerical values which he assigned to both sexes, he suggested that man's relation to woman was physically 3:2 and that this ratio must also prevail in initiative, educability, potential, and so forth: man was master and woman must obey.

'Genius,' he proclaimed, 'is virility of spirit and its accompanying powers of abstraction, generalisation, creation, and conception; the child, the eunuch, and the woman lack these gifts in equal measure.'

According to Proudhon, woman has been chosen by nature merely as an instrument of reproduction; that is, her only use to society is to function as a bearer of children and in herself she does not otherwise have a reason for being. To man, she costs more than he earns and her existence, therefore, is sustained by the perpetual sacrifice he makes.

Only two careers were open to woman, said Proudhon: 'housewife or harlot'. '. . . every woman who dreams of emancipation has lost, *ipso facto*, the health of her soul, the lucidity of her intellect, the virginity of her heart.' To guard against such corruption, Proudhon recommended that grounds for wife-killing include 'adultery, impudence, treason, drunkenness or debauchery, wastefulness or theft, and persistent insubordination.' Why not? Woman was only a 'pretty animal'. To listen to the 'literary eunuchs' who argued for woman's equality was reprehensible: '. . . its inevitable consequences are free love, condemnation of marriage, condemnation of womanhood, jealousy and secret hatred of men, and, to crown the system, inextinguishable lechery: such, invariably, is the philosophy of the emancipated woman.'[4]

A historian of French socialism and feminism, M J Boxer, summed up the social roots of Proudhon's ideas accurately:

> Proudhon, the son of a cooper and a cook, represented very well the typical French worker, peasant, or artisan, who distrusted the power of centralised hierarchical command. Within the province of the family, French Catholic tradition overshadowed anticlericalism. Proudhon's maxim, 'No family, no civilization, no republic', expressed the sentiment of many French workers.[5]

His attitude to women was part and parcel of his general petty bourgeois world outlook. Reflecting the ideals of independent artisans, owners of property and patriarchal rulers of the household, he stressed co-operation rather than class struggle, opposed state ownership of industry, and was against strikes. He was against the rich, but also against the workers who fought them:

> . . . the poor exploit the rich, the workers their employers, the tenant his landlord, the company promoter his shareholders, no less than the capitalist exploits and puts pressure on the industrialist, the industrialist his workers, and the landlord his tenants.[6]

The International Workingmen's Association — later known as the First International — was founded in 1864 and its General Council, led by Marx, voted to admit women to membership. But the French delegation voted against this by a 'large majority', on the grounds that 'the place of woman is by the home fire, not at the Forum . . . To men belong labour and the study of human problems; to women, child care and adornment of the worker's home'. The conflict was resolved by allowing each section to define its own membership.[7] (The French decision was not retroactive, so some women were allowed to continue as members.)

The French delegates wanted to end women's work. The 'greatest name on earth is the name of father,' the earner, they asserted. Woman nevertheless played an important role in society, since her 'department', the family, constituted the 'cornerstone of the entire social edifice . . . the soothing refuge of saddened hearts, anguished and distressed souls . . . We do not believe it useful for society to give her yet another vocation. If the wife of a worker became a deputy . . . who would salt the worker's soup?' She must also serve as educator of his children, 'on the express condition (however) that the father acts as directing force.' Industrial labour would prevent her from 'obeying her natural disposition.' They would not accept it, they declared, 'either in present society or, especially, in the reorganised socialist society.'[8]

The majority of the members of the Paris Commune of 1871 who were also members of the International Workingmen's Association were adherents of Proudhon. The life of the Commune — 72 days — was too short to overcome the contradiction between its revolutionary impetus and the dead burden of the past which weighed upon it.

Women in the Commune

There are many witnesses to the crucial role played by women in the Commune. One reactionary writer declared:

> The weaker sex behaved scandalously during these deplorable days . . . Those who gave themselves to the Commune — and there were many — had but a single ambition: to raise themselves above the level of man by exaggerating his vices . . . They were all there, agitating and squawking . . . the gentleman's seamstresses; the gentleman's shirt-makers; the teachers of grown-up schoolboys; the maids-of-all-work . . . What was profoundly comic was that these absconders from the workhouse unfailingly invoked Joan of Arc, and were not above comparing themselves to her . . . During the final days, all of these bellicose viragos held out longer than the men did behind the barricades.

And from Dauban, also an extreme reactionary:

> The women were like the men: ardent, implacable, frenzied. Never had they turned out in such great number, braving peril and defying death. They dressed the horrible wounds made by case-shot, shells, and cylindrical bullets; they ran to the side of those who, under the pressure of unheard-of tortures, were howling, sobbing, and bellowing with pain and rage; then, their eyes filled with blood, their ears full of those cries torn from the last living shreds of flesh, they resolutely took up the *chassepot* [a kind of gun] and ran toward the same wounds and the same agony. And what dauntlessness at the barricades, what ferocity in combat, what presence of mind, against the wall, before the firing squad . . .

'If the French nation were composed only of French women,' wrote the correspondent of **The Times** on 19 May 1871, 'what a terrible nation it would be.'[9]

On the first day of the Commune, 18 March, women played a crucial role in neutralising the troops sent by Thiers to seize the cannons of the National Guard. At Montmartre General Lecomte gave the order to fire. At this the women spoke to the soldiers: 'Will you fire upon us? On your brothers? Our husbands? Our children?' General d'Aurelles de Paladine describes what happened:

> The women and children came and mixed with the troops. We were

greatly mistaken in permitting these people to approach our soldiers, for they mingled among them, and the women and children told them: 'You will not fire upon the people'. This is how the soldiers of the 88th, as far as I can see, and of another line regiment, found themselves surrounded and did not have the power to resist these ovations that were given them. People were shouting, 'Long live the line!'

Faced with this unexpected intervention, the soldiers hesitated. A warrant officer stood in front of his company and shouted: 'Mutiny!' Thereupon the 88th battalion fraternised with the crowd. The soldiers arrested their general.

In the rue Houdon crowds of women assembled. General Susbielle gave the order to charge. 'But, intimidated by the women's cries, the cavalry, "backed up their horses", which made people laugh. Everywhere . . . the crowd, mostly composed of women, surrounded the soldiers, stopped the horses, cut the harnesses, forced the "bewildered" soldiers to fraternise with their "brothers" in the National Guard.'[10]

The *Union des Femmes*

One of the most important and by far the most clearsighted revolutionary organisation of women was the *Union des Femmes pour la Défense de Paris et les Soins aux Blessés* (Women's Union for the Defence of Paris and for Aid to the Wounded). This was the women's section of the French section of the First International. It was founded in April 1871 by Elizabeth Dmitrieff (1851–1910), the daughter of a Russian nobleman who had made a fictitious marriage in order to escape from Russia and study in Switzerland. When she came to London she met Marx and became friendly with his daughters. After the fall of the Commune she escaped back to Russia, married a prisoner condemned to deportation in Siberia, accompanied him, and died there. The composition of the *Union des Femmes* was strongly working-class.

Out of 128 members, we know the professions of 60. All women's trades are represented there: fifteen seamstresses, nine waistcoat-makers, six sewing-machine operators, five dress-makers, five linen-drapers, three makers-up of men's clothing, two boot-stitchers, two hat-makers, two laundresses, two cardboard-makers, one embroiderer of military decorations, one braid-maker, one tie-maker, one school-teacher, one perfume-maker, one maker of jewellery, one gold-polisher, one bookstitcher, and one bookbinder. The Central Committee, which in principle was made up of twenty members representing the twenty *arrondissements* of Paris, accurately reflected this social composition.

The *Union* was 'a responsible organisation of Paris *citoyennes* who are resolved to support and defend the cause of the people, the

Revolution, and the Commune.' In each *arrondissement* committees were set up to recruit women to serve at ambulance stations, at field kitchens, to administer funds from voluntary collections, to summon the women of the *Union* 'at any hour of the day or night', on the orders of its Central Committee and at the request of the Commune commissions. 'In short, the *arrondissement* committees were charged with the mobilisation of women.'[11]

In its first call to battle, issued on 11 April, the *Union* boldly declared its socialism and internationalism:

> Paris is being blockaded. Paris is being bombarded. *Citoyennes* . . . Do you hear the roaring cannon, the tocsin ringing out the sacred call? To arms! The homeland is in danger! Were those foreigners who were coming to attack Paris threatening those triumphs called 'liberty, equality, and fraternity'? No, these enemies, these murderers of the people and of liberty, are Frenchmen.
>
> *Citoyennes* of Paris, descendants of the women of the Great Revolution, the women who, in the name of the people and justice, marched upon Versailles and carried Louis XVI off as a captive — we, the mothers, wives, and sisters of the French people, will we go on allowing poverty and ignorance to make enemies of our children? Allowing them to kill each other — father against son, brother against brother — under our very eyes, for the whim of our oppressors, who want Paris handed over to foreigners and annihilation? . . . '*Citoyennes*, the gauntlet is down. We must win, or die.'[12]

The *Union des Femmes* summed up its goal as

> total social revolution, for the abolition of all existing social and legal structures, for the elimination of all privileges and forms of exploitation, for the replacement of the rule of Capital by the rule of Labour — in short, for the emancipation of the Working Class by the Working Class.[13]

There were many other clubs which organised women, but none were politically so advanced.[14]

Action

Women were also central in the production of arms needed for the defence of the Commune.

> Three thousand women seem to have been employed making cartridges. Lissagray describes the workroom in the Corps Législatif building where fifteen hundred women were sewing sandbags for the barricades: 'A tall and beautiful girl, Martha, distributed the work; she wore a red, silver-fringed scarf that her friends had given her. Happy songs alleviated their tasks. Every evening, the wages were paid out, and the workers received full payment for their work, 8 centimes per bag. The middleman of former days would have left them 2 centimes at the most.'[15]

Dmitrieff saw the co-operative production, which was taking over as owners neglected their enterprises and ran away from Paris, as the beginning of the socialist re-organisation of the economy. In a report to the Commission of Labour and Exchange set up by the Commune she wrote:

> Any re-organisation of labour tending to assure the producer of the proceeds can be effectuated only by means of free productive associations making advantageous use of the various industries to their collective profit. In taking work away from the bondage of capitalist exploitation, the formation of these organisations would eventually allow the workers to run their own business.
>
> It would modify not only the social relations of production, but also the forms of work which were inhuman. It was absolutely necessary that there be variety, for 'the continual repetition of the same manual movement has a deadly influence upon the organism and the brain.' The shortening of the working day should also be taken into consideration, for 'the exhaustion of physical strength inevitably brings about the extinction of moral strength.' Finally, it would be a good idea to abolish 'any competition between workers of different sexes', since, in the struggle they were waging against capitalism, their interests were identical. Wages ought to be equal for equal work.[16]

Women were active in running ambulances to nurse the wounded. They bore the main responsibility for organising soup kitchens and helping the poor.

Women played an important part in formulating and partially implementing a series of progressive educational reforms. One Parisian child in three did not get any formal education at all. Of those who did more than half had to go to church schools. Girls' education was even more under church control than boys'. The Commune took significant steps to change the situation, towards a state-funded system of compulsory education, free of clerical influence, balancing humanities and sciences and combining them with useful technical training. Girls' education was given special attention, having been the most neglected area. A special commission with an all-female membership was formed to oversee attempts made to set up girls' schools. An industrial school for girls was established. As a means of helping working women, early efforts were made to establish day nurseries near the factories.[17]

These educational efforts of the Commune were the first steps towards women's equality and liberation. Unfortunately history did not allow the opportunity to achieve significant and permanent results.

Many women and their organisations had a hostile, reactionary attitude toward prostitutes. Thus

> The *Club de l'Ecole de Médicine* demanded 'that all women of suspect

> morality plying their shameful trade on the public thoroughfares' be immediately arrested, and likewise 'the drunkards who have forgotten their self-respect'; that the cafes be closed at 11 o'clock at night; that smoking at concerts be forbidden. This document was approved unanimously. The residents of the 1st and 2nd *arrondissements* congratulated the municipal council of the 11th for having taken measures concerning prostitutes and drunkards, and asked that a decree of the same sort be applied to their neighbourhood . . . The members of the Commune in the 15th *arrondissement* had prostitutes and drunkards arrested.[18]

But many other women adopted a different attitude, and many prostitutes revealed a courageous readiness to fight for the Commune. Amanda, a prostitute, suggested at the Club Saint-Séverin that the Commune should form a special battalion of prostitutes.

Louise Michel, a leading woman Communard, went out of her way to reject any moral condemnation of the prostitutes. 'Who had more of a right than they, the saddest victims of the old world, to give their life for the new one?' Therefore she directed them to a committee of women (the 18th *arrondissement* Vigilance Committee of the *Union des Femmes*) 'whose spirits were generous enough to let these women be welcomed.'

'We shall never bring shame down upon the Commune,' these prostitutes said. Many, indeed, died courageously on the barricades during the bloody week in May when the Commune was suppressed.[19]

According to Edith Thomas, however, most prostitutes were not reliable supporters of the Commune: '. . . most of them, degraded for good by their "profession", much more often than not collaborated with the police, and were "respectful" of the established order.'[20]

The Commune also saw the first growing shoots of a new sexual morality and women's emancipation. Marriage came in for strong condemnation. The Commune decreed on 10 April a pension for the widows and children of 'all citizens killed defending the rights of the people', whether the children were legitimate or not. This in effect meant putting the free unions common among the working-class population of Paris on an equal footing with marriage. 'This decree,' said Arnould afterwards and rather hopefully, 'delivered a mortal blow to the religio-monarchical institution of marriage as we see it functioning in modern society.'

Some women wanted to go further. A woman in one popular club in the church of Saint-Jacques declaimed against marriage as 'the greatest error of past humanity', and proposed tht only the unmarried companions of National Guards killed in the fighting should receive the pension. 'Everything for the free women, nothing for the slaves.'[21]

The strong traditions of Republicanism had exercised a powerful influence over the political and intellectual life of France since 1789. Because the Catholic Church had fought against the revolution, the Republican tradition put anti-clericalism in a central position in the political debate and gave great importance to education, for whose control it struggled against the church throughout the nineteenth century.

In the course of the French revolution, when working women and their children were starving, they had swung from an extreme revolutionary position to counter-revolutionary Catholicism. Because of this the Republican tradition had become anti-feminist. It was based on a general mistrust of women politically, because it was believed they were much more under the influence of the priests than men. Hence the Commune did not even think of giving women the vote.

> . . . the goals of the Commune, set forth in a Declaration to the French people, took no account of women's existence. The men of the Commune did not foresee for a single instant that women might have civic rights, any more than did their 'great forbears' of 1789 and 1793, or the revolutionaries of 1848.[22]

Thus we have onc of the strangest paradoxes of the Commune: that working-class women played a massive role in a revolution which did not even allow them to vote. This must be seen, however, not just as anti-feminism, but as part of the Commune's general political immaturity. Elections to the Commune were held on the basis of the existing franchise and even the overwhelmingly hostile wealthy *arrondissements* took part. The Communards never understood the role and nature of the State and insisted on 'rebelling constitutionally'.

The final days

But the days of the Commune were numbered. The revolutionary changes that were taking place in Paris remained largely isolated from the rest of France because of the siege by German troops, while, with the connivance of the Germans, Thiers was able to build up an army. The troops gathered at Versailles without any attempt by the Communards to stop them. They first shelled the city, then invaded. The Communards fought back, barricade by barricade. When the Communards were eventually defeated and disarmed, the vengeance of the government was bloody and appalling. Thousands of men, women and children were simply lined up and shot.

Until the last moments women showed exceptional courage in defending the Commune.

> National Guards, women and children, workers in their *blouses*, worked all day and into the night constructing the defences on which many of

> them were to die. On the Place du Panthéon a barricade was built by women, wearing long scarves and red cockades, and children singing the *Chant du Depart* and the *Marseillaise*. In the Place Blanche on the Boulevard Clichy a battalion of 120 women erected the legendary barricade which they defended vigorously on the Tuesday, many being massacred after it fell. In the eastern part of the 18th *arrondissement* Josephine Courtois, who had already earned the title, 'Queen of the Barricades', for her role in the Lyon uprising in 1848, and a member of the clubs in her district, was requisitioning empty casks to help build a barricade at the corner of the rue Doudeauville and the rue Stephenson. She handed out cartridges and sent her little girl to take ammunition to the fighters. Edith Thomas in her book on women during the Commune lists many other similar figures, afterwards arrested and tried for their part on the barricades.[23]

When the Commune fell, women and children followed their husbands and their fathers, crying to the soldiers: 'Shoot us with them!' And they were shot. Women were seen to come down into the streets, enraged by these butcheries, strike the officers and then throw themselves against a wall waiting for death.[24]

The heroic activities of the women of the Commune, combined with the fires started by Versailles shells and by counter-revolutionaries trying to destroy evidence of their past corruption, gave rise to a mass hysteria about women incendiaries, the

> legend of the *pétroleuses*, which, born of fear and propagated by the press, cost hundreds of unfortunate women their lives. The rumour was spread that furies were throwing burning petroleum into the cellars. Every woman who was badly dressed, or carrying a milk-can, a pail, an empty bottle, was pointed out as a *pétroleuse*, her clothes torn to tatters, she was pushed against the nearest wall, and killed with revolver-shots.[25]

After the defeat of the Commune 1,051 women were brought before the Councils of War:

> The Parisian working and artisan class claimed 756 of them, seam-stresses, embroiderers, journeywomen, laundresses, linen-drapers, dressmakers, bookbinders, and so forth. We find only one woman of property, four schoolteachers, thirty-three proprietresses of hotels or cafes, eleven shop- or workroom-owners; 246 are 'without profession'.[26]

Thes women showed magnificent courage. A woman replied to the accusation of having killed two soldiers: 'May God punish me for not having killed more. I had two sons at Issy; they were both killed. And two at Neuilly. My husband died at this barricade — and now do what you want with me.' She was undressed and shot.[27]

Louise Michel, in her court appearance, assumed total responsibility, before the tribunal and before history, for her acts:

> I have been told that I am an accomplice of the Commune. Certainly, yes; for the Commune wanted, above all else, the Social Revolution, and the Social Revolution is the dearest of my desires. Even more, I am honoured in being one of the promoters of the Commune . . . Since it seems that every heart that beats for freedom has no right to anything but a little slug of lead, I demand my share. If you let me live, I shall never cease to cry for vengeance.[28]

The vengeance of Versailles was terrible — especially the vengeance of the Versailles ladies. When the Commune fell, Lissagray writes, 'Elegant and joyous women, as in a pleasure trip, betook themselves to the corpses, and, to enjoy the sight of the valorous dead, with the ends of sunshades raised their last coverings.'[29] 'One sees,' said the liberal-conservative newspaper **La Siècle** on 30 May 1871, 'elegant ladies insult the prisoners on their passage, and even strike them with their sunshades.'[30] At the anniversary of the Commune a historian remarked: 'According to reports, the elegantly dressed ladies were the most violent, especially against their own sex.'[31]

In Conclusion

The Parisian workers, women and men, revealed — for a moment — a glimpse of human potential, of human freedom. Women demonstrated fantastic courage and initiative on the barricades, in the new co-operatives and education and in the new ideas concerning sexual morality. The Commune showed, however, that though working-class brothers and sisters fought and died together, they did not achieve complete unity.

The revolutionary tradition of France and Paris was double-edged: it encouraged the revolutionary actions of the workers — men and women — but also acted as a conservative mould to their thoughts and actions. The artisan nature of industry strengthened this mould. The ideas of Proudhon were the result and the cause of contradictions and splits between men and women. The Commune gave us a glimpse of women's liberation, as if through an opaque glass.

For women Communards, the winning of women's rights depended on the winning of workers' rights. Both were won only very partially. The Parisian working class was still immature and lacked a clear political leadership; the conditions of siege hemmed it in. Above all, the lifespan of the Commune was far too short.

While between women Communards and men Communards complete unity was not achieved, between the women Communards and the bourgeois women there was no common ground whatsoever: a life-and-death struggle took place to settle accounts. The vengeance and venom of the bourgeois women towards their working-class 'sisters' knew no bounds.

4

The nineteenth-century American women's movement

American feminism was born out of the movement for the abolition of slavery. The classic work on the history of American feminism, Eleanor Flexner's **Century of Struggle**, put it this way:

> Thousands of men and women were drawn into the work; among the latter were the first conscious feminists, who would go to school in the struggle to free the slaves and, in the process, launch their own fight for equality. It was in the abolition movement that women first learned to organise, to hold public meetings, to conduct petition campaigns. As abolitionists they first won the right to speak in public, and began to evolve a philosophy of their place in society and of their basic rights. For a quarter of a century the two movements, to free the slave and liberate the woman, nourished and strengthened one another.[1]

Among the most prominent women active first in the abolition movement, then in the feminist movement, were Susan B Anthony and Elizabeth Cady Stanton. Elizabeth Cady Stanton was destined to become the leading intellectual of the movement for over half a century, and Susan B Anthony its main organiser.

The first gathering of feminism as a movement was the Seneca Falls Convention on 14–15 July 1848. Strictly speaking it was not a convention at all, since there were to be no delegates. Elizabeth Cady Stanton drafted a statement of aims for the convention which followed closely the American Declaration of Independence:

> We hold these truths to be self-evident; that all men and women are created equal; that they are endowed by their creator with certain inalienable rights: that among these are life, liberty and the pursuit of

happiness . . .

The history of mankind is a history of repeated injuries and usurpations on the part of man toward woman, having in direct object the establishment of a tyranny over her. To prove this, let facts be submitted to a candid world.

The facts presented ranged over every aspect of women's status. In conclusion, departing from its model, the Declaration stated:

In entering upon the great work before us, we anticipate no small amount of misconception, misrepresentation, and ridicule; but we shall use every instrumentality within our power to effect our object. We shall employ agents, circulate tracts, petition the State and national legislatures, and endeavour to enlist the pulpit and the press on our behalf. We hope this Convention will be followed by a series of Conventions embracing every part of the country.[2]

The convention also passed the following resolution moved by Elizabeth Cady Stanton:

Resolved, that it is the duty of the women of this country to secure to themselves their sacred right to the elective franchise.

The resolution was carried by a small margin. At the conclusion of the proceedings, sixty-eight women and thirty-two men signed their names to the Declaration of Principles.[3]

At this time the American bourgeoisie was still in its progressive, revolutionary phase. The slave-owning South was an obstacle to its development of a capitalist economy based on wage labour. The feminist movement, as one wing of the bourgeois-revolutionary forces, also played a progressive role. However, at the end of the Civil War of 1861–5, which unified the country under the domination of Northern industrial capital, both the bourgeoisie as a whole and its feminist limb became opposed to further radical change.

A split occurred between the women's movement and that for the abolition of slavery. The feminists were incensed at the injustice of the Fourteenth Amendment of 1866 which granted the vote to black men while denying it to all women, white as well as black. Susan B Anthony indignantly pledged: 'I will cut off this right arm of mine before I will ever work for or demand the ballot for the Negro and not the woman.' Elizabeth Cady Stanton made derogatory references to 'Sambo', and the enfranchisement of 'Africans, Chinese, and all the ignorant foreigners the moment they touch our shore.'[4]

As the century wore on, the women's movement became more and more respectable and conservative. The historian Aileen Kraditor explains:

When woman suffrage was a radical cause, a handful of pioneers who

> were willing to brave public censure were its leaders. During the period in which suffragists could expect to be pelted with eggs and fruit in various stages of decay, an unconventional mind was indispensable to the women who dedicated their lives to pleading their case before a hostile public. The treatment they received in turn encouraged their tendency to question all that their society held sacred in the realm of religion, as well as in the field of politics. But, by the last decade of the nineteenth century, woman suffrage had become respectable, and women who held orthodox opinions on every other issue could now join a suffrage organisation without fear of ostracism.[5]

With the transformation of the American bourgeoisie from a progressive force to a reactionary force towards the end of the century, its women members, who shared opinions and values with its male members on every issue other than that of women's suffrage, were bound to become racist, xenophobic, and viciously anti-working-class. Neither women nor men can escape the social, political and ideological milieu in which they live.

Some factors strengthened the move to the right. One was the rise of a militant working-class movement from the 1870s onwards, which engaged in widespread strikes, one of which, the Great Railroad Strike of 1877, involved nearly 100,000 workers from the Atlantic coast to the Mississippi valley. Another was the spread of the women's movement to the South. Black women had almost always been excluded from the feminist movement. But from the end of the nineteenth century the movement started organising white middle-class women in the south who were openly racist.

The right had a number of phobias: blacks, foreign-born people, slum dwellers, militant workers. Hence, while the demand of the feminists for women's suffrage did not change over the decades, the arguments advanced in its support changed radically. They became racist and xenophobic. Thus Susan B Anthony more and more stridently criticised the granting of the ballot to the 'brutish and ignorant Negro man'. Carrie Chapman Catt, one of the leaders of the National American Woman Suffrage Association (NAWSA) arraigned against 'the ignorant foreign vote' and the slum-dwellers' vote: 'Cut off the vote of the slums,' she declared, 'and give [it] to woman.' In the eyes of NAWSA the decisive attraction of giving the vote to women was that it 'would ensure the permanency of white supremacy in the South'.[6]

Thus, as Aileen Kraditor writes:

> The woman suffrage movement had ceased to be a campaign to *extend the franchise to* all adult Americans. Instead, one important part of its rationale had become the proposal to *take the vote away from* some Americans — Negroes in the south and naturalised citizens in the north.[7]

In this setting the women's movement attracted massive new support. It is estimated that NAWSA grew from 13,150 in 1893, to 17,000 in 1905; 45,501 in 1907; over 75,000 in 1910; 100,000 in 1915, and two million in 1917.[8]

In Different Worlds

American working-class women stood worlds apart from the bourgeois feminists. Their conditions of life were harsh. They earned a pittance, working 70–80 hours a week, and lived in dreadful slums with no medical or other services to speak of.

They found it even more difficult than the men to organise in trade unions. Besides the difficulties common to all young working classes the world over, there were added difficulties in the United States arising out of specific conditions: the large immigrant population in the cities, the continuous waves of immigration into a country of vast size with a decentralised structure. Trade union militants also had to face harsh repression and terror by employers and state.

Because of the conflict between the workers' urge to organise, and the seemingly impossible obstacles to achieving this, the history of American labour is largely a story of repeated advances and retreats played out on a grand scale. In the advance, workers try to organise in industrial or general unions, so as to include all workers, skilled and unskilled, men and women, white and black. This is followed by disintegration of the unions. A new advance follows, but this time the unions play for safety and organise only the skilled white workers, to the practical exclusion of women and blacks. This stage is followed by a rebellion of the unorganised workers, who become more radical, taking practically revolutionary steps to build industrial and general unions. Then a new, massive retreat takes place. And so it goes on.

The to-ing and fro-ing on the industrial front affects workers' organisation on the political front, so we see the political movement of the American working class oscillating between revolutionary syndicalism and extreme right-wing reformism.

Let us outline the story.

One of the earliest examples of women workers making great efforts to organise was in the campaign for the ten-hour day — in place of the 15-hour six-day week then worked. On 15 September 1845, 5,000 women employed in the cotton mills of Western Pennsylvania went on strike. They held out for almost a month before some, desperate, went back, only to be dragged out again by strikers who went from factory to factory, breaking open the gates and seizing the women at the machines. In the end they were forced back to work by hunger, gaining nothing.[9]

A generation later, after many strikes and efforts to build

unions, of which only a few tiny craft unions survived, a new step was taken. In 1866 the National Labor Union was founded. 'It was among the first organisations in the world to raise the question of equal pay for equal work for women and to place them in positions of leadership. It was the first American national labour federation to welcome Negro delegates,' writes one historian.[10] Sadly, it survived only till 1873.[11]

After half a century of sacrifice and struggle, the total number of trade unionists in the whole vast country in 1878 was only 50,000.[12]

The Knights of Labor

Nothing changed significantly until the rise of the Knights of Labor, which dwarfed all previous efforts. It originated in a secret fraternal order founded in 1869, which in 1881 discarded the bulk of its ritualistic features and turned seriously to organising workers on a mass scale. The goal of the Knights of Labor was 'to bring within the fold of organisation every department of productive industry,' and 'to secure to the toilers a proper share of the wealth that they create.'[13] A historian of the American labour movement, Philip S Foner, writes:

> The K of L provided a form of organisation and a common leadership for the American working class, skilled and unskilled, men and women, North and South, Negro and white, native-American and foreign-born, of all religious and political opinions.[14]

It engaged organisers to speak to workers in their native languages, formed assemblies based on nationality groupings, and also 'mixed' assemblies composed of workers of different nationalities. In this case organisers often needed to talk in Polish, Hungarian, German and English at the same assembly.[15]

The organisation grew by leaps and bounds. In 1878 it had 9,287 members; in 1879, 20,151; in 1880, 28,136; and in 1883, 51,914. Its period of greatest growth was during 1885–6, when more than 600,000 joined.[16]

The Knights of Labor made tremendous efforts to organise black workers in the south. The threat of lynching was ever present, and they had to act secretly. But in spite of these difficulties and the great opposition to their organisation, tens of thousands of black workers joined who had never been brought into the trade union movement before.[17] Probably as many as 90,000 black workers were members in 1887. Black workers were elected to positions of leadership at all levels — local assemblies, district assemblies, state conventions, and the General Assembly, in the vast majority of cases when the black members were a minority.[18]

The Knights of Labor carried their efforts on behalf of black people on to the streets in large mixed demonstrations. In Louisville

6,000 black and white people entered the National Park, which was closed to blacks, and 'thus have the Knights of Labor broken the walls of prejudice.' Birmingham, Alabama, and Dallas, Texas, saw large demonstrations, and for the first time, black speakers.[19]

The Knights of Labor also made real efforts to organise women, and the women reacted with spirit:

> The 1884 strikes of women members of the Knights in the textile mills of Fall River and Worcester and in the hat factories of South Norwalk were outstanding for the militancy and perseverance of the strikers. In 1885 one of the most memorable strikes of the decade was conducted by 2,500 carpet-weaving women members of the Order employed by Alexander Smith's Sons in Yonkers, New York.[20]

It has been estimated that in 1886, when the Knights' membership was at its highest, there were about 50,000 women members, forming 8–9 per cent of the total.[21]

The Knights of Labor fought for equal pay for women. The New Jersey Commissioner of Labor in 1886 stated that 'Since the girls have joined the Knights of Labor here they make the same wages as the men.' The Los Angeles **Union** concluded a survey of the national labour scene in the mid-1880s: 'The Knights of Labor is the only organisation we know which encourages the membership of ladies, demands for women exact equality, and insists on equal pay for equal work.'[22]

With all its achievements, however, the Knights of Labor could not survive. It displayed a number of serious weaknesses.

It was not a purely working-class organisation. Employers were encouraged to join. By the mid-1880s, non-working-class members were beginning to dominate the policies of its assemblies and direct them against the intersts of the vast majority of the membership. Instead of concentrating on strikes for union recognition, higher wages, shorter hours and better working conditions, the Knights concentrated on organising producer co-operatives which, they hoped, would 'make every man his own master and every man his own employer,' thus doing away with the wages system.

Last but not least, the Catholic Church played a crucial role in blunting the industrial militancy of the Order.

In the years 1886–7 the employers went on the offensive, exploiting the weakness of the Knights of Labor leadership and the then economic recession. There were more than 200 lock-outs and 161,610 workers (most of them members of the Knights of Labor) were thrown out of work.[23] Precisely at that point the Knights of Labor leadership turned its back on any serious fight on behalf of its members. In 1886 the leadership forbade striking unless there was a two-thirds majority in a secret ballot. If outside financial aid was required, striking was forbidden unless a member of the general executive board had tried to arbitrate. If this was unsuccessful, striking was still forbidden unless the general executive board gave the go-ahead.

Following this, the ranks of the Knights of Labor thinned from a maximum of over 700,000 in the summer of 1886 to 510,351 in July 1887. A year later the membership had sunk to 221,618; in 1890 it was 100,000; in 1893, 74,635; and in 1895, a mere 20,000.[24]

The Knights of Labor was murdered by its own bureaucracy. The grand efforts to establish workers' unity strong enough to surmount differences of skill, race, religious belief, sex or national origin came to an end. In the vacuum created, a new national organisation of trade unions arose — but this time excluding unskilled workers, women and blacks.

The American Federation of Labor

The American Federation of Labor (AFL), founded in 1881, grew slowly but steadily as the Knights of Labor disintegrated. Its leadership learnt from them not the need for greater militancy, but for more caution. It cringed before the ferocity of the employers' offensive, convinced that to attempt to unite the workers into powerful industrial unions by broadening the base of the existing craft unions was to invite head-on collisions with the big corporations and the government, and court the destruction of the existing labour organisations. It sought to make peace with the employers on certain terms which would keep the craft unions alive even if this meant increased victimisation of the unskilled and semi-skilled workers,[25] which included the vast majority of black, foreign-born and women workers.

When a few black workers managed to get into unions, they were organised in separate locals or branches. The AFL was a 'Jim Crow', white supremacist organisation, and this was nowhere more openly expressed than by Samuel Gompers, its president, who fanned race hatred against blacks, referring to them as 'darkies', as superstitious, dull, ignorant, happy-go-lucky, improvident, lazy, and immoral. On such vital issues as disenfranchisement, lynchings, the exclusion of blacks from jury service, segregation in schools, colleges, railroads and other public places, he was completely silent.[26] Foreign-born workers received the same treatment, plus the opposition of the AFL leaders to their very entry into the country, and subsequently to their membership of the AFL.

Women, also overwhelmingly unskilled or semi-skilled, were not wanted in the AFL. Their exclusion was achieved through long apprenticeship requirements, high fees for admission, and special examinations for women. Some unions admitted women employed in certain branches of industry only. Usually in such cases women were excluded from the best-paid branches of the trade.[27] Where they were admitted, the tendency was to set up separate unions. It was not uncommon for AFL organisers to form two unions in a shop or factory, one for women and one for men, and to arrange for negotiations with employers to be conducted by a joint committee representing both. The women workers frequently complained that they came off worse in such an arrangement, since 'the men think that the girls should not get as good work as the men and should not make half as much money as a man.'[28]

No other organisation anywhere engaged in strike-breaking as did the AFL. Philip Foner writes:

> 'scabbing on the job' became a common occurrence in the A F of L. Craft scabbed on craft; union workers broke strikes of brother workers, and there was even the amazing phenomenon wherein A F of L building trades unions built the barracks for scabs to live in who were hired to break the strikes of other A F of L unions.[29]

Nor was there anywhere corruption on the scale of that in the AFL. Officers derived incomes from robbing union treasuries, from gifts, fees, unrepaid loans, kickbacks, bribes from union members and employers; from large pay-offs for preventing or calling off strikes, negotiating 'reasonable' contracts and neglecting contract clauses; for co-operating with employers to form monopolies in a particular trade; for calling strikes against competitors who refused to join the monopoly or do its bidding.[30]

The AFL bureaucrats resorted to extreme measures to keep control. They built cliques of supporters; organised fraudulent elections; packed conferences with delegates who were full-time officials; used hired thugs to fight all opposition in the unions.

The main victims of the AFL bureaucracy were the unskilled workers, black workers, the foreign-born, and women. The fate of all these groups was tied together — now negatively, as they had been tied together positively under the Knights of Labor.

Industrial Workers of the World

The awakening of the great mass of disfranchised immigrants and floating workers, unskilled workers, men and women who found the doors of the AFL shut in their faces, led to the rise of the Industrial Workers of the World (IWW), known as the 'Wobblies'. Its establishment was also spurred on by the Russian revolution of 1905. At its founding conference in June 1905, 'Big Bill' Haywood, destined to become the foremost leader of the IWW, said that he hoped to see the new movement 'grow throughout the country until it takes in a great majority of the working people and that those working people will rise in revolt against the capitalist system as the working class in Russia are doing today.'[31]

The IWW believed that *all* workers should be organised in 'One Big Union', which should wage the class struggle through the workers' basic weapon, the strike, rising to the revolutionary weapon of the general strike, which would bring capitalism to an end and establish a workers' state run by trade union organisation.

Initially all the leading members of the IWW were members of the Socialist Party, whose left-wing members were enthusiastic supporters of revolutionary industrial unionism, and the IWW constantly intervened in political struggles: for civil rights, for free speech, against vagrancy laws, in defence of rights for prisoners, and many other issues.[32] 'Big Bill' Haywood did not remain aloof from electoral politics either. He was one of the most vigorous and effective Socialist Party campaigners in the 1904 and 1908 Presidential and Congressional elections and was the party's candidate for Governor of Colorado in 1906.[33]

But the Socialist Party purged its left wing in 1912 and Haywood was removed from the party executive for leading the IWW. He then left the party and was joined by many thousands of left-wingers who were either expelled or left of their own accord. The IWW then more and more adopted a non-political stance, rejecting political action.

The IWW made a special appeal to the migratory workers of the West. This was a roaming army of several million young, wifeless, homeless, semi-skilled or unskilled workers who moved from job to job in empty freight carriages. They worked in lumber mills, mines, construction projects, and in the fields. In their travels they mingled freely regardless of racial, nationality and religious differences.[34]

The IWW also took pride in its appeal to immigrant workers. An extensive foreign language press was organised specifically to attract the foreign-born. At the end of 1912 it published 13 papers in different languages: English, French, Italian, Spanish, Portuguese, Russian, Polish, Slavic, Lithuanian, Hungarian, Swedish, Jewish and Japanese. Most of these papers were short-lived.[35]

Special efforts were made to organise black workers. The IWW stood squarely for the organisation of black workers on the basis of complete equality. It practised what it preached even in the deepest south, where it raised the banner of 'No Race, No Creed, No Colour', and united black and white workers in a common struggle.[36]

While the western members of the IWW were mainly men, women were important among the semi-skilled and unskilled factory workers of the east. The Wobblies had a keen appreciation of the fighting qualities of women. M Tax, in her book **The Rising of the**

Women, wrote:

> The advent of women side by side with men in strikes will soon develop a fighting force that will end capitalism and its horrors in short order . . . in the language of Kipling, 'The female of the species is more deadly than the male'. It is also well to observe that the male becomes more 'deadly' in the presence and with the aid and encouragement of the female. The industrial union movement seeks to develop the fighting quality of both sexes.[37]

Wobbly papers paid special attention to any news of 'the activity of girl workers' and reports of the main IWW strikes always stressed the role played by women either as strikers or supporters of the men on the picket lines.

Probably the first case in history of a union organising prostitutes to strike was that by the IWW in April 1907 in New Orleans. Philip Foner tells the story:

> A large number of prostitutes in the city were inspired by Wobbly activity in the area to walk out of the brothels and demand better conditions. The madams in several houses had attempted to double the rent of the 'cribs' the girls used for entertaining. The girls, after a discussion of how things were done by the Wobblies, organised, elected officers, and 'picketed the offending employers'. In keeping with its principle of calling on all members to show solidarity with their rebellious sisters, the IWW reacted by boycotting the struck houses. The strikers won their battle.
>
> The ladies were happy to reciprocate. At a later date, the **Voice of the People**, the IWW organ in the deep South, reported, 'Girlies Boycott Yellow-legs'. The paper noted that 'the girls in the red light refuse to prostitute their bodies for the scab herders', the militia sent to suppress the strikers in Butte.[38]

Elizabeth Gurley Flynn

Some of the top IWW organisers were women, and Elizabeth Gurley Flynn could be considered the most prominent of them. Joe Hill, while in a Utah prison in 1915 awaiting execution on charges trumped up because of his union activities, wrote the song, 'The Rebel Girl', and dedicated it to Elizabeth Gurley Flynn. The nickname stuck. At the age of 16, in 1906, she joined the IWW, and a year later had her first strike experience at Bridgport Tube Mill in Connecticut. After that she was here, there and everywhere. She was with the striking miners of the Masabi Iron Range; with the Passaid textile workers who for seventeen months withstood gassing and clubs, ice-cold drenchings and the jailing of hundreds of workers; with the 23,000 textile workers of Lawrence in their bitter two-month long strike; with the Paterson silk weavers and ribbon makers, who endured five months of police brutality, arrests and near starvation. The list is practically endless.

Eizabeth Gurley Flynn followed a consistent revolutionary class line. She never made any concessions to bourgeois feminism. Thus in an article entitled 'The IWW Call to Women' she wrote:

> To us, society moves in grooves of class, not sex. Sex distinctions affect us insignificantly and would less, but for economic differences. It is to those women who are wage earners, or wives of workers, that the IWW appeals. We see no basis for feminist mutual interest, no evidence of natural 'sex conflict', nor any possibility — or present desirability — of solidarity between women alone . . . The 'queen in the parlor' has no interest in common with 'the maid in the kitchen'; the wife of a department store owner shows no sisterly concern for the seventeen-year-old girl who finds prostitution the only door open to a $5-a-week wage clerk. The sisterhood of women, like the brotherhood of men, is a hollow sham to labour. Behind all its smug hypocrisy and sickly sentimentality look the sinister outlines of the class war.[39]

She considered the women's suffrage movement dominated by 'rich faddists', and complained that working-class women were 'made the tail of a suffrage kite in the hands of women of the very class hiring the girls to lives of misery and shame.'[40] The key to the awakening of women workers, Elizabeth Gurley Flynn argued, was the struggle in the workplace. Women and men should organise and fight side by side.

> The IWW appeals to women to organise side by side with their men folks, in the union that shall increasingly determine its own rules of work and wages — until its solidarity and power shall the world command. It points out to the young girl that marriage is no escape from the labour problem, and to the mother, that the interest of herself and her children are woven in with the interests of the class. How is the IWW to overcome conservatism and selfishness? By driving women into an active participation in union affairs, especially strikes, where the mass meetings, mass picketing, women's meetings and children's gatherings are a tremendous emotional stimulant. The old unions never have considered the women as part of the strike. They were expected to stay home and worry about the empty larder, the hungry kiddies and the growling landlord, easy prey to the agents of the company. But the strike was 'a man's business'. The men had the joy of the fight, the women not even an intelligent explanation of it . . . Women can be the most militant or most conservative element in a strike, in proportion to their comprehension of its purposes. The IWW has been accused of putting the women in the front. The truth is, the IWW does not keep them in the back, and they go to the front.[41]

Women's liberation cannot be achieved without a socialist revolution, argued Elizabeth Gurley Flynn: 'Much more than the abstract right of the ballot is needed to free women: nothing short of a social revolution can shatter her cramping and stultifying sphere of today.'[42] The socialist revolution is also the precondition for women to break the shackles of sexual oppression:

> The only sex problem I know is how are women to control themselves, how be free, so that love alone shall be the commandment to act, and I can see but one way, through controlling their one problem of how to live, be fed and clothed — their own economic lives . . . Sexual enslavement . . . follows economic enslavement, and is but a gentle way of saying prostitution, whether it be for one night or one whole life.[43]

'Mother Jones'

Another giant of a woman who started leading workers some two decades before Elizabeth Gurley Flynn, and went on doing so for sixty years, was 'Mother' Mary Jones. Elizabeth Gurley Flynn wrote about her:

> The greatest woman agitator of our time was Mother Jones. Arrested, deported, held in custody by the militia, hunted and threatened by police and gunmen — she carried on fearlessly for 60 years . . .
>
> She was born in Cork, Ireland, and came here as a girl. She lost her husband, an iron moulder, and her four children in a yellow fever epidemic in Memphis, Tennessee. The union buried them (1867). Alone and desolate, she went to Chicago. She did dressmaking for the rich. While she sewed in the magnificent mansions along the lake front, she saw poverty and misery in the city. After the Chicago fire she attended meetings of the Knights of Labor in their scorched building. Following the first of May massacre of workers in 1886, outside the McCormick Harvester Works, and the subsequent Haymarket frame-up of labour leaders, she became a restless labour pilgrim, going from strike to strike — agitating, organising and encouraging. She began in West Virginia, going on to the anthracite area, and from then on she was with the coal miners in practically every struggle for the next 20 years, in the East, in Colorado — everywhere.[44]

'Mother' Jones was an organiser for the Knights of Labor, then one of the founders of the IWW, and one of its main leaders throughout. (She was also a founding member of the Socialist Party.) Her main activity was as an organiser for the United Mine Workers. 'Whenever trouble broke out against the miners,' Haywood wrote, 'Mother Jones went there. When a bridge was patrolled by soldiers she waded the river in winter. When trains were being watched the train crew smuggled her through. She organised "women's armies" during mining disputes to chase strike-breakers with mops, brooms, and dishpans. "God! It's the old mother with her wild women!" the coal owners would groan when confronted with this formidable array.'[45]

She led the miners in strikes in Virginia in 1891; in the anthracite region in 1900 and 1902; in Paint Creek and Cabin Creek, West Virginia, in 1912–13; in Ludlow, Colorado, in 1913–14; and in Kansas in 1921, among others.[46] She took part in organising railwaymen in strikes in 1903, 1904, 1905 and 1911; she led masses of women workers in the textile industry in strikes in 1901, 1903, 1905; in 1910 she led women bottlers on strike against Milwaukee breweries.[47]

Mother Jones was arrested in practically every strike. When she left prison, she agitated and organised, and so landed again in jail. When she was 82 years old, in 1912, she was arrested in West Virginia during a miners' strike and sentenced to 20 years' imprisonment. The uproar of protest from American workers forced the Governor of West Virginia to order her release.[48] One of the last strikes she participated in, when she was nearly 90, was the great steel strike of 1919.

Like Elizabeth Gurley Flynn, Mother Jones was an opponent of bourgeois feminism. Once she told a meeting of suffragettes in New York: 'You don't need a vote to raise hell! You need convictions and a voice! . . . The women of Colorado have had the vote for two generations and the working men and women are in slavery.' In her view women's suffrage was a trick of the rich to divert women from the real issues and keep them busy with 'suffrage and prohibition and charity.'[49]

She died in 1930 at the age of 100. She was buried along with the Virdin union martyrs in the Miners' Cemetery at Mount Olive, Illinois.

'Bread and Roses'

The greatest women's strike was the Lawrence textile strike of January to March 1912. The 23,000 strikers came from 25 nationalities, speaking 45 different languages. Philip Foner writes: 'The truth is that at no time previously in American labour history were so many diverse nationality and language groups so effectively united in a strike.'[50]

> In all the picketing and parades, the women strikers themselves, or wives of strikers, played a vital role. They trod the frozen streets besides the men, and often occupied the front ranks in demonstrations and parades, expectant mothers and women with babes in their arms marching with the others, and like the other mill girls, carrying signs which read: 'We Want Bread and Roses Too.' . . . more women than men appear to have been arrested for intimidating scabs while picketing . . . they refused to pay the fine, choosing rather to go to jail. This was particularly true of the Italian, Polish, Russian and Lithuanian women.[51]

The IWW always showed a genius for improvising new strike tactics. They introduced the idea of mass picketing, mass parades and demonstrations. The Lawrence strike showed unsurpassed ingenuity.

> To get around the prohibition against gathering in front of the mills, the strike committee developed . . . the famous moving picket line. Day after day, lines of pickets moved in an endless chain around the mill district to discourage strike-breakers . . Every day a parade would be held, with from 3,000 to 10,000 people marching to the music of bands and drum corps singing 'The Internationale', 'The Marseillaise', 'Solidarity Forever', and other radical and Wobbly songs.[52]

The acknowledged leader of the strike was the ex-miner 'Big Bill' Haywood. Elizabeth Gurley Flynn worked with him. The strike ended in an overwhelming victory.

But while strong in leading struggles, the IWW was weak in maintaining its organisation thereafter. Before the strike the IWW had about 300 members in Lawrence; in September 1912 the membership rose to 16,000, but by summer 1913 it had fallen back to 700.[53] This pattern of quick recruitment during a strike and quick loss after it was typical of the IWW.

The Lawrence textile workers' strike was followed in 1913 by the 25,000-strong Paterson silk workers' strike. This ended after five gruelling months in complete defeat. Two other defeats of IWW-led strikes — rubber workers in Akron and Studebaker car workers in Detroit — followed a few months later. Never again were IWW organisers able to rally a significant number of textile workers, and the IWW in the east was completely destroyed.

Largely controlled by the members in the Western states, the IWW reflected both the strengths and weaknesses of its composition and ideas. It was impossible to build stable unions among migratory workers. Elizabeth Gurley Flynn admitted: 'Most of us were wonderful agitators but poor union organisers.'[54]

The IWW was doomed to be a small revolutionary organisation, and never to achieve mass membership. At its zenith in 1912 it had 25,000 members. It declined in 1913 to 14,851; in 1914 to 11,365.[55]

The Women's Trade Union League

The failure of the AFL to organise women on the one hand, and the instability of the IWW on the other, opened the door for the formation of the Women's Trade Union League, which was founded in 1903 by a group of liberal women doing social work, and a few trade unionists. The leaders of the League looked upon it as an answer to the challenge of revolution. Thus one of them, Alice Henry, wrote in 1911:

> If the whole burden of remedying unfair industrial inequalities is left to the oppressed social group, we have the crude and primitive method of revolution. To this the only alternative is for the whole community through cooperative action to undertake the removal of industrial wrongs and the placing of industry on a basis just and fair to the worker.[56]

Another leading lady of the League, Louisa Perkins, wrote:

> . . . the perfect engine with which to bring about radical reforms is to be composed of strong disinterested men and women, representatives of the varied industries and interests of society, grouping money, trained intellect, practical experience and noble insight.[57]

The League saw itself as an all-classes alliance. 'Workingmen . . . cannot afford to cherish a class bitterness,' said Jane Adams, first Vice-President of the League. It made efforts 'to set up independent organisations for the women, but all eventually fell to pieces,' writes its historian, G Boone.[58]

Failing to go it alone, the League looked for trade union allies. it could not expect anything but a cold shoulder from the revolutionary IWW, which saw 'women's trade union leagues' widening 'the separation of men and women workers.'[59] So the League turned to the AFL, despite the latter's neglect of women workers.

The League achieved some prominence in New York in November 1909 with a waistmakers' strike, called the 'uprising of the Thirty Thousand'. It is worth quoting some details from Meredith Tax's description in **The Rising of the Women** to get the flavour of the League's participation and ultimate treachery. Initially the leaders of the League actively supported the strike. They

> organised a car caravan to publicise the strike. The cars, lent by various millionaire women, honked their way through the narrow streets of the Lower East Side, 'taking on and leaving off pickets . . . Within the autos rich, fashionable women and poor frail striking girls . . . were making merry over this exceptional affair. It was amusing to see rich women carrying cards on which was proclaimed the need for organisation for labour and which demanded shorter hours and increased pay.'
>
> No aspect of the strike attracted as much attention in the press as the support given it by certain wealthy women, notably Alva Belmont and Anne Morgan. Alva Belmont was the daughter of an Alabama plantation owner and one of New York's most prominent society matrons. She married William K Vanderbilt and embarked on a lavish campaign to break into New York society's 'Four Hundred'. After building a $3 million chateau on Fifth Avenue and a $2 million mansion in Newport, she finally achieved her goal, after which she divorced Vanderbilt and married Oliver Hazard Ferry Belmont, heir to the New York subway system . . .

Anne Morgan was the daughter of 'robber baron J P Morgan'.[60]

The arbitrators proposed what they thought a compromise. The leaders of the Women's Trade Union League welcomed this. The strikers, however, angrily voted it down, considering it a complete sell-out — the union was not recognised, for instance. The leaders of the League thereupon denounced the women workers' 'extremism' and the Socialist influence among them.

When it came to strikes led by the IWW, such as the 'Bread and Roses' strike in Lawrence in 1912, or the massive strike of women in Paterson in 1913, the League stood completely aside.

In the second decade of its existence the League gave more emphasis to legislation than to organisation. It looked more and more to the federal government for support. William O'Neill estimates that by 1919 members of the League held thirty-eight government posts.[61]

In drawing up a balance sheet of a quarter of a century of work by the AFL, IWW and Women's Trade Union League, one cannot fail to come to the sad conclusion that the results were unimpressive. In 1910 the total number of women in unions was only 76,748. Only 1.5 per cent of all women wage-earners, and 5.2 per cent of women in manufacturing industries, were organised.[62]

The Socialist Party — muddle, ambiguity and disarray

The Socialist Party of America had more than 150,000 members at the height of its power, published hundreds of newspapers, gained almost a million votes for its US presidential candidate, won the support of one-third of the AFL membership, and was instrumental in organising the IWW. To understand its attitude to women workers one must start with its attitude to trade unions.

Daniel de Leon, leader of the sectarian and small Socialist Labor Party, argued that 'the party must dominate the trade union movement'. The Socialist Party, on the other hand, advocated the neutrality of the party in trade union affairs. Even the left of the Socialist Party, led by Eugene V Debs, while refusing to accept the complete distinction between party and trade union work, still 'continued to adhere to the principle that the trade unions and the Socialist Party were separate entities, each with a specific duty to perform, and each to refrain from interfering in any way with the other.'[63]

It was accepted that Socialist Party members were to leave the work in the economic field to the union leadership and devote themselves to educating their brothers and sisters in the need to vote Socialist. In line with this the party sought support at annual conventions of the AFL for resolutions that it sponsored, which in the main dealt with the overthrow of the wages system and the establishment of a society based on the collective ownership of the means of production. It rarely dealt with the question of organising the unorganised. Despite supporting industrial unionism, it consorted with the AFL and refrained from outright condemnation of craft unionism.

But many left-wing members of the Socialist Party did not follow the line of non-interference in trade union affairs. Up to 1912 many of the leading activists of the IWW, such as 'Big Bill' Haywood, were also members of the Socialist Party.

On the right of the party many of its leaders were unabashed racists. Thus Victor L Berger, the first Socialist congressman, declared: 'There can be no doubt that the negroes and mulattoes constitute a lower race.'[64] One of the most prominent women leaders of the Socialist Party, Kate O'Hara, wrote in a document titled 'Nigger Equality' that 'Socialists want to put the Negro where he can't compete with the *white man*.' There could be but one solution to the race question — 'Segregation'.

> One Oklahoma socialist even insisted that there would be a segregated afterlife. He envisioned a 'Negro heaven' that was 'one vast watermelon patch', dotted with shady trees, dancing platforms, and numerous other recreational facilities, 'where they can play and dance and shout themselves throughout eternity'. This vision appeared in a pamphlet entitled **Why I am a Socialist**.[65]

At the 1910 conference of the Socialist Party, Ernest Untermann (the translator of Marx's **Das Kapital** into English) went so far as to assert that any attempt to combat 'race prejudice' would be a betrayal of socialist principles!

Even the left, despite their theoretical stand for black equality, made virtually no effort to use the party in a struggle for black rights, according to Ira Kipnis, historian of the party.

The middle-class composition of the Socialist Party made non-intervention in trade union affairs the easiest option. At the 1912 conference, the largest groups among the 193 delegates were 32 newspapermen, 21 lecturers, 20 lawyers, 12 mayors, and 11 full-time party functionaries. Categories such as manufacturers, real estate brokers, retail merchants, authors, ministers, physicians, and dentists provided another 60 delegates. There were also 11 white-collar workers, ten farmers and seven housewives. Most of the rest were skilled workers such as carpenters, machinists, and electricians.[66]

In 1906 the Socialist candidate for mayor of Milwaukee, William A Arnold, declared: '. . . the business interests of Milwaukee will be safer in the hands of an administration made up of Social Democrats than they have been under the Republican and Democratic administrations.' Arnold assured the voters that he was a property-holder and taxpayer himself, so obviously had no desire to harm the city's business. Victor L Berger, noted above for his racism, assured the city's industrialists that a vote for his Socialist Party was a vote against strikes. Milwaukee had had fewer strikes in the past six or seven years than any city one-half its size, due, he asserted, to Socialist influence in Milwaukee unions. 'I can say from actual experience that the Social-Democrats in this city have opposed almost every strike that has ever been declared here.'[67]

In this desert, those members of the Socialist Party who wanted to organise the mass of disfranchised workers turned to the IWW. 'Big Bill' Haywood's expulsion from the Socialist Party executive and resignation from the party led to the desertion of thousands of left-wing members, reducing the party's numbers from 150,000 before its May 1912 convention to 78,000 in June 1913.[68] Many more thousands of left-wingers were expelled in the following months, and the party lost all its vigour.

The Socialist Party was not particularly interested in working women — they had no vote. Ira Kipnis claimed that it 'gave far more attention to winning the support of Protestant ministers than it gave either to youth or women.'[69] It had, indeed, more than 300 clergymen in membership. Its orientation on the AFL rather than the IWW also made it difficult to relate effectively to women workers in struggle.

Women around the Socialist Party were largely the wives of party members. They formed themselves into autonomous groups sympathetic to the party.[70] The key activists of the socialist women's groups were veterans of women's clubs, where they were accustomed to sit side by side with bourgeois ladies in small discussion groups. Congeniality within the group held priority over any potential recruitment for active political work. The socialist women of San Francisco formed the William Morris Club and adopted as its motto: 'We strive to build the Comrade World, in Freedom, Art, and Fellowship.' They promoted education as their ideal, focussing on the development of women's appreciation of 'a full expression of life'.[71] While they expressed a loyal sympathy with the Socialist Party, they preferred 'to arouse and deepen among themselves the consciousness of their own individuality.'[72]

The standard arrangement was for a fortnightly parlour meeting held in a member's house. The activities of the groups depended on the proclivities of the district: children's choruses, boys' debating clubs, socialist Sunday Schools (where children were taught socialist songs and exercises), circulating libraries, were common to most areas of the country. In urban areas, the activities usually involved public agitational and political work. Socialist women attended as fraternal delegates the meetings of Temperance, Woman Suffrage, and

Women's Club organisations.[73]

By and large, members of the groups were not members of the Socialist Party, although many of the activists were. To prevent a drift away, the party called in November 1901 in its weekly paper **Appeal to Reason** for a radical organisation of socialist women. The statement of aims was rather insipid:

> Organisation is demanded, organisation to teach the principles of a higher industrial system than now obtains; a system that will be based upon the Golden Rule of the identity of all human interests . . . All women whose souls throb responsible to freedom and duty, all who seek to be loyal to God and humanity are requested to take part in this world struggle for elevation of mankind and to enrol themselves as members of the Women's National Socialist Union.[74]

An effort in 1904 to establish a federation of all the groups failed. A journal **Socialist Woman** (later renamed **Progressive Woman**) was started in 1907, to provide a focus for the groups. It was designed to be a popular magazine, like 'the **Ladies Home Journal** with a dose of socialism'. At its height its circulation reached only 12,000.[75]

A year later, in 1908, the groups did federate. The Socialist Party conference of that year established a Women's National Committee of the Socialist Party which nearly all the groups joined. The same conference consolidated the bloc between the right and centre, when the party gave up all pretence to be revolutionary, and started a campaign to eliminate the left. Decorating the conference hall were portraits of Marx and Engels draped with the American flag.[76] It also held the first full-scale debate on immigration, in which the extreme racists made the running.

The socialist women's movement related to women not as workers, but as housewives, as consumers. Thus the Socialist Party paper **Progressive Woman** wrote:

> The home, the child, the family purse and the family larder, are matters that appeal to every woman of the working class . . . The average woman knows that Johnny has to have so many pairs of shoes a year, that so much sugar must be used on the table, and that she has fewer and fewer dresses for herself as time flies and prices go up. If you can show her exactly what relation Senator Bing's conduct had with her household economics she will deign to take an interest in him.[77]

The kind of 'socialism' that the socialist women's movement preached had nothing to do with the class struggle — it was the product of women's feelings, of love:

> Sister Comrades, did you ever think that it is woman's part especially to love the world into goodness. Can we have neglected and withheld our love, and the effect combined with man's lack of wisdom, have brought

us to this recent condition of affairs?[78]

The main political activity of the socialist women's movement was campaigning for women's suffrage. In this they collaborated with NAWSA, the bourgeois feminist organisation that at that time was openly racist, xenophobic and anti-working-class. In collaborating with NAWSA, the American socialist women flouted the decision of the Stuttgart Congress of the Socialist International of 1907 which said:

> The Socialist women shall not carry on this struggle for complete equality or right to vote in alliance with the middle-class women suffragists, but in common with the Socialist Parties, which insist upon woman suffrage as one of the fundamental and most important reforms for the full democratisation of political franchise in general.

The leaders of the American socialist women's movement, however, argued that the vote was not a class issue.

After the betrayal of the waistmakers' strike in November 1909, leading members of the socialist women's movement in New York decided that they should break with the bourgeois suffragists. So in December 1909 a conference of New York socialist women 'Resolved, that the work of socialist women for the suffrage must be carried on along separate and independent lines through and by the economic and political organisation of the working class', and withdrew from NAWSA.[79] This action was endorsed by several women's branches across the country, but rejected by many others. At the National Congress of the Socialist Party in May 1910, the leaders, not wishing to antagonise either group of women, passed an ambiguous resolution allowing every branch of the party and the women's movement to decide its own tactics regarding collaboration with NAWSA. Many of the branches continued to belong to NAWSA.[80]

In Conclusion

We have seen how the bourgeois suffragists, catapulted into activity by the movement for the abolition of slavery, slid into reaction, racism, xenophobia and hatred of slum dwellers, following the sharp class polarisation in American society in the last few decades of the nineteenth and beginning of the twentieth centuries.

We have seen how working-class women, who could not but feel outsiders in this movement, nonetheless found it difficult to integrate into the industrial and political organisations of the working class. The American working class failed to build stable trade union organisations encompassing the unskilled — women, blacks and foreign-born workers. Both the Knights of Labor and the IWW — the latter after blazing the most heroic trail in American working-class history —

faltered and perished. What survived was a corrupt caricature of trade unionism — the AFL.

This industrial situation radically affected working-class political activity. The IWW by and large expressed the demands of a mass of militant, revolutionary workers. But its anti-political stance, its mistrust of all 'politics' and 'parties' as a reaction to the opportunitism of the Socialist Party, showed its narrowness. The Socialist Party, by turning away from the IWW and towards the AFL, continued to be a party of skilled workers and the lower middle class. The result was the blunting of the struggle against racism, and the exclusion of women workers from the unions.

The women in and around the Socialist Party, mainly wives of skilled workers and the lower middle class, faced a choice between the bourgeois feminism of Elizabeth Cady Stanton and Susan B Anthony of NAWSA on the one hand, and the working-class militancy of 'Mother' Jones and Elizabeth Gurley Flynn of the IWW on the other. The Socialist Party women could not bring themselves to side with the latter, so they inevitably fell under the influence of the former, and developed a mishmash of muddled ideas. Unable to forge the class unity of *all* workers — men and women, black and white, skilled and unskilled — they drifted to 'sex' unity, the unity of ladies with their maids.

5
The socialist women's movement in Germany

After the defeat of the Paris Commune the centre of gravity of the international labour movement shifted to Germany. Up to the outbreak of the First World War, the German Social Democratic Party, the SPD, was the main socialist force internationally and dominated every aspect of the labour movement inside Germany. Unlike in Britain, where the Labour Party was yet to be established by the trade unions, in Germany the SPD preceded the unions and was central in building them.

For twelve years the SPD survived illegally under the Anti-Socialist Law. Even when this was repealed in 1890, the party still had to operate under heavy restrictions. Yet it was by far the largest socialist party in the world and stood in sharp opposition to the economic, social and political order. In 1914 it had more than a million members, gained more than 4½ million votes in parliamentary elections, produced ninety daily papers, ran massive trade unions and co-operatives, sporting and singing clubs, a youth organisation, a women's organisation and had hundreds of full-time officials.

Before we deal with the organisation of women by the SPD we must deal with the general nature of the party's 'Marxism'.

The German state was not a conventional bourgeois democracy. The German middle class had failed miserably to carry out its own revolution in 1848, and had capitulated to the Prussian monarchy. The result was that the old monarchic state structure run by the Prussian land-owning aristocracy — the Junkers — continued to govern, although more and more it came to serve the economic needs of the bourgeoisie. The SPD, faced with legal limitations in Prussia and other states of Germany and an impotent Reichstag (parliament), was forced into a position of intransigent opposition.

At the same time the prolonged growth of German capitalism and continued rise in the living standard of workers over half a century, accompanied by a low level of industrial struggle, led the party into a numbing passivity. The SPD was like a 'state within a state'. It was bureaucratically run by trade union and party officials and party executive.[1] From birth to death, except when working for their employers, workers could be almost completely enclosed by party institutions. The party member could eat food bought in a Social Democratic co-operative, read nothing but Social Democratic papers and magazines, spend leisure time in Social Democratic cycling or gymnastic clubs, sing in a Social Democratic choir, drink in a Social Democratic pub, and be buried with the aid of a Social Democratic Burial Society.

So the SPD combined a *formal* revolutionary Marxism with *actual* reformism. The synthesis between the two was expressed clearly in the party's programme, the Erfurt Programme, which came largely from the pen of Karl Kautsky, the 'Pope of Marxism'. It was divided into two hermetically sealed parts, a minimum programme dealing with day-to-day reforms and a maximum programme which was useful for May Day oratory. This synthesis held for a long time. As the best historian of the SPD, Carl Schorske explains:

> So long as the German state kept the working class in a pariah status, and so long as the working class, able to extract a share of the material blessings of a vigorous expanding capitalism, was not driven to revolt, the Erfurt synthesis would hold.[2]

This division between economics and politics, minimum and maximum programme, theory and practice, was the cause of further atrophy in the SPD. Wage struggles became the exclusive property of the unions. Politics was limited to putting a cross on the ballot paper and accommodation to the capitalist state.

The synthesis of reformist content and 'revolutionary' form received its clearest expression in the debates in the German labour movement during the aftermath of the Russian revolution of 1905. On the wave of enthusiasm generated by the revolution, the tactic of using a general strike as the first step towards socialist revolution was endorsed by the SPD congress in Jena in 1905, only to be overturned a year later at the congress in Mannheim on the insistence of the powerful and aggressive trade union leaders. The party leaders, above all Bebel and Kautsky, accepted that the unions were *independent* of the party and should always remain so.

SPD 'Marxism' had atrophied, kept the form but lost the spirit of the revolutionary ideas of Marx, basically because the link connecting the struggle for economic reforms *inside* capitalism with the revolutionary struggle *against* capitalism had been cut.

The only people who fought against the split, and constantly opposed Kautsky's 'Marxism' from a revolutionary standpoint, were the small group inside the SPD around Rosa Luxemburg. But even Rosa Luxemburg and her comrades did not act as an independent organisation, but only as a tendency inside the SPD. Hence they did not intervene separately in the day-to-day struggles of workers.

Organising Women in Trade Unions

In the field of women's organisation the SPD had a number of positive achievements to its credit. First among them was the organising of women in the trade unions.

In 1892 the total number of women in the SPD's Free Trade Unions was only 4,355, only 1.8 per cent of the unions' membership and far below the proportion of women in the labour force — which was 34.9 per cent according to the 1895 census.[3]

That year the Halberstadt Congress of Free Trade Unions directed the craft unions to transform themselves into 'mixed craft' organisations, admitting unskilled women into the same unions as skilled men. It had previously been illegal for a trade union to organise both men and women, but even when this became legal, other legal barriers to organising women were not lifted. Women were forbidden in most states of Germany — Prussia, Bavaria, Saxony and others — from taking part in any associations which dealt with political issues, and this was given a very broad interpretation. For instance:

> In 1886 a women's association engaged in trade union work was dissolved by the police because it had discussed the institution by the state of a normal working day, a Bill on the protection of workers which had been submitted to the Reichstag, and a proposal for the introduction of government supervision of factory premises. Another association was dissolved because it had addressed a petition to the local authorities of the town for the appointment of women assessors in the industrial courts.[4]

After 1890 both the political and trade union wings of the socialist movement incorporated into their structures committees dealing with women's issues. All committees were in close contact with each other, and often had common membership. The results were impressive. Total membership of the trade unions grew from 237,094 in 1892 to a peak of 2,573,718 in 1913; but women's membership grew relatively even more rapidly, from 4,355 to 230,347 in the same period — from 1.8 per cent to 8.9 per cent of trade union membership.[5]

The unionisation of women proved far less successful in traditional women's jobs than in industries where women worked with men. Thus in 1914 more than 44 per cent of women working in engineering were in the union, while only 1 per cent in the tailoring trade.[6]

The socialist women's movement in Germany was almost synonymous with one person — Clara Zetkin (1857–1933). Zetkin also played a vital role in organising women into the unions. She herself was a member of the Bookbinders' Union in Stuttgart for 25 years; played an active part in the Tailors' and Seamstresses' Union, attending many of its congresses; was one of the representatives of the German Tailors' and Seamstresses' Union at its second international congress in London in 1896 and was elected the union's provisional international secretary.

Other leading socialist women also played an important role in organising women into unions. Louise Zietz (1865–1916) was for many years a member of the Unskilled Factory Workers' Union and was often elected secretary of the union's congresses. Ottilie Baader (1847–1925) was a leading member of both the socialist women's movement and the Tailors' and Seamstresses' Union. Members of the women's socialist movement served on the *Kartels* — a form of trades council but more influential. From 1905 the *Kartels* appointed their own women organisers in cities such as Hamburg and Nuremberg. They generally controlled strike funds, and therefore affected strike policy.[7]

The need for trade union unity between women and men was central to Clara Zetkin's thinking and action. While in Russia the unions included men and women from the beginning, in Germany it took a generation to open the doors of the male-dominated unions to women. (In Britain in took up to three generations: for instance the Amalgamated Society of Engineers, established in 1852, did not admit women until 1943, after 91 years — and then only into the lowest section.)

In no case did working women want to build a separate union. Weak groups of the working class are not inclined to sectionalism. Where this did happen it was under duress, either from a capitalist law imposing separation, because of liberal bourgeois feminist influence such as the Women's Trade Union Leagues in Britain and the United States, or because of craftism and bureaucracy in the men's unions. All the women-only unions were weak, unstable, and dissolved into the male unions at the first opportunity.

When it came to getting women into the SPD itself, Clara Zetkin and her friends came up against a big legal hurdle. Until 1908 the law in most of Germany forbade women from joining any political party.

The SPD was forced to adopt various means to try to circumvent this. In 1889 an Agitation Commission composed of several women was set up in Berlin to provide a centre for trade union and SPD activity. Other cities followed suit. Some of these replaced working women's organisations which had been closed down by the police. They arranged lectures, meetings and other activities and maintained contact with local party organisations. All the Agitation Commissions were independent of each other so as not to break the law. But the state still took measures against them. In 1895 they were all banned.

In 1894 the SPD conference decided to adopt a system of *Vertrauenspersonen*, or spokespeople. Responsibility for political propaganda was put into the hands of one individual, in which case the law against political association did not apply. The *Vertrauensperson*, the individual spokesperson, could therefore take any political initiative on her own. The number of *Vertrauenspersonen* rose from 25 in 1901 to 407 in 1907.[8]

In November 1895 a *Zentralvertrauensperson* was appointed to serve as a connecting link for the organised working women of the whole of Germany. At the same time Zetkin was elected to the national executive of the SPD.

Women also found other ways to circumvent the law, such as forming electoral clubs during the period set aside for active campaigning before elections, which was permitted by a gap in the Prussian law. Louise Zietz recounted how she circumvented the law of Thuringia which did not allow women to be speakers at public meetings: 'I was prevented from speaking. A male comrade spoke for ten minutes, and then I participated in the discussion from the floor, by speaking for 1½ hours.'[9]

When the Law of Association was abolished in 1908 the need for *Vertrauenspersonen* disappeared.

For many years socialist women had played a big role in recruiting women into the trade unions. Now the increase in women members of the trade unions gave a boost to the winning of women members for the SPD. The law made for a time lag between the two, but the female membership of the SPD caught up quickly. In 1906 the number of women in the SPD was only 6,460, while the number of women in the free trade unions was 118,908. In other words less than 1 per cent of women trade unionists were also members of the SPD. But by 1907 this had risen to 8 per cent; by 1908 21.3 per cent; 1909, 46.5 per cent; 1910, 51.2 per cent; 1911, 56.3 per cent; 1912, 58.5 per cent; 1913, 61.3 per cent; and by 1914 this was 83 per cent.[10]

Large public meetings provided opportunities for recruiting women to the party. Thus in Hamburg on 6 November 1905, at a meeting attended by 280 people, 26 women joined the party. In 1907 the figures for three big meetings were: 20 February: 700 attended, 45 joined; 18 March: 110 attended, 13 joined; 7 September: 1,200 attended, 50 joined. The following year, on 11 February 1908, another big meeting won 39 new members from an audience of 500.[11]

Zetkin on Bourgeois Feminism

To recruit women into the socialist movement, Zetkin argued, one had to oppose the bourgeois feminists. In a speech delivered to the Gotha congress of the SPD in 1896 (and later published as a pamphlet entitled 'Only with the Proletarian Woman will Socialism be Victorious'), she declared:

> There is no such thing as a 'women's movement' in and of itself . . . [A] women's movement only exists within the context of historical development and . . . there is therefore only a bourgeois and a working-class women's movement, which have nothing more in common than does Social Democracy with bourgeois society.

Elsewhere in the same speech, she said:

> The woman of the working class has achieved her economic independence but neither as a person nor as a woman or wife does she have the possibility of living a full life as an individual . . . For her work as wife and mother she gets only the crumbs that are dropped from the table by capitalist production.
>
> Consequently, the liberation struggle of the working-class woman cannot be — as it is for the bourgeois woman — a struggle against the men of her own class . . . The end goal of her struggle is not free competition against men, but bringing about the political rule of the working class. Hand in hand with the men of her own class, the working-class woman fights against capitalist society.[12]

Bourgeois feminism concentrated on the demand for 'women's suffrage' (indeed, for restricted women's suffrage). But even if women were granted political equality, nothing would be changed in the actual relations of power. Working-class women would simply be 'equally' exploited with working-class men, while the bourgeois women would have 'equal' privileges with bourgeois men.

Zetkin argued that socialist women should not confine themselves to the demand for the vote, as the bourgeois feminists did, but should fight for the right to work, equal pay, paid maternity leave, free child-care facilities, and education for women. She repeatedly scorned the label 'feminist', translating it into *Frauenrechtlerinnen* — in a clumsy English translation 'Women's Rightists'.[13] She ended:

> Women's activity is difficult. It is laborious, it demands great devotion and great sacrifice. But this sacrifice will be rewarded and must be made. For, just as the working class can achieve its emancipation only if

it fights together without distinction of nationality or distinction of occupation, so also it can achieve its emancipation only if it holds together without distinction of sex.[14]

To understand the development of the German socialist women workers' movement under Zetkin's leadership, one must understand its adversary — the bourgeois feminists. The non-socialist women's movement in Germany straddled a wide spectrum, from extreme right to radical left, the latter bordering on the right wing of the SPD.

Let us look at the radical feminists, the section nearest to the SPD. In 1904 a League for the Protection of Motherhood and Sexual Reforms (*Bund für Mutterschutz und Sexualreform*), also known as the New Moralists, was founded under the leadership of Helene Stöcker. It sought legal equality for husband, wife and children, easier divorce and legal recognition of 'free marriages', so that police interference should cease, and that the children of such liaisons should have the same legal rights as the children of legal marriages.[15] It campaigned for the spread of contraceptives and also for the repeal of an abortion law which imprisoned a woman for between six months and five years, even if the pregnancy was the result of rape. It was on this subject that the League made its influence most strongly felt within the women's movement. R Evans, in his book **The Feminist Movement in Germany 1894–1944**, assesses the place of the New Moralists:

Victoria Woodhull and Annie Besant, Margaret Sanger and Marie Stopes campaigned for similar aims. What was unique was the fact that Stöcker's programme enjoyed the broad support of the radical feminist movement. The exponents of free love and of contraception were generally ostracised by the feminist movement in England and America; even Josephine Butler had been treated by them with obloquy and distrust. Helene Stöcker and the movement she led were by contrast *part* of the feminist movement in Germany.[16]

The radical feminists also engaged in trade union activities, competing with the SPD women. In 1889 they founded a women's sales clerks' association whose membership rose to 11,000 over the next ten years. The organisation for sales clerks in the Free Unions, even as late as 1908, had only 3,807 men and 4,997 women members. The radical feminists also organised domestic servants.[17] They published a paper called **The German Working Women's Paper** (*Deutsche Arbeiterinnenzeitung*).

The social base of this trend of feminism was petty bourgeois — teachers and white-collar workers, who at that time were much more distant from the manual working class than they are today. In these classic petty bourgeois occupations, competition for jobs and status led to a war of the sexes. There were separate and hostile unions for men and women teachers, and a male clerks' alliance, among others.

The radical feminists also held conferences for working women in 1904 and 1907, and invited the SPD and Free Trade Unions to send delegates. They showed a much more serious attitude to working women than, say, **Spare Rib** exhibits in Britain at the present time. Their language was often almost indistinguishable from that of the socialists. Thus, for instance, one of their leaders, Minna Cauer, wrote on 15 November 1913: 'Only with the mass of working women can we some day fight the battle, only together with them, with the masses of employed and working women, will women receive the vote.'

However, lacking the cohering influence of a working-class base, the radical feminists, in the few years before the First World War, quarrelled violently over personal issues, split again and again, and finally wrecked the League.

Zetkin always tried to steer clear of the radical feminists. Joining forces, she said, could not lead to real action, but would lead to a blunting of the sharp edge of socialist policy. It was not always easy to stay clear, since the radical feminists spoke in persuasive 'social' language and even initiated campaigns which themselves were radical. As part of the 1895 campaign for the abolition of the Law of Association banning women from joining political organisations, a petition was drafted by the radical feminists Minna Cauer and Lily von Gizycki and a member of the SPD, Adele Gerhard. The SPD's central newspaper, **Vorwärts**, published the petition together with a statement of support, recommending party members to sign. Zetkin also printed the petition in her own paper, **Gleichheit**, but accompanied it with a warning in bold type: 'We decidedly advise every class-conscious member of the working class against this petition in any manner.'[18] A sharp exchange took place in the columns of **Vorwärts** between Zetkin and the veteran socialist Wilhelm Liebknecht, who tended to bend over backwards towards the radical feminists. Zetkin asked the opinion of Engels, who agreed with her completely.[19]

Time after time the radical feminists called on the socialist women to join their demonstrations, but the invitations were always rejected by Zetkin. This pattern of non-co-operation with bourgeois women to obtain goals for which both formally strove was never altered. It was with the greatest difficulty, however, that Zetkin managed to separate the working-class women from the radical feminists. Again and again she had to explain that, as Eleanor Marx put it, 'whenever working women meet together with bourgeois [or petty bourgeois] women it is the former who come under the influence of the latter.'

Gleichheit

One of the most important weapons of education and organisation for women was the women's fortnightly journal **Gleichheit** (Equality). Its subtitle was 'For the Interest of the Woman Worker'. It was founded in 1891 and edited by Zetkin for 25 years. Zetkin, while always emphasising the need for the complete political and organisational unity of the socialist movement, believed that socialist propaganda should be made to fit the specific audience at which it aimed. As she said in a letter to her Dutch colleague Heleen Ankersmit on 7 September 1913:

> If the women of the people are to be won for socialism then we need in part special ways, means and methods. If those who are awakened are to be schooled for work and struggle in the service of socialism theoretically and practically, then we must have special organisations and arrangements for it . . . we will not manage without special measures whose driving and executive forces are predominantly women.[20]

Zetkin set forth her conception of **Gleichheit** in an editorial addressed 'To the Readers' which was published with few changes at the beginning of each year throughout the 1890s.

> **Gleichheit** is directed especially to the most progressive members of the working class, whether they are slaves to capital with their hands or with their heads. It strives to school these theoretically, to make possible for them a clear understanding of the historical course of development, and an ability not only to work consciously in the battle for the liberation of the working class, but also to be effective in enlightening and teaching their class comrades and training them as fighters with a clear goal.[21]

According to Zetkin **Gleichheit** was 'written for the women who are spokespersons; it was not meant for the masses, but rather for the advanced.'[22] Much space was devoted to a description of working conditions in the textile, garment, food processing industries, in the bookbinding trade, in home industries and in all other branches of the economy in which women were particularly active. Detailed information on factory legislation was provided to help women take full advantage of its protection, however minimal. Strikes and labour unrest among working women in Germany and in other countries were always given prominent coverage.

In the earliest years of the paper's existence Zetkin not only edited it but also wrote most of the articles. During the first 14 years the circulation was small, although it rose consistently from 2,000 in 1891 to 11,000 in 1903–4. The nature of the paper changed considerably when the socialist women's movement expanded rapidly, reaching 75,000 in 1907.[23]

In 1904 **Gleichheit** began to be distributed free to women members of the socialist movement and to wives of SPD members. This is the main reason for the enormous expansion of its circulation from 11,000 in 1903–4 to 44,000 in 1905–6, 77,000 in 1908–9 and 125,000 in 1914.

In 1904 Zetkin was obliged by the SPD leadership to make the first in a series of changes in the format and character of **Gleichheit** designed to give the paper wider appeal. At the 1904 SPD women's conference she announced that beginning the following year a supplement would accompany **Gleichheit** intended to 'serve the education and interests of woman as housewife and mother', as well as providing good reading material for her children. This started in January 1905, the supplements being alternately 'For our Housewives and Mothers', or 'For our Children'. Zetkin made the best of a situation which had to a certain extent been forced upon her, by developing in particular those viewpoints neglected in the schools attended by working-class children, and giving selections from outstanding revolutionary writers and writers of fiction.

Another important field of activity of the women's socialist movement was education, in which most of its leaders were engaged. Zetkin gave lectures on cultural history at the Stuttgart Women's Education Club. Zietz ran the education club in Hamburg and Baader was active in such work in Berlin. In 1905 three thousand women were organised in these clubs.[24]

From 1908 the party sponsored women's reading and discussion sessions — *Leseabende* — all over Germany, which were mainly devoted to teaching Marxism. The number of women involved was large: in Berlin in 1910 about 4,000, or a third of the women members of the party. An estimated 150 localities ran such sessions.[25] The course of lectures in the Teltow Beeskow district of Berlin in late 1913 gives some idea of what they were like. These:

> centre on one theme: the scientific foundation of the modern working-class movement. Participants were introduced to such topics as the relationship between social reform, democracy, and socialism; idealism and materialism; and utopian and scientific socialism. These materials were followed by analyses of pre-capitalist economic development, the origins of the capitalist mode of production, the formation of the working class, and the nature of capitalist exploitation. After eleven weeks, the class ended with a discussion of method and goals of the class struggle.[26]

Zetkin and the international socialist women's movement

Clara Zetkin did a lot to influence and direct socialist women beyond the borders of Germany. In 1907 she took the initiative in convening the first international conference of socialist women in Stuttgart at which 59 women from fifteen countries participated. This conference decided to create an international organisation of all socialist women's organisations.[27]

The conference was far from homogeneous. On the key issue of the vote for women the Austrian, Belgian, British and French delegates agreed that the demand for restricted suffrage, in other words suffrage based on property or income qualifications, was more 'realistic' than universal suffrage. Similarly the British and French argued against the 'sectarianism' of Zetkin and her supporters towards the bourgeois feminist movement.

But Zetkin was completely unyielding on the two issues. She was supported by the Russian delegate, Alexandra Kollontai, among others. Zetkin won the day. The conference passed strong resolutions stating that 'socialist parties of all countries have a duty to struggle energetically for the introduction of universal suffrage for women' and 'socialist women must not ally themselves with the bourgeois feminists, but lead the battle side by side with the socialist men'. Zetkin was elected secretary of the International Women's Socialist Organisation, and **Gleichheit** was designated the central organ of the movement. Kollontai was elected to the secretariat.

A second international conference of socialist women held in 1910 in Copenhagen reaffirmed the demand for 'universal suffrage'. Zetkin then proposed the adoption of 8 March as International Women's Day. Both the date and the idea were taken from a demonstration of American socialist women in New York on 8 March 1908 in opposition to the bourgeois suffrage movement there. The proposal was approved with enthusiasm by the conference. Beginning in 1911 and continuing until the outbreak of the war in 1914, International Women's Day demonstrations were organised in practically all the main cities of Europe. (Of course the most important was the one which took place *during* the war — and launched the Russian revolution).

Right-wing Opposition to Zetkin

In the socialist women's movement, as well as inside the SPD as a whole, there was a right-wing opposition to Zetkin. The SPD was split into three tendencies: on the extreme right the 'revisionists', followers of Eduard Bernstein; on the extreme left the followers of Rosa Luxemburg; and in the centre the followers of Bebel and Kautsky. The same three tendencies appeared in the Socialist Women's Movement. Here the right was ready to practise class-collaboration with the liberals even more willingly than its counterpart in the SPD.

The most prominent spokeswoman of this tendency was Lily Braun (1865–1916). She came from a noble family and never lost her roots. She argued against the class struggle, declaring that socialism would be achieved not through the revolutionary activity of the working class alone, but also through the activity of a number of progressive forces, including feminists. All feminists, according to her, were by definition progressive, as they were against sex inequality just as socialists were against class inequality.

In 1895 Lily Braun collaborated with bourgeois feminists in drawing up a petition for the reform of the Law of Association. Together with Minna Cauer, the radical bourgeois feminist, she edited a paper titled **Die Frauenbewegung** (The Women's Movement). The first issue summarised its principles: support for all women regardless of political persuasion and fight for the common goal of full equality of the sexes. 'We want to be as fair to the struggle for equal education as for equal wages.'

Lily Braun complained about the attitudes of men to women in the labour movement, and argued that it was an illusion to believe that the class struggle would overcome the conflict between the sexes. In 1901 she published a pamphlet entitled **Frauenarbeit und Hauswirtschaft** (Female Labour and Household Co-operatives), which was a plea that women should be freed from houschold burdens by the organising of household co-operatives. Zetkin raged against this idea for being both utopian and opportunist, as only middle-class women with secure and regular incomes could benefit from such an undertaking. She called the suggested co-operatives 'bourgeois reform work'. Lily Braun was supported by a number of prominent people in the Socialist Women's Movement and a number of leading men in the SPD.

Lily Braun and her supporters were not without some successes. Between 1898 and 1902 in Hamburg as well as in Berlin, several joint meetings of working-class women and bourgeois feminists considered the possibilities of collaboration. Only with great and consistent effort did Zetkin manage to overcome Lily Braun's influence, and finally, in 1903, to push her to all intents and purposes out of the Socialist Women's Movement.

Another strand opposing Clara Zetkin was anti-feminist, represented by the Reichstag deputy Edmund Fischer. In an article entitled 'The Woman Question', published in the **Sozialistische Monatshefte** in 1905, Fischer asked: 'Is it unnatural, socially unhealthy, and ful for women generally to work, a capitalist evil which will and must disappear with the abolition of capitalism?' His answer was unequivocal: 'The so-called emancipation of women goes against the nature of women and of mankind as a whole. It is unnatural, and hence impossible to achieve.'[28] 'The first and highest good in life for the woman, buried deep in her nature,' he maintained, 'was to be a mother and live to educate her children.'

At the Mannheim Congress of the SPD in 1906 the left, led by Rosa Luxemburg, was beaten. The guns of the right were then directed against Clara Zetkin, who was a close personal and political friend of Luxemburg.

When the Law of Association was repealed in 1908 the women's conference in Nuremberg decided that women's associations should join the SPD local branches, with at least one woman included in each local and district executive committee, responsible for propaganda among women workers. The central bureau of the women's movement was transformed into a women's bureau subordinate to the national executive of the party. Only one woman was admitted to the executive, despite the women's protests. This was Louise Zietz. She was not on the extreme left of the party, like Zetkin, but supported the Kautskian centre.[29] The same year that Zetkin was pushed aside, 1908, the far more radical youth organisation was also purged.[30]

The integration of the women's movement into the SPD led to mass recruitment of women into the party, from 29,468 in 1908 to 174,474 in 1914 — in the short space of six years a growth of nearly 150,000![31]

1908 also saw Zetkin's editorial control of **Gleichheit** loosened. As we have seen, the nature of the magazine had already been changing. Its size was now doubled from 12 to 24 pages, and every issue was accompanied by both a children's and a mothers' and housewives' supplement. In 1910 the ultimate was requested — that she publish a fashion supplement. It was indicative of Zetkin's loss of power after 1908 that she complied with this demand to some extent, in that she regularly published articles on fashion and cooking as well as recipes and dress patterns. At the 1913 party congress she even promised that henceforth greater heed would be paid to 'the entirely unschooled', to those who 'do not yet know the ABC of our views.'[32]

Thereafter the unions officially took bulk orders of **Gleichheit** to distribute free, thus in 1914 accounting for as much as three-fifths of the total circulation, which rose considerably, from 11,000 in 1903–4 to 125,000 in 1914.[33] In 1914 the number of copies of **Gleichheit** distributed was equal to 71.6 per cent of women in the SPD, or 59.4 per cent of women in the free trade unions.

August 1914: The Watershed of War

The outbreak of the First World War was a great watershed.

A few days after the outbreak of war, on 5 August 1914, Zetkin published an article in **Gleichheit** entitled 'Working-class Women,

Be Prepared!', attacking the war.[34] She told her readers that Germany was fighting the war for 'the interests of the reactionary Hapsburg dynasty, for the gold and power hunger of the unfeeling, conscienceless great landed property owners and big capital.'[35] The article concluded with a thinly-veiled call for revolution:

> For the working class, brotherhood between people is not a hollow dream, world peace not just a pretty word . . . What must be done? There is a single moment in the life of the people when they can win all if only everyone is set. Such a moment is here. Working-class women, be prepared.[36]

Again and again Zetkin came into conflict with the censorship in her opposition to the war. This was shown by the increasing number of blank spaces in **Gleichheit** columns which were demonstratively left empty.

Gleichheit became for a few months the internationally recognised journal of women opposing the war. Zetkin, together with Rosa Luxemburg, organised an International Women's Conference against the war in March 1915 in Berne. In August 1915, Zetkin was arrested, for the first of many times.

It would be wrong, however, to assume that many in the German Women's Movement supported the position taken by Luxemburg and Zetkin. In fact they were isolated in their opposition to the war.

> Both Rosa Luxemburg and Clara Zetkin suffered nervous prostration, and were at one moment near to suicide. Together they still tried, on 2 and 3 August [1914] to plan an agitation against war; they contacted twenty SPD members of the Reichstag with known radical views, but got the support of only [Karl] Liebknecht and Mehring . . . Rosa sent 300 telegrams to local officials who were thought to be oppositional, asking for their attitude to the vote and inviting them to Berlin for an urgent conference. The results were pitiful. 'Clara Zetkin was the only one who immediately and unreservedly cabled her support. The others — those who even bothered to send an answer — did so with stupid or lazy excuses.'[37]

So thin was the SPD's veneer of Marxism that the majority of the party leadership abandoned internationalism overnight and voted their support for the German war effort. The trade unions cut their bulk orders for **Gleichheit** and circulation dropped dramatically from the 125,000 of 1914 to 40,000 in December 1915.[38] Zetkin was forced out of the editorship.

The war brought the women of the SPD into collaboration with the bourgeois feminists. Bourgeois women moved into municipal administration, forming a national women's service and organising a women's auxiliary army for municipal officials. In her capacity as head of SPD women, Louise Zietz spoke before middle-class groups in Berlin to explain socialists' welfare efforts and raised the possibility of collaboration. Socialist feminists followed the SPD itself in suspending the class struggle during the war.

The actual decision to co-operate with bourgeois women was left to the local clubs, but the war had created new political options. The reaction to contact with middle-class women varied greatly, some groups working together with bourgeois women, some continuing to avoid collaboration. **Gleichheit**, now out of Zetkin's hands, wrote on 20 July 1917: '. . . in practical matters we can learn many things from bourgeois women.'[39] The unions had also launched in January 1916 the fortnightly **Gewerkschaftliche Frauenzeitung** (Women's Trade Union Paper), edited by Gertrud Hanna, which reached a distribution of 100,000 after only a year, and 350,000 by January 1919.[40]

After a year of enthusiastic SPD support for the war, Louise Zietz finally found the party position hard to swallow. She sided with Kautsky, Bernstein and the leaders of the future Independent Social Democratic Party, the USPD. In summer 1915 she was expelled from the executive of the SPD.

Gleichheit now got a new subtitle: 'Magazine for the Interests of Workers' Wives and Women Workers'. The new editors explained the programme as: 'Political education, simple teaching and valuable entertainment'. In 1922 the subtitle was to change again, this time to read: 'Magazine for women and girls of the working people, organ of the United SPD.'

Clara Zetkin, along with Rosa Luxemburg and a small minority of those who had been on the left of the SPD, never flinched in her opposition to the war. And as the horror and bloodshed grew year by year, so did general opposition to the war among the German working class, bringing Germany to the brink of revolution in 1918 and 1919.[41] Yet even after four years of war the number of women collecting around Rosa Luxemburg and Clara Zetkin — the one by far the greatest genius of the German socialist movement, the other the most prominent socialist women's movement leader — was tiny. In 1918, in the new German Communist Party, the party set up by Rosa Luxemburg, only 9 per cent of the members were women, as against 15 per cent in the USPD and 20.5 per cent in the SPD.[42] In absolute terms the Communist Party had fewer than 300 women members while the SPD in 1919 had 207,000.

The failure of Rosa Luxemburg, Clara Zetkin and their supporters to create a significant socialist organisation among women — as among men — was the consequence of both *objective* circumstances and *subjective* defects of the left in Germany. The objective circumstances were an expanding capitalism leading to the bureaucratisation of the labour movement and its transformation into a deeply reformist movement. The subjective failure of the revolutionary left was that it did not intervene in the day-to-day struggle, thus failing to build a bridge between the workers' struggle for reforms and its own revolutionary politics; did not, in other words, develop revolutionary practice, but limited itself to general propaganda. It had no organisation to speak of. One might ask what on earth Zetkin was doing being editor of **Gleichheit** in the years before the war when the reformists effectively took it over.

The revolutionary left was in fact a group of loosely-connected individuals. When Rosa Luxemburg's Spartakus League was established during the war, it had only weak links with workers in industry. Its main activity was not in the workplace, but on the streets and at public meetings. If revolutionaries found few ties with workers' struggles, this applied even more to women revolutionaries when women workers were by and large less well-placed than men in the most militant, key sections of industry.

The Sorry End of the SPD Women's Movement

During the war the number of working women rose from 9.5 million to about 15 million.[43] After the war the SPD murdered the German socialist revolution. Some solution to the dangers of mass unemployment following demobilisation from the armed forces was crucial if the capitalist economy and state was to be stabilised. The remedy was simple: sack the women. Employers were obliged by decrees of 18 March 1919 and 25 January 1920 to dismiss anybody who was not unconditionally dependent on wages, in the following order of priority:

1. Women whose husbands had a job.
2. Single women and girls.
3. Women and girls who had only 1–2 people to look after.
4. All other women and girls.[44]

Women leaders of the SPD justified these measures. Thus Gertrud Hanna, who was a member of the Women's Secretariat of the General Federation of German Trade Unions, said:

> What is the lesser evil, female or male unemployment? It is quite extraordinarily difficult to answer this question . . . I am in the uncomfortable position of being unable to offer any suggestions as to how the woman question can be solved at the present time . . . I have only one suggestion: women must work to gain more influence over who is employed and who is dismissed.[45]

The SPD women's organisation was forced to become a body

which undertook merely social work. In December 1919 the SPD founded the *Arbeiterwohlfahrt* (Workers' Welfare Bureau) as the main organisation of women's activities. The 1921 SPD conference justified this by declaring that 'women are born protectors of humanity, and, therefore, social work corresponds so well with their nature.'[46]

The women in the SPD got a paper that fitted its new politics. The title **Gleichheit** had too revolutionary an overtone. The new title was **Die Frauenwelt** (Women's World) with mainly edifying stories, dress patterns and fashion illustrations, cookery, recipes and very little politics. When at the Berlin women's conference in 1924 one delegate requested that the paper should deal a little with the real distress of women workers' lives, she was told by the male editor, Dr Lohmann:

> My own opinion on the matter, at any rate, and I know that I am supported here by the majority of women comrades in distress, who have emphasised the same to me in a whole series of letters, is that they do not want to have the misery of their domestic life before their eyes even in their leisure time. They want to be shown the sun which some day in the future will shine into their lives because of socialism.[47]

Extremist Right Takes Control of Bourgeois Feminist Movement

Meanwhile, what happened to bourgeois feminism?

The radical League for the Protection of Motherhood and Sexual Reforms got a thrashing in 1908 at the conference of the umbrella organistion of bourgeois women — the Federation of German Women's Organisations (*Bund Deutsche Frauenvereine* or BDF). The BDF united women's associations of various sorts: cultural, religious, charitable and recreational, as well as political pressure groups, female suffrage societies, and moral and social reform associations. It was a purely women's organisation, not a feminist one.

The right was on the march, speeded on by the affiliation to the BDF of societies such as the German-Colonial Women's League (*Deutsche-Kolonialer Frauenbund*), which was dedicated to the preservation of the purity of the white race in the German colonies through the export of white women from the mother country, founded in 1907 and numbering some 12,000 members by 1911; the German Association against the Misuse of Alcoholic Drinks, founded in 1883 and numbering 37,000 (mostly men) in 1911; and the most powerful conservative organisation, the German Evangelical Women's League.[48]

The membership of the BDF rose to some 250,000 by the outbreak of the First World War. The government began to find it convenient to consult the BDF to obtain 'the women's point of view' on questions in which it thought women had a special interest.

The person best representing the rightward shift was Gertrud Bäumer, who was to be president of the BDF for nine years — 1910–1919. She argued that the women's movement had to be national, in the sense of supporting an aggressively imperialist foreign policy, and it had to be social, in the sense of devoting itself to reducing social tension and class conflict through social reform and organised welfare work. The ultimate aim of female emancipation, according to Bäumer, 'is not formal equality, but the equally living, equally full and rich influence of all female values on our culture, a richer flow of specifically female forces into the total of the world's activities.' Translating the 'specifically female forces' into reality, Bäumer declared that if woman 'limits herself to house and family, she is under certain circumstances acting in this way more in accordance with the ideal of the women's movement than if she goes into any male profession.'[49]

Between 1911 and 1914 the BDF ran a campaign against the New Morality. It firmly supported the view that abortion should be a criminal offence punishable by imprisonment. The outlawing of abortion stimulated 'a sense of moral responsibility in sexual matters' which was 'the best way of raising the general level of morality in the country at large.'[50]

The right-wing trend in the women's movement was aggressively imperialist. Maria Lischnewska, a spokeswoman of this trend, argued that in order for Germany to win the struggle for world supremacy, 'we need people to defend our achievements against the vast hordes of our enemies . . . we need people to populate the colonies we have, and the colonies we still have to conquer . . .' It was also racist. While staunchly upholding the institutions of marriage and the family, one of its spokeswomen demanded that 'racially mixed marriages be made illegal'. 'Half-castes,' she declared, were 'mostly inferior'. The dangers of a 'bastard population' in the colonies must be avoided. Another demand that gained in popularity in these years was that 'drinkers be sterilised'. Concern about prostitution as a source of social disorder gave way to a more urgent preoccupation with prostitution as a danger to the strength and purity of the race. From this point of view state regulation was a disastrous policy, and the view that it should be eliminated as a major source for the spread of venereal disease gained ground.

As early as 31 July 1914 the BDF set up a National Women's Service in co-operation with the Ministry of the Interior to carry out welfare tasks on the home front during the war.[51] When the war ended and the Weimar Republic was founded, the BDF continued to assert its nationalist priority, stating that it united 'German women of every party and creed, in order to express their national identity.'

During the 1920s the leadership continued its rightward drift, with the parties most hostile to women's rights firmly in the saddle. The parties that had been most inclined to favour women's rights, the German Democratic Party, and to a far greater extent the SPD, the Independent Socialists and the German Communist Party, received little support from women at elections.[52] But the BDF grew into a mass organisation, claiming, in 1931, 1,500,000 members, and, even taking into account double counting, it must have had around 750,000.[53]

During the years of depression, 1929–33, the petty bourgeoisie deserted the bourgeois parties in millions to join the Nazis. This shift to the extreme right was followed by the BDF. Hitler repaid his debt. The BDF's official organ, **Die Frau**, still under Gertrud Bäumer's editorship, survived almost to the end of the Third Reich.[54]

6
Russian Marxists and women workers

The bourgeois and socialist women's movements in Russia, compared with those in Germany which battled with each other over a long period, were much smaller and had a much shorter life. But their conflicts were even sharper than in Germany.

The Gentry Feminists

Until the revolution of 1905 there was no women's movement to speak of in Russia, although there were groups of feminists. In the atmosphere created by Tsar Alexander II's abolition of serfdom in 1861 and other limited reforms, people began to dream of other liberties. Among those affected were women of the nobility, and in 1859 a group of women gentry formed the first feminist group in Russia. This published a magazine called **Razvet** ('A Journal of Science, Art and Literature for Adult Women'), devoted to a cautious struggle for higher education for women 'in accord with the spirit of Christian teachings'.[1] Such a call could hardly fire the mass of Russian women at a time when no more than five or six people in every hundred could even read and only one of those had any higher education.[2] Although literacy spread, to reach 21 per cent by the turn of the century, as late as 1909 only one girl in three hundred went to secondary school.[3]

In the same year that **Razvet** was founded, a philanthropic women's group by the name of 'The Society for Cheap Lodging and Other Aid to the Residents of St Petersburg' was formed. Its most ambitious project, begun in 1868, was a sizeable clothing workshop employing between 300 and 500 workers. This mainly fulfilled orders for uniforms for the Ministry for War.[4] The Society also organised communal kitchens and a school for working mothers.[5]

Other philanthropic causes gave rise to other societies, one 'for Helping Needy Women', another 'for Circulating Useful Books', another 'for Stimulating a Love for Work'.

From these small philanthropic beginnings came bigger developments. In 1893 the Russian Women's Mutual Philanthropic Society was founded,[6] which had about 2,000 members in 1900. It operated a sixty-room hostel for educated women, another for transients, a cafeteria, an employment service, and a child care centre for working women. It also organised talks on the 'physical, intellectual and moral upbringing of children', and special committees for aid to victims of floods and famine.[7]

In 1900 the Russian Society for the Protection of Women was founded to counter prostitution. Headed alternately by two princesses, Evgenii Oldenburgskaia and Elena Saksen-Altenburgskaia, it was well staffed with titled patricians and wealthy philanthropists such as Baron Ginsburg and Countess Panina.[8] Stites, the historian of Russian feminism, writes:

> Fearful pity and hopeful piety were the main ingredients in the feminists' attitude towards prostitutes, and their response was to care for the fallen women and to provide them with the spiritual strength to resist a return to the streets . . .
>
> Traditional 'charity' among Russian ladies was embellished by the conspicuous leadership of tsarinas, empress-dowagers and princesses. Activities usually were limited, refined, and impersonal.[9]

Bourgeois Feminists

1905, the year of revolution, awakened millions of women, working-class, bourgeois and petty bourgeois. Alexandra Kollontai wrote, looking back: 'In 1905 there was no corner in which in one way or another, the voice of a woman speaking about herself and demanding new rights was not heard.'[10] In Moscow and St Petersburg, Minsk, Yalta, Saratov, Vilna and Odessa, public women's rights meetings were held for the first time.[11]

Late in February 1905 a feminist political organisation was established, composed mainly of middle-class women and *intelligentki*. It was called the Women's Equal Rights Union. Leading members had close ties with the Teachers' Union and included a number of journalists. Their ranks were strengthened by two women members from the political circles that became the Kadet Party — Anna Miliukova and Ariadna Tyrkova.[12]

The Women's Equal Rights Union grew rapidly. On 7 May 1905

twenty-six branches from nineteen cities and towns sent seventy delegates to the three-day meeting of its First Organisational Congress in Moscow.[13] At this a number of working women put forward a resolution which emphasised the needs of industrial and peasant women, such as equal pay for equal work and welfare for mothers and children. But women of the bourgeoisie, who were the majority at the Congress, rejected this proposal. They then put forward a resolution which called only for the unity of women of all social strata in the struggle for a republican form of government and universal suffrage without distinction of sex, nationality or religion.[14] In addition the programme demanded national autonomy; equality of the sexes before the law; equal rights of peasant women in any land reforms; laws for the welfare, insurance and protection of women workers; equal opportunity for women; co-education at every level; the reform of laws relating to prostitution; and abolition of the death penalty. It was a classic programme of radical bougeois reform.

When the second congress of the Women's Equal Rights Union convened on 8 October 1905, at the height of the revolution, it went as far as to call for the boycott of the elections to the Duma, or parliament, following in the footsteps of the Bolsheviks, Mensheviks and Socialist Revolutionaries. At the congress members 'recognised that the goals of the socialist parties were closest to those of women.' Carrying a banner reading 'Universal Suffrage Without Distinction of Sex', Moscow Union members marched in the funeral demonstration for Nicholas Bauman, a Bolshevik murdered by the police. A Union member was wounded when police shot at the demonstrators. Though members did participate in other demonstrations and work on strike committees, much of their activity involved support work, such as establishing soup kitchens, first aid stations and services for the unemployed. During clashes with the racist gangs of the Black Hundreds, or the police and army, Union activists served as medical aides.[15]

The Women's Equal Rights Union's most militant phase coincided with the height of general revolutionary activity, from the October general strike to the Moscow uprising in December 1905. It was, however, a loose organisation, and a number of its branches disregarded the call for a boycott of the Duma, and followed the Kadets. At the third congress of the Union, on 21 May 1906, the boycott was lifted.[16] The Union's membership in 1906 reached 8,000.[17]

Another bourgeois feminist organisation founded in 1905 was the Women's Progressive Party, led by Dr Maria Ivanovna Pokrovskaia. She represented the most extreme feminist separatism. From 1904 to 1917 Pokrovskaia spent a good deal of her time and money on the journal **Zhenskii Vestnik** (Women's Herald), editing and publishing it almost single-handedly from her apartment. Far more than other feminist journals, it consistently devoted space to the situation of women factory workers, domestic servants, prostitutes and peasants, for, as it said:

> It is clear that women aspiring to equal rights cannot place their hopes in the bourgeoisie and the aristocrats. The working people have experienced and experience now the full weight of lack of rights — these are the ones we can count on now.[18]

Pokrovskaia paid detailed attention to women workers, calling not only for general factory reform but specifically for women factory inspectors, a ten-month fully paid pregnancy leave, nursing facilities in the factories, and equal wages for equal work. The Women's Progressive Party was one of those liberal Russian groups whose outlook was far more social reformist than their opposite numbers in Europe. It called for the 'elimination of the unfair distribution of wealth and the just payment of labour', and improved public health measures, but was against protective legislation for women workers. A call for 'the destruction of militarism', the replacement of armies by militias, and 'the unification of all the peoples of Russia in the name of general humanitarian ideas', rounded out the programme, save for one important item. All this was to be accomplished while coming to terms with the Romanoff monarchy — by reforming it and making it constitutional![19]

However, Pokrovskaia objected to working-class militancy, on both feminist and pacifist principles. She opposed strikes because of their consequences for women:

> We ask: who bears the chief burden of the strike? The wife and mother . . . Let the men stay at home with the hungry children during strikes, and let the women be free to leave the cries of hunger![20]

Pokrovskaia's party, unlike the Women's Equal Rights Union, excluded men. She opposed the socialists, 'since they, like other political parties, were led by men, this only perpetuating male control and female passivity'. She had no sympathy for the class struggle:

> Every woman aspiring to equality ought to be called a feminist — be she landowner or peasant, wife of the factory owner or working woman, privileged or not. For feminism there are no classes, legal castes, or educational levels. It is an idea which equalises all.[21]

She deplored revolutionary violence, and wrote at the time of the Moscow uprising of 1905: 'It is not through violence and slaughter that we can recreate life but only through peaceful reform.'

The Women's Progressive Party attracted no more than a handful of members from the middle or upper classes. Kollontai noted that the members' behaviour, dress and conversation at meetings alienated working-class women.[22]

During the 1905 revolution, the Russian Women's Mutual Philanthropic Society ran frantic campaigns petitioning important individuals and institutions. In 1905 alone, the Society made 398 requests to regional assemblies (*zemstvos*) and 108 requests to municipal government for support for women's rights, posted 6,000 appeals to different social and government agencies, and sent petitions to five governors-general, 80 governors and 46 marshals of the nobility asking for their endorsement of equal rights.[23]

Women in the Revolutionary Movement

The most reliable list of revolutionary activists available is of people arrested. For the 1860s this shows that of 2,000 people arrested, 65 were women, about 3 per cent.[24] In the 1870s the proportion of women was significantly higher: around 700 out of 5,664 revolutionaries arrested, over 12 per cent. Like the men, the women in the movement were almost all between twenty and thirty. To a much greater extent than the men, they came from the gentry — some two-thirds of those most deeply implicated in the years 1873–77, and at least four of these were daughters of generals. All but a handful had been given a good education, many in European and, after 1876, Russian universities.[25]

The proportion of women in the Socialist Revolutionary Party, which arose out of the Populist movement, was 14.3 per cent between 1901 and 1916.[26] Women were most heavily involved in carrying out terrorist missions, where being female offered considerable tactical advantages. They also paid a high price for their activities: of forty-three revolutionaries sentenced to life imprisonment with hard labour for terrorist activities between 1880 and 1890, twenty-one were women.[27]

Among the Marxists who became significant in the 1890s and beginning of this century the proportion of women was much smaller. Unfortunately information is scanty. At the Sixth Bolshevik Party Congress held in August 1917, out of 171 delegates ten were women, or roughly 6 per cent. The first comprehensive census of party members was not taken until 1922, when women constituted just under 8 per cent of the total membership of the Communist Party.[28] The Populist and terrorist movements, with their emphasis on heroic individual actions, attracted more women, largely from the intelligentsia. The Marxists' main activity was agitating and organising among industrial workers, where they found it difficult to organise women.

Women and the industrial struggle

Women did come into action with the entry of the working class into the arena of industrial struggle. The story of women workers' industrial struggle between the 1870s and 1905 is best told by Kollontai, a leading participant in the revolutionary movement:

> The movement of women workers is by its very nature an indivisible part of the general workers' movement . . . In all the risings and in all the factory riots which were so distasteful to tsarism she took an equal part, alongside the working man . . . Working women played an active role in the unrest at the Krengel'mskaya factory in 1874; women were involved in the 1878 strike at the Novaya Pryadil'na factory in St Petersburg, and in 1885 they led the textile workers in that famous strike in Orekhovo-Zeyevo, when the factory buildings were destroyed and the tsarist government was forced to hurry through, on 3 July, a law banning night work for women and young people.
>
> The 'April Rebellion' of 1895 at the Yaroslav factory was carried out with the help and under the influence of the women weavers. The women workers of St Petersburg did not desert their comrades during the sporadic economic strikes of 1894–96, and when the historic strike of textile workers broke out in the summer of 1896 the women workers joined the men in a unanimous walk-out.
>
> At a time of unrest and strike actions the proletarian woman, downtrodden, timid and without rights, suddenly grows and learns to stand tall and straight . . . participation in the workers' movement brings the woman worker towards her liberation, not only as the seller of her labour power but also as a woman, a wife, a mother and a housekeeper.

Kollontai does not glorify working-class women. She paints them warts and all. She notices their lack of perseverance and the weakness of the political socialist element among them:

> . . . as soon as the wave of strike activity died down and the workers returned to work whether in victory or in defeat, the women would be scattered and isolated once again.

The few women in the underground party organisations were from the intelligentsia. Working women could not be persuaded to attend either the illegal or the 'legal' meetings where Marxism and revolutionary socialism were 'presented under the guise of harmless lessons in geography and arithmetic. The working women were still avoiding life and struggle, believing that their destiny was the cooking pot, the washtub and the cradle . . .' However, she wrote,

> the picture changes swiftly once the red flag of revolution is hoisted high above Russia . . . In the revolutionary years of 1905 and 1906 the woman worker . . . was everywhere . . . to give full justice to the

self-sacrifice of the proletarian women and their loyalty to the ideals of socialism, we would have to describe the events of the revolution scene by scene.[29]

Both wings of the Social Democratic Party — the Bolsheviks and the Mensheviks — and the Socialist Revolutionaries did their best to attract women into the trade unions. The Bolshevik-dominated textile union of the Moscow district considered in 1906 that 'the only solution to the problems of improving the position of the working class in general, and of women in particular, is organisation of the proletariat.' Given that 'women, because of their economic and domestic situation, are much less capable of defending themselves against the bondage and exploitation of capital', it proposed that 'all measure be taken to attract women on an equal basis with men into unions and all other workers' organisations.'

> Strike demands throughout 1905–7 more often than not reflected women workers' needs. There is scarcely a strike document in industries employing women that does not mention, in some form, demands for paid maternity leave (usually four weeks before and six weeks after childbirth), for time off for feeding infants, and for construction of nurseries at the factory.[30]

Unlike Britain or Germany, the doors of the unions were wide open to women from the beginning in Russia. But the difficulties of organising women workers were extreme. First there was the low level of literacy and culture, much lower for women than men; then women's low wages — about half of men's in manufacturing industry in 1913[31] — also the double burden of being both workers and housewives. So women lacked confidence. One woman worker expressed the feelings of women workers towards participation in workers' groups:

> Well, I do want to express myself, but then I think it over — so many people, they will all be looking at me and what if someone laughs at what I say. I grow cold with these thoughts, I'm filled with terror. So — you will silently, but your heart is inflamed.[32]

The result was a very low level of trade union organisation of women in a country where trade unionism lagged anyway. Those industries which employed many women were particularly backward. Thus in 1907 only 1.2 per cent of the workers in the garment industry and 3.9 per cent of those in textiles were members of trade unions, as against 43 per cent of print workers and 8.6 per cent of engineers.[33] The proportion of women trade unionists was tiny. In the Moscow textile industry, for example, women made up only 4.4 per cent of trade union membership. In St Petersburg and the central industrial region the proportion was higher, but still very low.[34] In the Soviets

— or workers' councils — which arose in 1905 women were again very under-represented. While women were about two-fifths of the Petersburg working class, there were only six women among the 562 delegates.[35]

In the Wake of the 1905 Revolution

Only in 1905, when the government retreated before rising popular unrest, did the large-scale organisation of working women become possible. The Marxists found themselves in sharp competition with bourgeois feminists. Because of the greater difficulty of organising women and their consequent weakness compared with men, women were more profoundly influenced by bourgeois women's organisations than men workers were by the liberal party of the Kadets, whose influence on them was very small.

The bourgeois feminists made the effort to attract working women. To start with they were successful. In 1905 in St Petersburg they founded four women's political clubs aimed at working women, which functioned for nearly two months before being closed by the police.[36] Many working women, however, resisted recruitment by Social Democratic organisers. A group from the Andreev factory in Moscow requested that the local branch of the Women's Equal Rights Union send some feminist agitators, as the Social Democrats had proved 'too severe'.

Sometimes Social Democratic Party organisers worked with feminists. In one case a male Social Democrat who organised women workers used feminist literature and received Women's Equal Rights Union help and advice. Women workers went to feminist meetings and invited speakers from the Women's Equal Rights Union to their factories.[37]

But though groups organised by the bourgeois feminists rose quickly they also disintegrated rapidly. One reason was the abyss between the bourgeois and petty bourgeois ladies on the one hand and the working women on the other. The case of servants is a good illustration. The Women's Equal Rights Union helped to establish a servants' union in Moscow and some other towns. S K Ispolateva, a member of the Union's central bureau, reported that her cook, also a Union member, organised servants' meetings, usually in her kitchen. Ispolateva led these meetings. When the meetings grew too large, they were moved to the staircase of the servants' entrance. They were always confined to the servants' quarters.[38]

Kollontai commented: 'They tried to construct an idyllic, mixed union of grand-lady employers and domestic servants . . . They strove to organise domestic servants under the vigilant eyes of their mistresses.'[39]

In Kharkov the local branch of the Women's Equal Rights Union organised a special committee to study the situation of domestic servants. In response the Social Democrats called servants' meetings to point out 'the unacceptability of a project worked out with the close participation and leadership of their employers.' At these meetings the servants developed their own proposals, including a minimum wage, a standard working day and a day off. The majority of servants welcomed this project; the majority of feminists were, according to Kollontai, 'disappointed'. They came to the conclusion that their efforts to organise working women had failed, and they changed tack. Members of the Women's Equal Rights Union decided to limit their activities among working women to general propaganda, such as Sunday schools, workers' courses at individual factories, work at cafeterias and soup kitchens, and gathering signatures for petitions.[40]

Social Democratic women intervened in meetings for working women that had been organised by the Women's Equal Rights Union, but their attitude to the Union varied. The Socialist Revolutionary and Menshevik women believed in the need to create a broadly-based alliance including socialists and liberal women.[41] The Bolsheviks opposed this.

Kollontai, who had joined the Marxists in 1896, did not undertake organisational work among women till the winter of 1905. Then, although she had not yet joined the Bolsheviks, she was one of the most vociferous opponents of any alliance.[42] She argued for the maintenance of 'strict class lines', the organisation of working-class women within the trade unions and the Social Democratic movement,[43] and total opposition to the feminists. She always referred to the word 'feminist' in a derogatory way. She defined it thus: 'Feminism — the struggle of bourgeois women to unite, to rely on one another and thus to rebuff the common enemy — men.'[44]

During 1905 she attended many feminist meetings in order to denounce their leaders and call on women workers to separate themselves from them. She did not have a smooth passage. Cries of 'Hooliganism!' 'You play into the hands of the Black Hundreds!' 'Strangling is too good for you!' were not uncommon.[45]

Bolshevik and Menshevik women tried, despite opposition from some leading socialists, such as Vera Zasulich, to establish clubs for working women. Kollontai's first attempt, sanctioned by the party's Petersburg committee, proved disastrous. Though the party had promised to provide a meeting place, when Kollontai and several workers arrived, they found a sign on the door reading, 'The meeting *for women only* has been cancelled. Tomorrow there will be a meeting *for men only*'.[46]

The results of establishing working-class women's clubs were very small indeed. The first socialist-sponsored club for women workers, called the Working Women's Mutual Aid Society, opened in St Petersburg in the autumn of 1907. It was legal and its organisers included Kollontai and a group of women workers. Its activities included lectures and a library. It was open every night and had between 200 and 300 members (of whom about two-thirds were women and one-third men). It was deliberately not identified with any faction: both Bolsheviks and Mensheviks attended its functions. In the spring of 1908 a faction fight divided the club, one vociferous group wanting to exclude all *intelligentki*. Kollontai, as one of the *intelligentki*, dropped out.

While all the working women's clubs in St Petersburg had dissolved by the end of 1908, fifteen workers' clubs which included men and women in their membership survived. They had some 6,000 members in all, of whom around one-fifth were women. These women were overwhelmingly young (about two-thirds below the age of 25) and literate — in the two clubs for which there is information, one had a literacy rate for women of 96.6 per cent, the other 99.5 per cent.[47]

The First All-Russian Women's Congress

As the revolutionary tide ebbed, so did the activity of the women's movement. A final attempt to revitalise it was the First All-Russian Women's Congress held over a week in December 1908. A survey of the congress illuminates the relationship of socialist women with bourgeois feminists.

Members of the Women's Mutual Philanthropic Society and the Women's Equal Rights Union joined forces to plan the congress over nearly a year, hoping that a new unified women's organisation would result. Anna Filosofova, one of the veteran founders of feminism in Russia, now in her seventies, especially wanted to cap her years of feminist activity by the creation of a National Council of Russian Women. She asked members of the congress: 'How can we gain political and social rights and influence, if we ourselves cannot unite and mobilise women's power?'[48] The congress slogan was: 'The women's movement must be neither bourgeois nor proletarian, but one movement for all women.'

In the autumn the textile workers set up an organising committee, contacted other unions, and finally won the full endorsement of the St Petersburg Central Bureau of the Trade Unions. The organising committee consisted of members of the sales clerks, typographers, seamstresses, bookkeepers, clerks and confectioners' unions, in addition to the textile workers. Later delegates from workers' clubs also joined.[49] This continued interest of workers in the congress influenced the Bolsheviks, who were opposed to it, and they decided to participate. One male Bolshevik who attended the congress wrote later of the pre-congress illusions:

> Every woman worker wanted to lay out her stored-up sorrows before this Congress, 'before the entire proletariat'. Though we said many times that this Congress 'would give us nothing', that 'we are going only for agitation', all the same we could see the illusions on the delegates' faces.

To expose these 'illusions' the Bolsheviks still wanted to keep participation to a minimum. At first they urged the workers simply to 'go to the Congress, show your banner, and march home!' But when this too did not dampen the enthusiasm, the Bolsheviks conceded that their delegates should take part but only to articulate the social democratic position. If their demands were refused, they proposed a walk-out.

More than fifty organisational meetings were held before the congress, attendance ranging from three to 150, the total number of working women participating being between 500 and 650, according to Kollontai. As a result of these efforts, a broad-based Workers' Group was set up to represent the working-class women at the congress. Kollontai differentiated three basic positions within the group: the Bolsheviks, who wanted to cut co-operation with the feminists to a minimum and to leave the congress as soon as possible; the Mensheviks, who took an opposite position, arguing against alienating the democratic elements of the congress and for creating a general democratic alliance; and Kollontai herself, who insisted on clarifying the contradictions between the feminists and socialists on all basic points concerning women's issues.[50]

The Bolshevik-controlled Petersburg Committee of the Social Democratic Party sent two leading Bolshevik women as delegates for the Workers' group, V Slutskaia, formerly a vigorous opponent of participation, and P F Kudelli; and a man, 'comrade Sergei', of whom we know nothing more, as its leader. When the congress convened on 10 December in St Petersburg City Hall the working-class women proved to be a tiny minority — 45 out of 1,053 delegates.[51]

There were three groups at the congress. On the stage, behind a long table, 'comfortably seated in two rows of chairs', sat the members of the organising committee, 'typical Petersburg "lady-patronnesses"', ' "cream" of the Petersburg and provincial aristocracy and bourgeoisie, the wives of ministers, high officials, factory owners, merchants, well-known lady-philanthropists.'[52] On the other side of the hall, sharply contrasting with the women on the platform, was a group of women workers, small in number as the congress was held in working hours. They included a sizeable proportion of Bolsheviks. By far the largest group consisted of members of the intelligentsia.

This impression is confirmed by the statistics available of those who took part, although this covers only 243 of the 1,053 officially represented and excludes most of the workers, who had left the congress before the questionnaire was distributed. A majority of those responding (60 per cent) were between the ages of thirty and fifty; 27 per cent were younger and 13 per cent older; 59 per cent were married, 28 per cent unmarried, 12 per cent widows, and only 1 per cent in 'free marriages'. More than half (54 per cent) had finished secondary school; 30 per cent had a higher education; 16 per cent had the equivalent of a grammar school education. Over half had their own careers; but a sizeable minority (42 per cent) either did not indicate their own work, or more likely, were not engaged in paid work. Of women who did have their own careers, those in the 'free professions' (doctors, teachers, writers, artists) predominated (75 per cent). Of the remainder, 14 per cent were employed in public or private institutions; 11 per cent were either students or workers. Of those who were married, the majority had spouses who were professionals.

Again and again class conflicts erupted. A leading member of the Women's Equal Rights Union, Z S I Mirevich, called for unity: 'In unity there is strength. Unity is possible only on the basis of complete lack of party affiliation'. The Bolshevik Anna Gurevich retorted:

> Women of different groups and classes of the population need different rights and must fight in different ways and their organisations must be different. Women workers must fight for all the needs of the working class.[53]

One member of the Workers' Group stated: 'Working women are fighting for their *full rights* . . .'[54] Bourgeois women were content merely to throw off the legal shackles which disabled them, while continuing to exploit the working class (particularly their maids). Marxists sought to destroy the 'single master of contemporary life — capital'.[55] Kollontai delivered her talk, 'The Woman Worker in Contemporary Society', on 15 December:

> The woman question, say the feminists, is a question of 'rights and justice'. The woman question, answer the proletarian women, is a question of a 'piece of bread'. The awakening of woman, the development of her special needs and demands, will come only as she joins the army of the independent labouring population.[56]
>
> There is no independent woman question; the woman question arose as an integrated component of the social problem of our time. The liberation of woman as a member of society, a worker, an individual, a

wife, and a mother, is possible therefore only together with the solution of the general social question, with the fundamental transformation of the present social order.[57]

One feminist underlined the differences between her wing of the congress and the Workers' Group with some honesty:

> The two principal modes of human activity are individual and collective. People like feminists, possessing greater scope, time, and the means to express themselves in individual action, do so, hoping to leave their personal stamp upon the activity they have engaged in. This, at bottom, was the underlying impulse of feminism.[58]
>
> The socialists, she said, put their emphasis on collective action.

Another feminist leader, Olga Shapir, stated: 'As regards unity . . . I regard it as impossible in a class society. I regard the constant appeals of the workers' party for disunity as useful in forcing us to renounce a vain hope.' She therefore suggested that the movement should concentrate on the inner emancipation of women through the 'raising of consciousness' (a phrase used frequently by feminists at that time) to free them from the shackles of a slave mentality.[59]

On the last day of the congress the Bolsheviks among the Workers' Group staged a demonstrative exit, making it clear that no co-operation could be maintained between the workers and the capitalists, but the Mensheviks stayed on.[60]

After the congress, its organisational committee arranged a banquet in a luxurious restaurant. A Bolshevik woman interrupted the proceedings with a loud question: 'Why aren't there working women, peasant women, and maids at this table?'[61]

A report of the congress in the Menshevik press criticised the Workers' Group's heavy emphasis on economic questions and insistence on 'demarcation' of class boundaries. Sympathetic openings to the working women, privately expressed, were not developed largely because of the extremism of the Workers' Group, said the report. Thus the workers made it hard, if not impossible, for a genuine coalition of left and liberal elements to develop. They 'broke the vital threads' of common, if temporary, political interests linking them with the democratic women, and created the impression of being against the entire women's movement. They made it seem as if socialism was the only way to cure social ills.

Kollontai's report in the same paper maintained that the congress had decisively shown 'that class antagonism, that opposition of socio-economic interests divides the world of women as it does that of men into two hostile camps . . .' It had, she claimed, decisively convinced women workers of the futility of unity with women of other classes.[62]

Reaction and the Revival

1907–12 were years of harsh reaction. When the working-class as a whole suffered a series of terrible defeats, women workers were pushed back even further. With the upward movement of the class thereafter women workers became active again and large-scale, militant and well-organised women's strikes took place. In the years 1905–20, wrote the historian Anne Bobroff,

> . . . strikers began to develop organisational skills, a determination not to return to work until genuine gains were won, and a willingness of women and men to support each other. It was not uncommon for a women's section of a plant to strike, and then to gain the support of other workers, including men, who would walk out in sympathy. For example, in October 1910, the administration at the Teikov textile factory increased the workload among the women in the water frame workshop. Even under the former conditions this work had been 'most difficult', resulting in two deaths from overwork. In addition, 'the extremely unceremonious treatment of them by the administration stirred up discontent among the women'. The women struck and were subsequently joined by the weavers, spinners and ultimately all 5,000 workers in the factory.

In the summer of 1913 2,000 workers in Palia textile factory, mostly women, went on strike for 47 days, demanding wage increases, paid pregnancy leave, use of the factory owner's bath house and laundry facilities. In late 1913, 5,500 workers, the majority women, struck at the Riga rubber factory. 'And disturbances at the Khludovsky textile factory were renewed following settlement of a walkout by 5,000 employees when three women were dismissed on suspicion of having incited the workers to strike.' Another strike of 3,000 took place in a Moscow pastry and perfume factory, where two-thirds of the workers were women.[63]

> Perhaps the most interesting development in the female strike movement during the 1910–14 period was the growth of consciousness among working women of their own needs as women. They would no longer accept rudeness and sexual exploitation by foremen and employers. And they also set forth strike demands relating to their particular needs.
>
> Strikes frequently began when women refused to tolerate the sexual abuse which was endemic. At the Grisov factory in Moscow in 1913 a strike began because 'The attitude of the factory administration is revolting. There is no other word for it than prostitution.' Among the demands was one for polite treatment of working women in particular, with prohibition of swearing. The immediate cause of the 1911 strike of 5,000 workers at the Khludovsky factory in Yartsev was the 'indelicate treatment' of women workers by one of the foremen, whose offences

> were even documented by the factory inspector. The strike demands included the dismissal of this foreman.
>
> At a plywood factory in Riga women worked with glue prepared from blood, curds, cement and lime. The glue stank terribly and ate away at their hands. But a second cause for discontent was that several foremen were 'not ashamed to curse in the most obscene words even to women'.

Demands were made at various factories which related to the problems of pregnant women and mothers: for pregnancy leave, against the firing of pregnant women, for half-pay during confinement leave, for relief from carrying heavy weights during pregnancy, for two one-hour breaks per day for nursing mothers, and an end to a policy of not hiring married women.[64]

International Women's Day

The first time International Women's Day was held in Russia was in 1913. It was held six days early, on 2 March (17 February by the old calendar then in use) for fear of police interference. The Bolshevik newspaper **Pravda** commemorated the day with a special six-page issue, and a holiday committee was set up by the Bolshevik-controlled Petersburg Committee of the Social Democratic Party, consisting of a group of women textile workers and Bolshevik activists. Celebrations took place in five cities: St Petersburg, Moscow, Kiev, Samara and Tblisi. The largest was in St Petersburg. Over a thousand people — out of a larger number who failed to get in — crowded into the hall, which was heavily policed both outside and inside, the police occupying the first two rows. One of the main speakers, a textile worker, Ianchevskaia, summed up the meaning of the assembly thus: 'The women workers' movement is a tributary flowing into the great river of the proletarian movement and giving it strength.'[65]

These words and the general spirit of International Women's Day grated on the nerves of the bourgeois feminist Dr Pokrovskaia. She wrote:

> As we expected, the women workers' day did not protest at all against the subordinate position of wives in relation to their husbands. They spoke primarily of the enslavement of the proletarian women by capital, and only in passing mentioned domestic subservience . . . Mme Kudelli was wrong in asserting that economic interests are the most important for the woman worker. Personal freedom stands higher.[66]

Her conclusion was: all men benefitted from male privilege; all women must join together to fight it.

In 1914 the government refused a request for ten meetings in the larger workers' quarters of St Petersburg to celebrate International

Women's Day on 8 March, allowing only one, and this was heavily policed. Three of the five planned speakers were arrested and the police refused to allow substitutes. Disappointed and angry, many of the large numbers present spilled out into the streets, singing revolutionary songs, only to be eventually dispersed by the police, who made mass arrests.

In both 1913 and 1914 there were deep differences between the Mensheviks, who wanted only women to participate in the celebrations, and the Bolsheviks, who insisted that International Women's Day should be celebrated not only by working women but by the entire working class.[67]

During the war it was far more difficult to celebrate International Women's Day. But despite a government ban the day was commemorated in 1915 and 1916 by small meetings and celebrations.

Rabotnitsa

Early in January 1913 the Bolshevik daily **Pravda** began publishing a special section entitled 'Labour and the Life of the Working Woman' which gave information about all the meetings and rallies to be held in preparation for International Women's Day and all the resolutions passed.[68] It also contained a correspondence page which by the winter of 1913 was receiving more correspondence from working women than it could handle. At Lenin's suggestion, therefore, the foreign bureau of the central committee of the Bolshevik Party decided to publish a separate journal aimed specifically at working-class women. It was called **Rabotnitsa** (The Working Woman).

Writing from abroad to his elder sister, Anna Ulianova-Elizarova, Lenin suggested that she organise the publication of the journal and select the editorial board. Her selections, which were confirmed by the central committee, were divided into two groups, one residing in Russia and one in exile abroad. The first group included P F Kudelli, K N Samoilova, L Menshinskaia and Anna Ulianova-Elizarova herself. The second, in exile, was Inessa Armand, Nadezhda Krupskaia, Lilina Zonivieva and Liudmila Stal, all scattered in various places of exile. The resident editors were to be responsible for the publication of the journal and any organisation connected with it.

To finance the first issue, the Russian members of the editorial board took on sewing jobs. A number of women responded with enthusiasm to **Pravda**'s appeal for funds for **Rabotnitsa**. A typical note, signed by a group of thirty working women, said:

> . . . warm greetings to our journal **Rabotnitsa**. We are sure that it will be a true mouthpiece of our needs and interests and we promise you our

> constant moral and material encouragement. We are contributing 2 roubles and 74 kopeks to the journal fund.

Krupskaia suggested an outline of contents, including current politics, general political and economic struggles of the workers' movement highlighting the participation of women, the protection of women's conditions in their workplaces, the struggles of working women abroad, and the family and the working woman.[69]

A few days before the first issue was due, all the members of the Russian editorial board except Anna Ulianova-Elizarova were arrested, and the majority of the articles for the issue confiscated by the police. Anna Ulianova-Elizarova persevered, finally succeeding in finding a printer. 12,000 copies did appear as planned on International Women's Day.[70] The lead article, written by Krupskaia, sharply differentiated between Bolshevism and bourgeois feminism. On the 'so-called "woman" question' she wrote:

> Bourgeois women advocate their *special* 'women's rights', they always oppose themselves to men and demand their rights from men. For them contemporary society is divided into two main categories, men and women. Men possess everything, hold all rights. The question is one of achieving equal rights.
>
> For the working woman the woman question becomes quite different. The politically conscious women see that contemporary society is divided into classes . . . That which unites the working woman with the working man is much stronger than that which divides them. They are united by their common lack of rights, their common need, their common conditions which are the exploitation of their labour, their common struggle and their common goals. 'All for one, and one for all'. This 'all' means members of the working class — men and women alike.
>
> The 'woman question' for working men and women — this question is about how to involve the backward masses of working women in organisation, how better to make clear to them their interests, how to make them comrades in the common struggle quickly. The solidarity between working men and women, the common cause, the common goal, and the common path to those goals. Such is the solution for the 'woman question' among workers . . . our journal strives to help working women become conscious and organised.[71]

Rabotnitsa dealt with a wide range of women's concerns: maternity insurance, female labour, child-care centres, hygiene information, the problems of working women and the family, children's stories, Women's Day, electoral rights for women. Seven issues were published between 23 February and 26 June 1914, when it ceased publication because of impossible obstacles imposed by the outbreak of war. Of the seven issues, two were confiscated by police.

Against Separatism

Anne Bobroff, a historian critical of Bolshevism, complains that Lenin always insisted on the party leadership controlling women's activities. She writes:

> The Bolshevik women who ran **Rabotnitsa** worked in close association with Lenin. And although the two editorial boards were both made up completely of women, the editor of **Sotsial demokrat** — Lenin — had the deciding vote in the event of a tie.

In addition, she says, equal voting rights for the Russian and foreign editorial boards was a device 'to guarantee majority control over editorial policy to Lenin and those women who were in closest contact with him.'

A blatant example occurred at the international women's congress in Berne in March 1915.

> Lenin sat drinking tea in a nearby restaurant while the women's congress was in session . . . The 'Bolshevik women, working under Lenin's direction, introduced a resolution which . . . called for an immediate organisational break with the majorities in the existing Socialist and Labour parties and for the formation of a new International'. Despite the overwhelming opposition of all the other delegates, the Bolshevik representatives refused to withdraw their motion. Because a show of international unity among socialists was desperately desired at that point, Clara Zetkin finally negotiated with the Russian women and Lenin in a separate room. 'Here Lenin finally agreed to a compromise.'[72]

This gives us 'further insight into the Bolsheviks' resistance to organising working women into all-female groups.'[73]

Sadly Anne Bobroff, like many non-Marxists, does not understand the reasons behind the role of the revolutionary socialist party and 'democratic centralism' as put forward by Lenin. In Marx's words, the working class is 'the subject of history'. In the struggle for its own emancipation, therefore, it must fight for the emancipation of *all* humanity, of all who are oppressed. For this reason, there can be no concessions to prevailing bourgeois ideas which divide workers on grounds of race, nation or sex — and this particularly applies to the party, whose role is to lead the working class in its struggle for power.

'Democratic centralism' is the principle on which the party operates, and does not mean the dictatorship of the central leadership, as Bobroff implies. When the central leadership is functioning properly it is not acting on its own, but rather it is carrying out decisions arrived at through the widest possible understanding of the working-class struggle. Thus democracy in the party is essential so that the party can put forward policies which meet the needs of the working class. But centralism too is essential. For the working class is continually divided by bourgeois prejudices, and the experience and understanding of the class struggle varies enormously from one group of workers to another. The party must overcome this unevenness and these divisions if the working class is to be united sufficiently to win the struggle for socialism. Centralism is also essential because this struggle is against a highly centralised enemy, the capitalist state.

Once the central leadership of the party has been democratically elected, all sectional organisations of the party need to be subordinated to it — in order to ensure that their activities mirror the needs of the working-class struggle as a whole and not the *divisions* of the bourgeois society in which we live. It was because Lenin took political work amongst women particularly seriously that he intervened in it in depth.

Towards October

The war deepened the abyss between socialist women and bourgeois feminists in Russia. The bourgeois feminists jumped on the patriotic bandwagon. Dr Pokrovskaia proclaimed:

> In such a great patriotic moment . . . we must reduce to the minimum our needs, abandon luxury, and sacrifice all on the altar of society . . . This is important . . . for the success of that equality which progressive women all over the world hope to achieve.[74]

The Mutual Philanthropic Society was no less enthusiastic in supporting the war effort, through voluntary organisations covering every home front activity. The Women's Equal Rights Union, in August 1915, called for a 'women's mobilisation' of the 'daughters of Russia' along the lines of that attempted by Christabel Pankhurst in England — a campaign to draw all Russian women into some kind of war work. 'This is our obligation to the fatherland, and this will give us the right to participate as the equals of men in the new life of a victorious Russia.'[75]

For Russian working women, however, the war meant added burdens on their already heavily laden backs. At the same time changes in employment during the war increased their economic strength. The number of women in employment swelled enormously. Mass conscription lowered the number of men working in inspected industries by 12.6 per cent between 1914 and 1917; for the same period the number of women rose by 18.8 per cent. Women made up a third of the labour force at the start of the war and about half by 1917.[76]

The war at first led to total disarray in the labour movement. The first nine months were very quiet on the industrial front — and it was women who triggered a change, beginning with bread riots. In

Petrograd on 6 April 1915, when the sale of meat was suspended for one day, women smashed and looted a large meat market; the scene was repeated in Moscow two days later over a shortage of bread. During the disturbances the commandant of the city was badly cut by flying cobblestones. Later in the summer this happened again in the turbulent Khitrova Market. Similar events occurred in the following year.

Women participated in a large number of strikes. A strike in Ivanovo-Voznesensk in June 1915 began as a 'flour strike'; a month later it erupted again as a political demonstration to end the war and free jailed workers; thirty people were killed. A simultaneous strike in Kostroma was met by armed repression and followed by a mass funeral; it erupted again, and this time the working women addressed a circular to the soldiers asking them for protection instead of bullets.[77]

News of the clashes led to major political strikes in August and September. In August 27,000 workers went on strike in Petrograd demanding the withdrawal of Cossack guards from the factories, the release of five exiled Bolshevik deputies to the Duma, and freedom of the press, among other things. Early in September 64,000 workers came out in Petrograd with political demands. Altogether in 1915 there were 928 strikes, of which 715 were economic, involving 383,587 workers, and 213 were political involving 155,941 workers.

The struggle continued in 1916. The commemoration of Bloody Sunday on 9 January 1916 brought 53,000 workers out (85 per cent of them in Petrograd). Throughout 1916, and especially in the second half of the year, not only were more and more workers involved in strikes, but these became more and more political in nature. Altogether in 1916, 280,943 workers were involved in political strikes, and 221,136 in economic strikes.

In January 1917 a police report noted that

> the mothers of families, exhausted from endless standing in line at the stores, tormented by the look of their half-starving and sick children, are very likely closer now to revolution than Messrs Miliukov, Rodichev and Company, and of course, they are more dangerous because they represent that store of inflammable material for which one spark will set off a fire.[78]

It was the women workers of Petrograd who started the revolution of 1917. On 22 February (7 March) a group of women workers met to discuss the organisation of International Women's Day the following day. V Kaiurov, the worker-leader of the St Petersburg district committee of the Bolshevik Party, advised them to refrain from hasty action:

> But to my surprise and indignation, on 23 February, at an emergency

conference of five persons in the corridor of the Erikson works, we learned from comrade Nikifer Ilyin of the strike in some textile factories and of the arrival of a number of delegates from the women workers, who announced that they were supporting the metal workers. I was extremely indignant about the behaviour of the strikers, both because they had blatantly ignored the decision of the District Committee of the party, and also because they had gone on strike after I had appealed to them only the night before to keep cool and disciplined. With reluctance the Bolsheviks agreed to [spreading the strike] and they were followed by other workers — Mensheviks and Social Revolutionaries. But once there is a mass strike one must call everybody into the streets and take the lead.[79]

Not until 25 February did the Bolsheviks come out with their first leaflet calling for a general strike — *after* 200,000 workers had already downed tools!

The massive wave of strikes and demonstrations was the culmination of years of accumulated anger. As one witness later recounted:

The working women, driven to desperation by starvation and war, came along like a hurricane that destroys everything in its path with the violence of an elemental force. This revolutionary march of working women, full of the hatred of centuries of oppression, was the spark that set light to the great flame of the February revolution, that revolution which was to shatter Tsarism.[80]

It was the women workers in the textile industry who elected delegates and sent them round to neighbouring factories with appeals for support. Thus was the revolution detonated. It was, as Trotsky said,

. . . a revolution begun from below, overcoming the resistance of its own revolutionary organisation, the initiative being taken of their own accord by the most oppressed and downtrodden part of the working class — the women textile workers.[81]

It was these same women who fraternised with the soldiers, persuading them to disobey the orders of the officers, and to hold fire:

They go up to the cordons more boldly than men, take hold of the rifles, beseech, almost command: 'Put down your bayonets — join us'. The soldiers are excited, ashamed, exchange anxious glances, waver; someone makes up his mind first, and the bayonets rise guiltily above the shoulders of the advancing crowd. The barrier is opened, a joyous and grateful 'Hurrah!' shakes the air. The soldiers are surrounded. Everywhere arguments, reproaches, appeals — the revolution makes another forward step.[82]

The newly resurrected **Pravda** acknowledged the revolution's debt to women in an editorial:

Hail the women!
Hail the International!
The women were the first to come out on the streets of Petrograd on their Women's Day.
The women in Moscow in many cases determined the need of the military; they went to the barracks, and convinced the soldiers to come over to the side of the Revolution.
Hail the women![83]

But the Burden of Centuries cannot be removed easily

But even the revolution could not shift the deep prejudices implanted over generations in the minds of both men and women workers. As Marx said: 'The tradition of all the dead generations weighs like a nightmare on the brain of the living.'

Take the question of equal pay. During the 1905 revolution, the demands for minimum wages were in most cases explicit in requesting lower rates for women than for men.[84] The same assumption underlay agreements after the February 1917 revolution. The first minimum wage agreement concluded between a society of factory owners and the Soviet of Workers' and Soldiers' Deputies established two minimum wages — one for men, who were to receive five roubles a day, and another for women, who were to receive four.[85] For Nevsky shoe factories the minima concluded were five roubles and three; for the giant Skorokhed shoe factory in Petrograd (13 March) five and three roubles and fifty kopeks; for unskilled Ekaterinoslav workers (14 June) three and two.[86]

The Bolsheviks fought against unequal wages. Kollontai had joined the Bolsheviks in 1915. In an article entitled 'A Serious Gap' which appeared in **Pravda** on 5 May 1917, she criticised the agenda of the coming trade union congress:

> There is a serious gap in the agenda of the conference. The question of equal pay for equal work, which is one of the most burning questions for the working class as a whole and for working women in particular, is not down for discussion. The low pay women receive is now even more impermissible since the war has thrown a large number of women on the labour market who are their family's sole 'breadwinner'.[87]

After the October 1917 revolution equal pay was established by law.

Another aspect of unevenness was, as in 1905, the extreme under-representation of women in the Soviets. Again and again in the most democratic elections in history, women workers voted for men to represent them. In the Moscow Province, where women made up half the working population, of 4,743 delegates to the Soviets on 26–7 March 1917, there were only 259 women. In Grozny, four out of 170 delegates were women; in Nizhnigorod, three out of 135; in Odessa, about 40 out of 900, in Iaroslav, five out of 87.[88]

The women who were in the vanguard of the revolution in February 1917 afterwards moved into the background of the historical arena. Hence in Trotsky's **History of the Russian Revolution**, women workers appear only in the first couple of chapters.

One of Lenin's first acts upon returning to Petrograd in April 1917 was to demand central committee support for political work among women:

> Unless women are drawn into taking an independent part, not only in political life generally, but also in daily service obligatory to everyone, it is idle to speak not only of socialism, but even of complete and stable democracy.[89]

The Executive Committee of the Petrograd Committee of the Bolsheviks made a special effort to organise women. On 10 March Vera Slutskaia was put in charge of agitation among working-class women. Her recommendations, submitted three days later, were the creation of a women's bureau as part of the Petrograd committee, and the revival of **Rabotnitsa**. Each district committee of the Petrograd committee was to select a woman representative to the bureau, whose immediate tasks were to take steps towards republishing **Rabotnitsa**, and issue leaflets 'directed specifically to the woman proletarian question'.

Slutskaia specified that 'no independent women's organisations whatsoever will be created'. The working women in general would be organised in the working-class political and trade union institutions. The bureau was to conduct only agitational work in full agreement with the decisions of the Petrograd committee. Agitation bureaux were accordingly established throughout all party districts. Clubs were also founded with the aim of drawing non-party working women into party activity.

On 10 May **Rabotnitsa** was started as a weekly with a circulation of between forty and fifty thousand. Its editors were Krupskaia, Elizarova, Kollontai, Samoilova, Nikolaeva, Kudelli and Velichkina. It dealt with such questions as the war, the eight-hour working day, the election to the district Dumas, child labour, the women's movement in Russia and abroad.[90]

When the Bolsheviks came to power in October 1917 the question of the involvement of the mass of non-party women took on new dimensions. Now the question was how to mobilise millions of women to participate in building socialism. Where they succeeded and where they failed will be examined in a later chapter.

In Conclusion

The story of the women's movement in Russia demonstrates clearly how the sharpening class struggle polarises women into two antagonistic women's movements: working-class and bourgeois. The greater the polarisation of women, the stronger the bonds between working-class women and men. This conclusion was central for the Bolsheviks, who were intransigent in their opposition to the bourgeois feminists. Against this, the Mensheviks, who advocated a political alliance with the liberals, were also for conciliation between working-class women and bourgeois feminists.

The Bolsheviks understood the difficulty of organising working-class women, who are held back as victims of a double oppression as wage slaves and household slaves. The conclusions they drew from this were fundamentally different from those of the feminist separatists. The Bolsheviks argued that women *and* men workers face the same bosses, the same capitalist state. It is in the workplace that women can overcome their passivity and their isolation from each other (which is imposed largely by the family structure of society), gaining confidence in their capacity to act collectively. As workers too, the needs of men and women are identical. Because of these things any separatism between men and women workers will damage both, and will damage women more than men.

Likewise, because the role of the party is to lead the struggle of the working class, the structure of the party — including any of its organisations relating to women — must fit the constituencies of the workers' struggle, not the political constituencies of bourgeois society. This again means focussing on the workplaces, where the interests of women and men stand together.

Conclusive proof of the correctness of the Bolshevik stand on the woman question was the revolution itself. It was women workers, who, together with men, inaugurated the 'festival of the oppressed' — and it was the October revolution that opened up the grandest chapter of women's liberation.

7
Women's movements in England

The sharp demarcation between women workers and bourgeois feminists that occurred in Germany and Russia was absent in England. There are a number of reasons.

First, in both Germany and Russia it was the socialist party which founded the trade unions, while in Britain the unions founded the Labour Party. These unions, except in the cotton industry, were for a long time closed to women.

Secondly, the political movement of the working class in England was extremely confused and conservative. Its leaders continued to hold a hotch-potch of conservative and liberal ideas mixed with narrow-minded trade unionism. The 'Marxists' were mainly in the sectarian Social Democratic Federation (SDF), some of whose leaders were anti-feminist (and racist) to an extreme. The socialists who were pro-feminist were by and large in the ILP, the Independent Labour Party, a muddled party which sought co-operation with the Liberals, and hence even more strongly favoured co-operation between working-class and Liberal women. Where working women rub shoulders with grand ladies, it is obvious who will influence whom.

Working Women in the First Half of the Nineteenth Century

In the first quarter of the nineteenth century women participated in the illegal trade union movement and were active in the campaigns for the repeal of the Combination Acts. The reform agitation which started at the time of the French revolution and was renewed after the end of the Napoleonic wars, took on a mass character in some manufacturing districts, particularly among the cotton workers of Lancashire. The movement included many women, who formed women's political unions with their own committees and officers. In the famous demonstration for parliamentary reform at St Peter's Fields in Manchester on 16 August 1819 many women took part.[1]

When, in the summer of 1834, Robert Owen founded his short-lived Grand National Consolidated Trade Union, a general union open to all irrespective of trade, craft or sex, tens of thousands of women joined it. Unfortunately it disintegrated some five years later.

When it came to working-class politics, which for the years 1837–48 meant the Chartist movement, women again played a significant role. They formed a number of Women's Charter Associations, and were very active in all three Charter campaigns. At the movement's largest mass meeting in Birmingham in 1842 as many as 50,000 women took part, besides tens of thousands of men.[2] But this was a short chapter of history, followed by a long period of reaction. To quote from Dorothy Thompson's excellent article 'Women and Nineteenth Century Radical Politics: A Lost Dimension':

> The gains of the Chartist period, in awareness and in self-confidence, the moves towards a more equal and co-operative kind of political activity by both men and women, were lost in the years just before the middle of the century . . . One of the losses of this process in the Victorian period was the potential contribution to politics and society generally of the women of the working-class communities.[3]

When, in the late 1840s and early 1850s, a formal structure was established for the emerging unions, it was skilled men who organised themselves, leaving behind unskilled workers in general, including women. The only exception was the Lancashire cotton union which not only made serious and successful efforts to organise and activate women, but also negotiated rates based on 'the rate for the job' and not a rate according to the sex of the worker doing the job.[4] The exclusion of women from other unions was aided by the fact that outside the cotton industry women were dispersed in very small workplaces: dressmaking in sweatshops or at home, lace-making, small pottery workshops and so on, where it was difficult to organise.

Emma Patterson (1848–86) began to organise those women not catered for by the unions. She was the daughter of a schoolteacher, and married to a cabinet-maker. In 1874 she founded the Women's Provident and Protective League, of which she became honorary secretary. This was an alliance of leisured and working-class women concerned with the problems of women workers. The name 'trade union' was deliberately rejected as being likely to antagonise middle-class supporters. It was 'anxious to disclaim any views of antagonism towards employers of female labour'. Striking was deprecated as 'rash and mistaken action', and arbitration was promoted.[5] While the experience of bourgeois ladies 'helping' working women to organise was the product of sexist divisions in the working class, it was itself a further cause of disunity, giving many working-class men the ideal excuse for reactionary views on the right to work or the vote.

The aim of the League was to establish women-only trade unions. Its achievements, however, were puny. Between 1874 and 1886 the League established between thirty and forty women's societies in England and Scotland. Few counted more than a few hundred members or survived longer than a few years. About half succumbed within a year. The most successful, such as the Dewsbury Woollen Weavers and the Leicester Seamers and Stitchers, subsequently joined the men's trade unions. In 1886 the combined membership of women's societies was probably less than 2,500 women. During the same period, the female membership of the cotton unions rose steadily from 15,000 in 1876 to 30,000 in 1886, and women shared with men in the progressive advance of wages.[6] The total membership of the League was less than 7 per cent of all organised women.

This failure led Emma Patterson to make a U-turn in the 1880s and seek collaboration with the men's unions. Another issue on which she and the League made a radical turn was the question of protective legislation limiting the length of the working day for women and children. Protective legislation was supported by many male workers and fought for by the trade union movement generally in the 1870s because men believed they would benefit from the proposed changes. They hoped that the restrictions would make it more difficult to hire women. Men therefore would not have to compete with women for jobs.

This it did not do. Indeed, after the introduction in 1847 of the first Act restricting the working day for women and girls in the textile industry, the percentage of women and girls above thirteen in the industry rose from 55.9 to 57, while that of adult men decreased from 26.5 to 25.8.[7] Instead what the protective legislation did achieve was a shortening of the working day for men too. As Thomas Ashton, secretary of the Oldham Spinners' Association, colourfully put it: 'The battle for the limitation of hours of adults in general was fought from behind the women's petticoats.'[8]

The middle-class feminist supporters of the League opposed protective legislation on the grounds that it was discriminatory against women. The League's stand had, of course, been warmly supported by the employers.[9]

The New Unionism

Until the rise of the New Unions only a tiny minority of workers was organised. The total membership of unions in 1888 was 750,000, some 5 per cent of all occupied people. Among adult male manual workers the proportion of trade unionists was about 10 per cent.[10]

In 1888–9 a wave of industrial unrest swept the country, which brought with it a new outburst of trade union organisation, this time of unskilled men and of women. The strike of the 700 matchgirls working for Bryant and May in East London 'was the small spark that ignited the blaze of revolt and the wildfire spread of trade unionism among the unskilled.'[11]

In March 1889 Will Thorne launched the National Union of Gas Workers and General Labourers. Without even a strike the union won an eight-hour day. The union's growth was phenomenal. By September 1890 it had 89 branches, including two composed entirely of women, with a total membership of 60,000.[12] The gas workers' militancy affected the dockers. In 1889 a dock strike started with 10,000 workers and grew to 100,000. The initial membership of 800 in the dockers' union — the Dock, Wharf, Riverside and Labourers' Union — grew to 60,000.

From the outset the New Unions did not exclude women from membership, but as they tended to organise mainly in transport and labouring, few women came within their orbit. Still, the spirit of new unionism inspired women, and in the years 1888 and after they engaged in considerable industrial action. Blanket weavers in Heckmondwike, female cigarmakers in Nottingham, cotton workers and jute workers in Dundee took action spontaneously in 1888. Women in a tin box manufactory in London struck and pelted men who continued to work there with red-ochre and flour.[13]

In 1889 a dozen little societies of women workers sprang up in London, and as many in the provinces. The strike of the Leeds tailoresses swelled the ranks of a local Society of Workmen from a mere handful to 2,000 in the space of a few weeks.[14] Many thousands of women joined trade unions in the years 1888–9.

But at the end of 1889 the employers started a general counter-offensive. A dock strike in Liverpool was badly beaten. In London in the early 1890s the dockers' union was forced out of the docks,[15] and its membership went from 100,000 in 1889 down to 56,000 in 1890, 22,913 in 1892 and 10,000 in 1896. A similar development affected the National Union of Gas Workers and General Labourers, its membership declining from 60,000 in 1890 to 36,108 in 1892, and 29,730 in 1896. The National Amalgamated Union of Sailors and Firemen, which had 58,780 members in 1890, dissolved in 1894. So did the

National Labour Federation which in 1890 had had 60,000 members.[16] Almost no women remained in the general unions.

But despite the ebb, the general trend was towards the greater organisation of women in the trade unions, above all by the opening up of the men's unions to women. The female membership of all trade unions increased from about 37,000 in 1886 to nearly 118,000 in 1896, and about 167,000 in 1906. Of this number 143,000 women belonged to textile unions, within which 125,000 were in cotton unions. By comparison the women-only unions at the time had probably no more than 5,000 members.[17]

The National Federation of Women Workers

The Women's Trade Union League served as an umbrella organisation uniting women-only unions from different trades. The mixed unions also collaborated with it, getting the services of a woman organiser in return for a small affiliation fee. But because of its mixed-class membership, the League was unable to become integrated into the trade union movement and affiliate to the Trades Union Congress.[18]

Because of this, Mary Macarthur, who had become the League's secretary in 1903, decided in 1906 to found the National Federation of Women Workers. This was formed on the model of a general labour union, and was open to all women in unorganised trades or who were not admitted to their appropriate trade union.[19]

Mary Macarthur opposed the separation of women from men. She 'had always looked to the day when women would be part of a large strong body representing both men and women'.[20] The Federation therefore co-operated as far as it could with the skilled men's unions, and its membership gave active support to the policy of joint organisation for men and women employed in the same trade or industry. Often a branch of the Federation was transferred to a men's union which had decided to open its doors to women.

The National Federation 'organised more women, fought more strikes and did more to establish women trade unionism than any other organisation'. It was

> rooted in the ideas and militancy of the early general labour unions. In its struggle to improve wages and conditions, it usually found that the strike was the only weapon at its disposal. Its record between 1906 and 1914 was largely one of strikes.[21]

Between 1904 and 1914 the membership of the Federation grew from 2,000 to 20,000.[22] By 1914 female membership of all trade unions had risen to 357,956, of which 210,272 were in cotton,[23] a growth of 190,000 in eight years.

The years 1910–14, a high point of working-class struggle, saw even closer relations between working women's and men's struggles than 1888–9. There were mass strikes of miners, seamen, dockers, railwaymen, engineers and transport workers. At the same time 500 women chainmakers in Cradley Heath, Birmingham, about half of all women in the trade, went on strike. After being locked out for ten weeks they won and the chainmakers' union membership rose briefly to 1,700.

The impact of the women chainmakers' victory was dramatic. The whole of the Midlands was affected: workers in the brick trade, in the metal hollow-ware trade, and thousands of unskilled and unorganised men who were labouring for less than £1 a week in the dingy factories and workshops of the Black Country revolted. All of them, like the Cradley Heath women, won recognised rates of wages and trade union organisation.[24]

In the summer of 1911, 15,000 unorganised women working in twenty-one Bermondsey firms came out on strike, leading to the organisation of women in eighteen of them: jam and pickle makers, biscuit makers, tea packers, cocoa makers, glue and size-makers, tin-box makers and bottle washers. The wave of militancy led to a swift rise in women membership of the unions, which doubled between 1910 and 1914.[25]

Nevertheless, despite the great achievements of women workers in the years 1888–9 and 1910–14, they still lagged very much behind men workers. The main cause was the general nature of the British labour movement.

The Conservatism of the British Labour Movement

In Britain the slow process of industrialisation permitted organisation to spread first among those with craft power, encouraging them to be exclusive, unlike Germany, where rapid industrialisation led to rapid organisation in general unions which included skilled and unskilled, men and women. Between 1891 and 1910 British trade union membership grew from 1,109,000 to 2,565,000, or two and a half times. In the same period the German Free Trade Unions escalated from 278,000 to 2,017,000, or seven times, virtually closing the gap with the British.[26]

The Amalgamated Society of Engineers took 50 years before it allowed semi-skilled workers into membership. By August 1914, semi-skilled workers were only 6.1 per cent of the ASE membership.[27] The German Metal Workers' Union (DMV) although a latecomer, was a much bigger organisation than its British counterpart. In 1914, while the ASE had only 174,000 members,[28] the DMV had 545,000.[29] While the ASE did not have *one* woman member until

1943, the DMV had, in 1914, 22,551 women members (about 7 per cent of all members of the union) and in 1917, 83,266 (or 21 per cent).[30]

Although the craft unions, to achieve economic security, had again and again to fight bitter battles against the employers, when seen in a broad historical context, craft unionism inflicted grave damage on the whole working class, women and men alike. Skilled men in strong unions, the 'aristocracy of labour', had virtually permanent employment while the majority of workers lived in a wonderful buyers' market for the employers. These skilled men enjoyed superior incomes, education and culture. They were socially nearer to the lower middle class than the working class. Hence, to the extent that they influenced the working class as a whole, they created a tradition of narrow-minded conservatism, which acted as a bulwark against Marxism gaining strength in Britain (and even largely distorted the 'Marxism' that did manage to dig roots, that of the SDF).

When a labour party was finally established in 1893 in the shape of the ILP, its leaders did their best to fudge over their differences with the open capitalist parties, the Liberals and the Conservatives. Thus in 1894, at the second annual conference of the ILP, its leaders, aiming not to frighten away the trade union leaders, defeated an attempt to bind its members

> to support and vote only for candidates at any election who have adopted the objects, policy and programme of the Independent Labour Party, and who are not members or . . . nominees of the Liberal, Radical, Conservative, Unionist or Irish Nationalist Parties.[31]

In 1900 the Labour Representation Committee, which later evolved into the Labour Party, was born out of the ILP and the trade union movement. Ralph Milliband aptly sums up its activities as 'largely the history of political manoeuvres to reach electoral accommodations with the Liberals'.[32]

In 1906 the Labour Party conference overwhelmingly rejected a constitutional amendment to make 'the overthrow of the present competitive system of capitalism and the institution of a system of public ownership' a definitive objective of the party. 'Was it desirable,' Keir Hardie asked, 'that those Members in the House of Commons who were not Socialists should be cleared out?' Flirting with the Liberals went on uninterrupted until the First World War.

It was the unique combination in Britain of class collaboration with indifference of the trade union and labour leaders towards unskilled workers in general, and women in particular, that led to the rise of such organisations as the Women's Trade Union League and the National Federation of Women Workers. Similar organisations could not have arisen in Russia or Germany. There a sharp class abyss separated the economic and political organisations of the workers from those of the employers. There was little place for lady philanthropists to organise women into women's unions.

In the political sphere the differences were even more marked. In Germany and Russia workers were mortal enemies of the state because workers' organisations there were mainly illegal and frequently subject to brutal suppression. So in both countries the question of suffrage was clearly a class issue. All socialist parties demanded general *adult* suffrage. No one dreamt of restricting the claim to men only.

Things were radically different in Britain. Here, by a long gradual process, men were given the vote: in 1832 the men of the middle classes, in 1867 many of the skilled men; in 1884 all skilled and all unionised working men. To be entitled to vote a man had to prove a property qualification as a householder, freeholder, copy holder, rent occupier paying £10, university degree or other entitlement. According to one estimate, this left about 70 per cent of the adult population of England and Wales excluded from voting — all women, sons living with parents, domestic servants living with employers and soldiers living in barracks. This included 42 per cent of men.[33] The final condition to qualify for the vote was to be registered at one place for 12 months. This was reckoned to be a particular disadvantage to the working-class voter, especially in London, because it was common for a man to have to move in order to be near his place of work at a time when the cost of public transport was a serious burden.[34]

For those who argued for the vote to be given to women there were two options, either to fight for it to be on the same terms as applied to men, or to fight for general adult suffrage.

The first option would mean that in practice only a tiny minority of women would win the vote. Sylvia Pankhurst explained:

> If the vote were to be extended to women on the same terms [as applied to men], the working-class mother would not be able to qualify, for her husband, not she, would exercise the single vote open to them as householders. The ill-paid workman who was a lodger had seldom sticks to furnish a room even if it were rated high enough to carry a vote. On the other hand, the wives, daughters and mothers of the rich would easily provide themselves with the required qualification.[35]

Mary Macarthur estimated that if women were enfranchised on the same terms as men, less than 5 per cent of working women would be eligible.[36]

The second option did not appeal to many in the Labour Party. So long as two-fifths of men did not have the vote, an 'impossibilist' call for votes for all — including women — appeared as an abrogation of the party's 'gradualist' philosophy.

There was of course a third position: total opposition to women's right to vote. All three were held by different sections of the ILP, the Labour Party, the Social Democratic Federation and the trade unions.

At the 1905 Labour Representation Conference a resolution demanding votes for women on the same terms as applied to men, on the grounds that there was 'no likelihood' of adult suffrage, was argued for by Keir Hardie and Philip Snowden. (Snowden was one of the pioneers of the ILP. He was to become Chancellor of the Exchequer in the Labour governments of 1924 and 1929, then joined the National Government with the Tories together with Ramsay MacDonald.) The resolution was opposed by Harry Quelch, delegate of the London Trades Council and a member of the SDF, who claimed that this would be in the interests of bourgeois women, so would increase the electoral chances of the Tories and Liberals. Quelch amended the resolution to demand adult suffrage, and the amendment was carried by 483 votes to 170. In the 1906 conference, Quelch's position was reaffirmed — but this time by a very small majority. Other prominent protagonists of adult suffrage were Mary Macarthur and Margaret Bondfield, a leading member of the Shop Assistants' Union.

In 1906 an Adult Suffrage Society was formed to co-ordinate opposition to the limited suffrage Bill, with Margaret Bondfield as president. But it was totally ineffectual.

Outright opposition to female suffrage was expressed by some leaders of the labour movement. The most extreme was Belfort Bax, a 'theoretician' of the SDF. (It must be stressed that many in the Federation took great exception to Bax's anti-feminism — and racism. There were many revolutionary socialists in the SDF who were deeply committed to women's liberation.) To quote just a few of Bax's outrageous statements:

> . . . in England whilst the woman is practically relieved of all responsibility for the maintenance of her husband, he can be compelled by poor law to maintain her under a penalty of three months' hard labour . . . I think, then, no one can deny that the existing marriage laws are simply a 'plant' to enable the woman to swindle and oppress the man.[37]
>
> The husband is compelled, by custom and by law, to do *corvée*, or to yield up such portion of his earnings as may enable his wife to live in comfort . . . The woman possesses the monopoly of . . . the means of sexual satisfaction, her body; and for allowing him access to which the law entitles her to demand a rent and dues in the shape of food, clothes, shelter — in short, provision in accordance with the station of life occupied by her 'villein', the husband, without any exertion on her part.[38]

To 'prove' that women should not get the vote, Belfort Bax argued from the assumption that women, like people of the black races, were inferior:

> . . . lower races stand in the same relation to higher races that children do to adults. Their minds are so far different from the former, that there is no basis of organic equality between the two.

Relating this to women, he goes on,

> I think it is clear, therefore, that we are justified in debarring any order of persons from the franchise if they, as an order, indicate an inferiority based on an organic difference which is likely to render their co-operation in political or administrative life a danger or disadvantage to the community as a whole . . . Now the question arises, are we to regard women as possessing a deep-lying organic difference, involving inferiority, to men? If so, we shall be *eo-ipso* justified in opposing woman-suffrage on the ground that the well-being of the community as a whole would be endangered thereby.[39]

Only a conservative movement, one intellectually as backward as the British Labour movement, could produce a Belfort Bax.

Problems for Working-Class Women

Lib-lab politics damaged the interests of women workers even more than men. The latent ability of working-class women to struggle was distorted, stunted and never allowed to develop, while being steered into class alliances and conservatism. The potential that *did* exist may be glimpsed from the story of the suffrage movement among women cotton workers at the turn of the century. This is told by Jill Liddington and Jill Norris in their excellent book, **One Hand Tied Behind Us**.[40]

In 1893 Esther Roper launched a suffrage campaign among the Lancashire textile workers which had considerable impact on the older suffrage societies, the growing Labour Representation Committee, and eventually upon parliament. From early 1900 until 1906 the campaign gained momentum and showed impressive successes.

On 1 May 1900 a petition was launched in Lancashire. By the following spring the number of signatures of working-class women on the petition was 29,359. On 18 March a deputation of 15 Lancashire women cotton workers took the petition to London to present it to the House of Commons. Fired by this success, the North of England Society activists decided to cast their net more widely, to the wool workers in Yorkshire and the cotton and silk workers in north Cheshire.[41] In February 1902, a deputation of Yorkshire and Cheshire women textile workers presented a new petition to the House.

The 90,000 women members of the cotton unions — representing in 1896 no less than five-sixths of all organised women members — were the backbone of the movement. They wanted general adult suffrage, as part of a list of social and economic demands:

> . . . they were not merely interested in the possession of the vote as a symbol of equality. They wanted it in order to improve conditions for women like themselves . . . What was the point of a vote without any idea of how it could be used? Without exception, they were all involved in wider campaigns for working women. As trade unionists they tried to improve women's wage levels and conditions at work. They campaigned for improved education for working-class girls, and better facilities for working-class mothers and their children.[42]

The way they went about their business was rooted in working-class experience: '. . . their methods were those they had learned elsewhere: factory gate meetings, pushing suffrage motions through union branches, organising through trades councils.'[43]

Unhappily the movement, in failing to get the support it deserved from the wider labour movement, came up against a number of insuperable obstacles. It fell into the arms of bourgeois feminists, and after a few years died away.

The Women's Social and Political Union

An organisation which left a much greater impression in the history books was that of Mrs Emmeline Pankhurst and her daughter Christabel. In 1892 Emmeline, wife of Dr Richard Pankhurst, barrister, member of the Manchester Chamber of Commerce and founder of the Manchester Liberal Association, left the Liberals to join the newly founded ILP. At the end of 1894 she was elected ILP candidate to the Chorlton Board of Guardians, and the following year campaigned for her husband as ILP candidate for Gorton in the general election. In 1898 Dr Pankhurst died.

During the 1890s and until late in 1903 Mrs Pankhurst was more preoccupied with Labour's progress than with votes for women. In that year she was elected to the national executive of the ILP. All the Pankhurst children — Christabel, Sylvia, Harty and Adela — joined the party. And in the same year, Emmeline and Christabel, the child closest to her mother, introduced a plea for women's suffrage, on the ground that 'it will advance the industrial condition of women.'[44] On 10 October 1903, following months of rising unemployment and short-time working among women cotton workers, Mrs Pankhurst, keen to better the lot of working women, set up a small group, mostly of working-class supporters of the ILP. This was the Women's Social and Political Union.[45]

> It was her intention to conduct social as well as political work; she

> envisaged the provision of maternity benefit, and other such amenities for the members of the new organisation, which at that time she intended should be mainly composed of working women, and politically a women's parallel to the ILP, though with primary emphasis on the vote.[46]
>
> There were tendencies in the early days of the WSPU towards the adoption of other objects than the franchise alone; indeed towards a general assistance to reform movements.[47]

It took an interest in and acted on behalf of the unemployed, of textile strikers in Yorkshire, of 'native races' in Natal, and other causes, besides women's suffrage. The main activity of the WSPU was to address ILP meetings, trade unions, trades councils, Labour Churches and Clarion Clubs. Though the WSPU was not officially affiliated to the ILP, in practice it was dependent on it for publicity, platforms, and audiences.

But the logic of a women-only organisation, dedicating more and more of its energies to the votes issue, started weakening the social content of its activities. In November 1903 Christabel, the first to seek concentration on the single issue, speaking to the newly-formed Sheffield Women's Suffrage Society, urged 'women not to be divided, to join together on one question — the vote.'[48]

July 1905 saw a march of 1,000 women from the East End of London to Westminster, and November another of 4,000 wives of unemployed men demanding 'Food for our Children', 'Work for our Men', and proclaiming 'Workers of the World Unite'.[49]

In 1906 the WSPU leaders moved from Manchester to London, where they continued at first to focus on working-class women. In the same year they organised the first suffrage demonstration. On 19 February, after a march of three hundred women from the East End, there was a meeting and lobby of parliament, attended also by wealthy ladies, some dressed in their maids' clothing to avoid recognition. On 27 February the 'Unemployed Women of South West Ham' voted to become the Canning Town branch of the WSPU, its first London branch.[50]

A short time later, however, Christabel, who became the dominant figure in the WSPU, decided that a working women's movement was of no value as working women were the weakest section of the sex: 'Surely it is a mistake to use the weakest for the struggle! We want picked women, the very strongest and most intelligent!'[51] Christabel redefined the aims of the WSPU in these terms:

> Ours is not a class movement at all. We take in everybody — the highest and the lowest, the richest and the poorest. The bond is womanhood! The socialists are fighting against certain evils which they believe to be attributable to the spirit of injustice as between man and man. I am not

> at all sure that women, if they had had their due influence from the beginning, would not have brought about a totally different state of affairs . . . It comes to this. The men must paddle their own canoe, and we must paddle ours.[52]

The pennies and shillings collected among the hundreds and thousands of the poor counted as little beside the substantial sums beginning to be donated to the WSPU by the affluent. For instance at an Albert Hall rally on 19 March 1908 one woman promised to give £1,000 a year until women could vote, and twelve other women gave £100 each. The treasurer of the WSPU, Mr Pethwick Lawrence, himself promised to donate £1,000 a year.[53] At that time the pound was worth probably thirty times its present value, so these were huge sums. The income of the WSPU grew massively, from £3,000 in 1906–7 to a peak of £37,000 in 1913–4. No comparable organisation, not even the Labour Party, commanded such resources.[54]

The running of the organisation became completely dictatorial. Emmeline and Christabel did not allow any national conference of the union after September/October 1907. They and Mr and Mrs Pethwick Lawrence ran the show, without any committee, until October 1912, when the Lawrences were unceremoniously expelled by Emmeline and Christabel.

Working-class women now found themselves out of place in the WSPU. Furthermore, the WSPU's slogan, 'Votes for Women', interpreted by Emmeline and Christabel Pankhurst as meaning votes on the same terms as applied to men, was described by women trade unionists as 'Vote for the Ladies', and repeatedly denounced.

The Road to the Cul-de-Sac

Towards the end of 1906 and throughout 1907 the WSPU demonstrations in many cities besides London grew larger and became more freqent. Every demonstration was followed by large scale arrests: 53 on 13 February 1907, 74 on 8 March, 65 on 21 March. The demonstrations grew bigger. On 15 July 1908, 20,000 came to the WSPU demonstration on Clapham Common in South London; on 19 July 150,000 came to Heaton Park, Manchester; and on 26 July, 100,000 demonstrated at Woodhouse Moor in Leeds. The annual report of the WSPU for 1 March 1907 to 29 February 1908 claimed that the Union had held 'upwards of 5,000 meetings' during the year, 400 of which had drawn audiences of over a thousand.

The WSPU demonstrations reached a climax on 21 June 1908, when a vast throng assembled in Hyde Park. **The Times** thought there were between 250,000 and 500,000, and the WSPU paper **Votes for Women** claimed: '. . . it is no exaggeration to say that the number of people present was the largest ever gathered together on one spot at one time in the history of the world.'[55]

Unfortunately all this led nowhere. The Liberal government did not budge on the question of women's suffrage. And the Pankhursts did not dare try a repeat performance of the 21 June Hyde Park demonstration, rightly believing that a larger demonstration could not be achieved. In frustration, a couple of WSPU members broke some windows at 10 Downing Street on 30 June 1908. Liberal Party meetings were broken up. From August 1909 a new tactic was adopted, with all those arrested going on hunger strike. The government reacted with 'cat and mouse' methods, first force-feeding, then releasing the prisoner after a grave deterioration in health . . . and re-arresting her after her health had improved.

At the same time WSPU politics became more and more anti-working-class. After the death of three strikers in August 1915, in transport strikes in Liverpool and Llanelly — two were shot — **Votes for Women** merely commented that 'several lives had been lost', but suffragettes had more reason to revolt than working men, for the latter had votes, and so 'could gain improvements in their condition without resorting to strikes.' When Tom Mann, Guy Bowman, and Fred Crowsley were imprisoned for an appeal to soldiers not to shoot their fellow workers on strike, the WSPU coldly commented that this offence was more serious than any committed by the suffragettes, and should have been more seriously punished.[56]

On the death of King Edward in 1910, Christabel vied with the Conservative papers in her expressions of devotion to the throne. The WSPU suspended all propaganda and mourned heavily in its paper.[57]

On the question of Home Rule for Ireland, as the Irish Nationalists in the House of Commons did not show any support for the WSPU demands, the WSPU organised a poster parade outside parliament with the slogan 'No Votes for Women, No Home Rule'. Instead they gave all their support to the Ulster Unionists who in September 1913 accepted the demand of votes for women.

Continued failure brought forth ever more desperate tactics. On 21 November 1911 Emmeline and Christabel organised a mass window-breaking in the West End of London. In January 1913 they started a long campaign of arson, directed against prominent rich people. On 3 June 1913 Emily Wilding Davison attended the Derby, dashed on to the course and was run down and killed by the King's horse.

Meanwhile mass activity in the form of public meetings and demonstrations almost entirely ceased. During the massive and critical strikes and lock-outs of 1910–14 the WSPU stood aside.

The campaign also developed an extreme anti-man psychology.

Christabel put her ideas forward in a book titled **The Great Scourge and How to End It**. The great scourge was VD, contracted, as was 'widely accepted by medical authorities' by '75 per cent to 80 per cent of men' before marriage, 'that is, out of every four men there is only one who can marry without risk to his bride.' The cure for venereal disease was 'Votes for Women, which will give to women more self-reliance and a stronger economic position, and chastity for men.' 'Young women . . . must be warned of the fact that marriage is intensely dangerous, until such time as men's moral standards are completely changed.'[58] The WSPU launched a campaign called The Moral Crusade to propagate Christabel's ideas.

By the time Britain declared war on Germany in 1914 the WSPU was about the most chauvinistic organisation in the country. Christabel proclaimed that 'the success of the Germans would be disastrous for the civilisation of the world, let alone for the British Empire.' In the following months the Pankhursts led a national drive to recruit women for the munitions industry, and on 15 October the **Suffragette** was renamed **Britannia**. Its subtitle was: 'For King, For Country, For Freedom'.

In 1915 the WSPU launched an 'industrial peace campaign' with the financial and moral backing of prominent industrialists (some of whose country mansions had been burned down by Pankhurst arsonists only a year or two previously). It had salaried officials, often ex-suffragettes. 'Bolshevik' shop stewards who were fomenting class struggle were denounced. Women, more proof against foreign theories, must see to it that men understood the dangerous, immature nonsense of socialism and where their duty and true interests lay. The campaign concentrated on the areas of greatest industrial unrest — the north of England, Glasgow and the mining districts of South Wales. Progress reports were sent regularly to the Prime Minister.[59]

It was the WSPU that introduced the practice of sending white feathers to civilians who did not volunteer to join the armed forces.

On 1 June 1917 Mrs Pankhurst asked the Prime Minister, Lloyd George, to send her to Russia. There she met Kerensky and advised him to take a firm line with the Bolsheviks. She reviewed the women's battalion, the Battalion of Death, which was created by Kerensky in a final desperate attempt to boost patriotism and shame men into fighting, and found it 'the greatest thing in history since Joan of Arc.'[60] The battalion was the last defender of the Winter Palace against the Bolsheviks in October. Emmeline Pankhurst called on Russian women to storm the soviets all over Russia and force the men to support Kerensky and the Provisional Government — although in private she expressed the view that Kerensky was a weakling and that only the counter-revolutionary General Kornilov could save Russia.[61]

Sylvia Pankhurst

The only Pankhurst who remained active in the Labour movement was Sylvia, who made a significant contribution to working-class struggles in the East End of London. Unfortunately she suffered from the influence of the conservative labour movement and the bourgeois-dominated feminist movement, and appears from her numerous writings to have had no knowledge of the ideas of the revolutionary thinkers from Marx onwards.

In Sylvia's first book, **The Suffragettes**, published in 1911 at the height of WSPU activity, she gave uncritical praise to the WSPU, and dimissed all other groups in a few off-hand remarks. She opposed the window-breaking and arson campaigns, but muted her criticism. She explained why she could not break with her mother and sister at the time in her book **The Suffragette Movement**, written later in 1931:

> I believed, then and always, that the movement required, not more serious militancy by the few, but a stronger appeal to the great masses to join the struggle. Yet it was not in me to criticise or expostulate. I would rather have died at the stake than say one word against the actions of those who were in the throes of the fight.[62]

She opposed WSPU support for a Bill giving women the vote restricted according to income, and 'Mrs Pankhurst admitted the truth of my contentions, but declared the matter was decided, and unity essential. I felt the force of the latter argument.'[63]

Despite her efforts at accommodation, and against her will, Sylvia was expelled from the WSPU in January 1914, after speaking at a mass meeting in the Albert Hall in support of the Dublin workers on strike, at which James Connolly was the main speaker.

While Mrs Pankhurst and Christabel lived in West London and spent their time in well-to-do circles, in 1912 Sylvia started organising in the East End, through the East London Federation of Suffragettes (ELFS). On 18 March 1916 this became the Workers' Suffrage Federation, then in May 1918 the Workers' Socialist Federation. Until the Russian revolution she was completely dedicated to the question of winning the vote. The first issue of her weekly paper, **Women's Dreadnought**, on 8 March 1914, defined its task thus:

> The **Women's Dreadnought** is published by the East London Federation of Suffragettes, an organisation mainly composed of working women, and the chief duty of **The Dreadnought** will be to deal with the franchise question from the working woman's point of view, and to report the activities of the Votes for Women movement in East London. Nevertheless, the paper will not fail to review the whole field of the women's emancipation movement.[64]

A 6,000-word editorial plus three more of the issue's eight pages, all written by Sylvia Pankhurst, were devoted to the suffrage. Even when the question of prostitution was dealt with — again in an article written and signed by Sylvia Pankhurst — although the cause was given as low wages and poverty, the solution suggested was: votes for women. International Women's Day, which coincided with the publication of the first issue of **Women's Dreadnought**, was not mentioned.

At the time of Sir Edward Carson's activities in stirring up Protestant opposition to Irish Home Rule, an article entitled 'Women and Ulster' in the **Women's Dreadnought** did not utter a word of criticism of the Ulster Volunteer Force. On 22 January 1916 it devoted 350 words to 'News from the Clyde' dealing with the persecution of shop stewards in the munitions industry in Glasgow, but about 11,000 words — practically four-fifths of the issue — to the question of suffrage.

When the ELFS changed its name to the Workers' Suffrage Federation the programme of the organisation was defined thus: 'The object of the Federation is to secure Human Suffrage: a vote for every woman and man of full age. Membership is open to every woman and man over 18 years.' And that was all.[65]

Totally opposed to the First World War, Sylvia Pankhurst professed pacifism, hoping that peace could be achieved through the agreement of the rival imperialist powers. Hence in **Women's Dreadnought** of 3 April and 5 May 1915 she enthused over the imminent Hague peace congress, and on 16 December 1916 called for 'peaceful negotiations' and 'the establishment of an international court'. In the issue of 27 January 1917 there is an ecstatic welcome for the peace terms put forward by the US President Wilson.

Together with the narrow politics of votes for women and pacifism went concentration on community services in the first two years of the war. Sylvia Pankhurst organised a communal restaurant 'supplying first-rate food at cost price' in the ELFS hall at Old Ford Road.[66] About one hundred nursing mothers received a quart of milk and dinner every night from the ELFS.[67] During 1915 nearly 1,000 mothers and babies were seen at the Federation's clinics, and more than £1,000 was spent on milk.[68] The ELFS also opened a nursery for forty children, and a couple of workshops producing garments and toys. The toy factory employed 59 people.[69] Xmas and New Year parties for children used up a lot of energy.

Wealthy patrons were sought out by Sylvia to fund these services. She thus spent a weekend with the Tories Lady Astor and former Prime Minister Arthur Balfour at Cliveden. She gives the following description:

> I spoke to them quietly of the hard, grey life in the East End; of the

> women and girls making toys in our little factory; drudges, errand girls, charwomen learning to paint, the sausage-filler turned designer. I strove to reveal to them within our poor ones the eternal psyche, striving for release from its dull prison . . . The collection taken, the crowd swarmed to a buffet laden with glittering delicacies.[70]

Within the same pattern of Sylvia's ideas was an appeal in the middle of the war to press baron Lord Northcliffe, who was on the extreme right of the Tory Party, to help in the fight for women's franchise.[71]

It is illuminating to compare Sylvia Pankhurst's attitude to social work with that of the Bolsheviks in the same period. In September 1916, well before the revolution, the Petersburg municipal council decided to open nine canteens with a daily capacity of 8,000 people — a much larger enterprise than anything Sylvia Pankhurst was involved in. The Bolsheviks considered this a mere palliative. So throughout the factories they moved the following resolution:

> . . . all piecemeal means of fighting the food crisis (for example co-operatives, wage rises, canteens) can only marginally mitigate the effects of the crisis and not eliminate the causes . . .
>
> The only effective means of struggle against the crisis is a struggle against the causes producing it, a struggle against the war and the ruling classes which plotted it; in taking all this into account, we call upon the Russian working class and all democrats to take the road of a revolutionary struggle against the tsarist monarchy and the ruling classes behind the slogan of 'Down with the war!'[72]

The ELFS also tried to improve conditions in the numerous sweatshops in the East End, without much success. It was also active in supporting rent strikes, successfully preventing evictions, and getting demands for increased rent withdrawn.

In 1915 and 1916 Sylvia Pankhurst started involving herself in the activities of the miners in South Wales, and **Women's Dreadnought** became a well-informed journal on the mass struggles there. There was little resonance, however, with the massive upsurges in Sheffield, Manchester, Belfast or Barrow-in-Furness.

Sylvia Pankhurst's eclecticism led to some odd pursuits. Imitating James Connolly's Irish Citizens' Army, she set up a 'People's Army' in August 1913 — 'an organisation men and women may join in order to fight for freedom. And in order that they may fit themselves to cope with the brutality of Government servants.'[73] The army drilled every Wednesday night after the Federation meetings in Bow and was observed and cheered on by several hundred men and women. Drilling usually consisted of 80 to 100 people marching in formation, carrying clubs. At its peak it was estimated that over 700 women took part.[74]

Sylvia's preoccupation with the single issue of universal suffrage, which she regarded as an end in itself, meant that she was unable to develop an effective strategy. She did not understand what Lenin and Luxemburg grasped clearly, that struggles around specific reforms such as the vote are of value, not in themselves, but as a means of raising workers' confidence and consciousness. Thus she did not grasp that other struggles, above all, those of the shop stewards' movement in the engineering factories, were essential to the success of any struggle against the war.

Though she totally opposed the war, she lacked Lenin's understanding that this was a war in which the strongest capitalist powers were competing for domination of the weak. Any peace on the basis of existing society could therefore only reinforce the exploitation and oppression of the mass of workers throughout the world. Lenin argued that workers had no interest in fighting for 'their' country — but every interest in fighting for their class. He called for workers to end the imperialist war by declaring civil war against their own governments. Such a position was foreign to Sylvia Pankhurst, who saw the class struggle in primarily moral terms, and wished to alleviate suffering and right wrongs. So she was unable to see, as Lenin did, that the world war represented an enormous opportunity to overthrow the entire system, and so to achieve peace through workers' revolution. It is hardly surprising that Sylvia Pankhurst's career as a socialist was so short and confused.

The impact of the Russian Revolution

The Russian Revolution was a major turning point in Sylvia Pankhurst's life. The federation organised two enthusiastic meetings in the East End to celebrate on 24 and 25 March 1917. Seven thousand people attended the first of these.[75] 'I am proud,' Sylvia declared, 'to call myself a Bolshevist.'[76] But even now her position contained basic inconsistencies. **Women's Dreadnought** of 2 July 1917, reporting the annual conference of the Workers' Suffrage Federation, wrote:

> The conference recognises that modern wars are of capitalist origin, and whilst private competitive trading continues, the danger of war will not be entirely wiped out. While working to secure a co-operative system of society which shall render wars impossible, the Conference urges:
>
> a) The establishment of an International Court for the settlement of international affairs . . .
>
> b) The establishment of international free trade and the abolition of 'spheres of influence', internationalisation of the trade routes and narrow seas and the freedom of the seas.

War is the product of capitalism . . . but the solution is an international court and free trade, arrangements within capitalism!

Still, with the October revolution Sylvia Pankhurst made a radical turn. She changed the name of her paper on 28 July 1917 from **Women's Dreadnought** to **Workers' Dreadnought**, 'as members realised that solidarity between men and women was essential if they were going to win their fight.'[77] It also got a new subtitle: 'Socialism, Internationalism, Votes for All', and became the most informed paper in Britain on the policies of Bolshevism. It was the first British revolutionary paper to grasp fully the implications of the Russian revolution. On 17 November, in an article by Sylvia Pankhurst entitled 'The Lenin Revolution', it stated:

> Had the revolution stopped short at Kerensky's premiership and Kerensky's policy, it would have meant little more to humanity than an echo of the French Revolution. Now it bids fair to be something very much more . . . The Russian Revolution is a Socialist Revolution.

The article concludes: 'Our eager hopes are for the speedy success of the Bolsheviks of Russia: may they open the door which leads to freedom for the people of all lands.' The paper was full of praise for the Soviets and juxtaposed them to parliament: 'Parliaments, as we know them, are destined to pass away into the limbo of forgotten things, their places being taken by organisations of people built up on an occupational basis' — meaning the Soviets.

In practice, with the October revolution, the suffrage question disappeared from the paper, together with any specific feminist agitation. Russia, the war, and strike reports in Britain completely dominated it.

In addition to its connections with the South Wales miners and East End women, the Federation established close relations with the shop stewards' movement in London from the beginning of 1918, and reported widely from elsewhere in the country. From March 1918 it regularly published good information about the industrial scene throughout the country — mainly in W F Watson's 'Workshop Notes'.

At the 1918 annual conference the Workers' Suffrage Federation adopted a seven-point programme:

1) The organisation to be renamed the Workers' Socialist Federation (WSF).
2) Opposition to all war, and the abolition of the armed forces.
3) Recognition of the Soviet Government and the opening of immediate peace negotiations on the basis of no annexations, and self determination.
4) An immediate International Socialist Conference to work out peace terms.
5) Self-determination for India and Ireland.
6) Abolition of the capitalist system — the workers to organise on an industrial basis and build up a National Assembly from local workers'

committees.

7) Release of anti-war prisoners.[78]

New branches of the WSF were set up in many parts of England and South Wales and to a small extent in Scotland. By the end of 1918 the WSF had 17 branches in London and 23 in the provinces. In 1918 the total membership was probably about 300. The members of both ELSF and WSF were both women and men, but men now made up the big majority.[79] From 20 July 1918 the subtitle of **Workers' Dreadnought** became 'For International Socialism'.

Sylvia Pankhurst played an important role in spreading the message of the October revolution, not only by using **Workers' Dreadnought** but also by establishing the Russian People's Information Bureau in July 1918. When the Comintern was established in March 1919, Sylvia Pankhurst was appointed an English correspondent of its monthly paper, **The Communist International**.

But Sylvia Pankhurst did not basically understand the nature of Bolshevism, and when she made contact with Lenin, in July 1919, the break became inevitable.

On 16 July 1919 she wrote to Lenin, arguing that of all the organisations in Britain which declared their support for communism only her group, the WSF, and the South Wales Socialist Society, were really communists, as they opposed all participation in parliamentary elections and were for keeping away from the Labour Party. Lenin replied critically on 18 August, that to oppose parliamentarism is one thing, but to refuse to participate in parliamentary elections is completely different:

> We Russians, who have lived through two great revolutions in the twentieth century, are well aware what importance parliamentarism can have, and actually does have during a revolutionary period in general and *in the very midst of* a revolution in particular.

We must, he said, use the parliamentary arena. '*Soviet propaganda* can and must *be carried on* in and from within bourgeois parliaments.'[80]

Sylvia Pankhurst was not to be persuaded. She was on principle against participation in parliamentary elections, against any united action with the Labour Party, for boycotting the existing trade unions. When the Unity Conference to establish the Communist Party of Great Britain took place in July 1920, Sylvia Pankhurst did not join but instead jumped the gun by renaming the WSF 'The Communist Party, British Section of the Third International'. This was severely rebuked by Lenin in a message to the convenors of the July conference.[81] From then on the break was irrevocable.

On 3 July 1920 **Workers' Dreadnought** published 'Provisional Resolutions towards a Programme' of the Communist Party (British

Section of the Third International): 'The Communist Party, believing that institutions of capitalist organisation and domination cannot be used for revolutionary ends, refrains from participation in parliament and in the bourgeois local government system'. Lenin made a sharp attack on the ultra-left section of British Communists, in particular Sylvia Pankhurst and William Gallacher, in his **'Left Wing' Communism — An Infantile Disorder**.

Sylvia Pankhurst's break with Lenin was not accidental. She never had a Marxist world view, and hence, although *formally* her support for the demand for adult suffrage was identical to that of Lenin, their *methods of approach* diverged radically. Sylvia Pankhurst had for two decades argued that the demand that parliament give votes for women was crucial in itself. For Lenin, on the other hand, all democratic demands were subordinated to the workers' class struggle for power and socialism. Hence he never raised the question of suffrage up to the level of being an *absolute*, which it was for Sylvia Pankhurst. Up to the October Revolution it was for her an absolute imperative — a totem — and after that an absolute abhorrence — a taboo. As a totem it justified Sylvia Pankhurst's collaboration with bourgeois feminists for many, many years; as a taboo it justified a break with Lenin, who consistently saw in the struggle for the vote not a principle, but a tactic.

In the next three years **Workers' Dreadnought** devoted itself almost exclusively to an attack on Lenin and the Communist International. From July 1921 to September 1922 it published a series of articles by and in praise of leading anarchists, and attacking Lenin. Workers' industrial struggles disappeared completely from the paper. Instead, from 26 November 1921 there was a regular series of Esperanto lessons as a key to fighting nationalism (Sylvia Pankhurst even wrote a small book on the subject, **Delphes, or the Future of International Language**).

Possibly the best pointer to Sylvia Pankhurst's complete loss of direction once she broke with the Comintern can be gauged from the changes in the paper's subtitles. On 2 December 1922 the subtitle 'For International Communism' was removed. Instead there were ever new ones, such as 'For Clear Thoughts and Plain Language', 'We Stand for End of Wagedom', 'For Mutual Service', 'For Independence of Thought and Solidarity of Action', 'No Taxes under Communism' or even 'The Happy are Always Good'.

What a muddle! **Workers' Dreadnought** ceased publication with the issue of 14 June 1924, but Sylvia Pankhurst travelled further. She ended her life as an apologist for the reactionary and tyrannical Emperor Haile Selassie, to whom in 1955 she dedicated a book, **Ethiopia: A Cultural History**, with the glowing praise: 'Guardian of

Education, Pioneer of Progress, Leader and Defender of his People in Peace and War'.

British Women Gain the Vote

In 1918 all men got the vote at 21, and women at 30. Women also won the right to be parliamentary candidates. In 1928 women gained the vote on the same terms as men, at the age of 21. Was the Act of 1918 the outcome of the activities of the suffragettes, of women such as Emmeline Pankhurst or her daughters Christabel and Sylvia?

Not at all. Seeing the revolutionary upheavals following the Russian revolution, the ruling classes decided to try to block the road to workers' power by diverting the growing militancy on to the parliamentary road. The British army faced a series of mutinies. Tanks had to be sent to Glasgow to crush the mighty 40-hour strike movement and Lloyd George was worried whether he could count on the troops to do his dirty work. If in general, as Lenin argued, serious reforms are the by-products of revolutionary struggle, the establishment of the Weimar Republic in Germany and the granting of universal suffrage in Germany, Austria, Hungary, Poland, the Baltic States . . . and Britain, was the by-product of the revolutionary struggle of workers and a measure to block this struggle. Votes were granted to women as a reaction to the struggle of the millions of workers led by Lenin, Trotsky, Luxemburg and Liebknecht, and not as a result of the pressure of the suffragettes in Britain or the women's movement in Germany.

In Conclusion

The story of the women's movement in Britain at the turn of the century, as well as the movement to organise working-class women industrially and politically, is not a happy one. Conservatism, craftism, sectionalism, dominating the labour movement, did massive damage to the working class as a whole, and especially to its women members. The outcome was a terrible mess. Working-class women were forced into an alliance with liberal ladies, while at the same time imitating all the vices of the bureaucracy of the trade unions and Labour Party. Working-class women's ability to struggle was badly stunted and distorted. Even Sylvia Pankhurst, the most advanced of the socialist women leaders, could not rise above the intellectual morass dominating the British labour movement. Her great courage and efforts ended in futility.

8
France's sad story

One of the paradoxes in the history of working-class women's movements is the pathetic record of French socialism in organising women, despite their outstandingly heroic role in the Great Revolution of 1789 and the Paris Commune of 1871.

Small enterprises dominated the industrial economy of France at the end of the nineteenth and beginning of the twentieth centuries. A census in 1896 showed that the 575,000 'industrial establishments' in the country employed on average 5.5 workers each. Only 151 of them had 1,000 or more workers, while over 400,000 had only one or two workers, and another 80,000 three or four. Of the 575,000 establishments, 534,500 had less than ten.[1] Even in Paris, the capital and main manufacturing centre, at the end of the nineteenth century most workers were employed in small workshops or on their own.[2]

This backwardness was reflected in pathetically weak trade unions, even in branches such as the mines and railways which in other countries were well organised. As late as 1900 only 2.9 per cent of the eligible workers were in unions, and in 1911, 4.9 per cent.[3] These figures include workers in Catholic or 'yellow' unions which in 1914 made up some two-fifths of all organised workers.[4] The workers who were organised were dispersed in a large number of tiny unions (*syndicats*). The average membership of the *syndicats* affiliated to the CGT union confederation was only 100 in 1902, rising to 200 in 1914. In the Loire, 3,497 out of 17,663 were organised in 1897, and these were divided among ten different unions, the largest having only 1,127 members.[5] The 30,000 unionised building workers were organised in no fewer than 357 different unions.[6]

The French unions were not only small, but also poor and unstable; most, except for the printers, had barely sufficient funds for their administrative expenses. As late as 1908 regular strike assistance was assured in only 46 out of 1,073 strikes. Only in 36 of these was assistance in the form of cash.[7]

National federations of trade unions hardly existed until the end of the nineteenth century, and were correspondingly poor and weak. Only the printers had a really effective national organisation. The CGT (*Confederation Generale du Travail*) — the equivalent of the British TUC — was founded in 1895. It was a loose, feeble body. Each union, whatever its size, had the same voting rights. The six smallest, with a combined membership of only 27, had as many votes as the six largest, which had some 90,000 members. The Executive Committee of the CGT held about one-third of the votes by proxy, from small unions unable to afford to send their own representatives to congress. In 1910 its income was only about 20,000 francs (£800). To support the general strike of 1 May 1906 it had appealed for funds — and received the ludicrous total of 5,000 francs (£250).[8]

Women were badly represented in the trade unions. In 1911 they made up some 38 per cent of all wage-earners, quite a high proportion compared with other countries.[9] Although the proportion of women among trade union members was practically the same in France (8.7 per cent in 1914) as in Germany (8.9 per cent in 1913), because the whole trade union movement was much weaker in France, the organisation of women workers was tiny (only 89,364 in 1914).[10]

A significant number of these were in women-only unions: in 1900, 15.3 per cent, and in 1911, 24.9 per cent.[11] This compares unfavourably with Germany where there were practically no women-only unions. Where women and men belonged to the same unions — as in textiles — the women were no less militant than the men, but in general the proportion of women among strikers was considerably lower than the proportion of women in the relevant branch of the economy.[12] Where there *were* big strike movements, however, there was an increase in the number of women strikers.[13]

The dead weight of Republican tradition

Ideological and organisational division was a hallmark of French socialism well into the 20th century. In 1905 the Second Socialist International tried to unite all the socialist parties and groups in France. As a result the six existing national socialist groups and a number of regional organisations fused to form the *Parti Socialist Unifié — section française de l'International ouvrier* (SFIO). It was very much under the influence of Jean Jaurés, and was through and through reformist. Jaurés summed up his own views thus:

> It is not by the violent and exclusive agitation of this or that social faction, but from a sort of national movement that justice must emerge . . . The masses and the working bourgeoisie must unite to abolish capitalist privileges and abuse.[14]

Accordingly, 'a wide variety of social types entered the party; artisans as well as factory workers, even small shopkeepers (17 per cent of the party, nearly half of them publicans) and peasants (7 per cent of the party, one-third of them proprietors).'[15] Even after the fusion, the Socialist Party did not succeed in gaining a mass base. Between 1905 and 1914 its membership rose from 34,688 to 93,210.[16] This pales beside the German SPD, which had more than a million members by 1914.

The republican tradition out of which French socialism arose was fundamentally anti-feminist. Its basis was fear that women were under the thumb of the Catholic Church. The heroism of the revolutionary working women of 1789–93, 1848 and 1871 seems to have been blotted from memory by the counter-revolutionary, pro-Catholic rebellion of the famished women in 1795. Soon after this event, as early as 1796, Gracchus Babeuf, in his 'Manifesto of the Equals', had accepted sex as well as age as grounds for denying political rights in the communist republic he visualised.

A century later the woman Communard Paule Mink argued against women's suffrage as long as women were subject to the influence of the Church.[17] The dead weight of the republican tradition dragged back the organisation of women in general.

The fragmentation of the socialist parties before 1905 constantly impeded the organisation of women even more than that of men. The early women socialists found themselves separated from each other by their affiliation to various of the splinter groups which characterised French socialism in its formative period. Each time a small women's group was involved in a split, it cost it its existence, whereas for the parties it only cost members.

The social composition of the socialist parties also impeded the recruitment of women. The narrow horizon of a worker in a small workshop informed his attitude to women. Proudhonism[18] was the ideology that perfectly fitted these workers, and dominated the French labour movement many decades after the death of its author. The reactionary ideas of Proudhon regarding women dominated the French labour movement.

When the first French Workers' Congress was held in Paris in October 1876, the question of women's work was the first item on the agenda. The men at the congress made it clear that they thought women should be dependent on their husbands: 'Man being stronger and more robust ought to earn enough to support his household.'

Since, however, they recognised that men could *not* earn enough, they thought it permissible for women to work, but only at home, doing piece-work. The committee on this question (which included two women) thus resolved that for women to work *in factories* meant 'the destruction of morals, (which are) the veritable religion of workers.'[19]

The second congress, held in Lyons in February 1878, came to the same conclusions. A woman should be able to support herself in order to be independent, but only 'until the day when, embracing a new role, she becomes wife and mother, that is a woman by the hearth (*femme au foyer*), to which she brings care and work which are at least equivalent to man's work and for whom the (entire) day will be needed for housework.'[20]

Ten years later, in 1888, the *Fédération national des syndicats* passed a resolution calling industrial work for women a 'monstrosity'. Another ten years later, after the formation of the CGT, nothing had changed. At its 1898 congress the CGT voted in the principle that 'men should feed women'.[21] Only in 1935 did the CGT accept the principle of full equality.

The Weak Challenge of Bourgeois Feminism

The organisation of women by the German SPD was spurred on by the challenge of bourgeois feminists, whose organisations boasted hundreds of thousands of adherents. In Britain too, the suffragettes could mobilise hundreds of thousands in demonstrations. This had no equivalent in France, where the bourgeois feminist movement was tiny.

The first feminist organisation, *Société pour la Revendication des Droits de la Femme* (Society for the Demand for Women's Rights) was founded in 1866. Four years later it was superceded by the *Société pour l'Amelioration du Sort de la Femme* (Society for the Improvement of Woman's Lot), with a membership of between 150 and 160 and meetings averaging an attendance of a mere 10 or 12. The authorities suppressed it in 1875. In 1882 the society was relaunched under the new name of *Ligue Francaise pour la Droit des Femmes* (French League for Women's Rights), which by 1883 had only 194 members, of whom 96 were men, and these played the major role in its activities. In 1885 the only branch outside Paris, in Nantes, defected, and many of the men left. By 1892 the League had 95 members, 33 of them men.[22]

Another more radical organisation was launched in 1878 by Hubertine Auclert, called *Société pour le Suffrage des Femmes* (Women's Suffrage Society), but by 1880 it had only 18 dues-paying members.[23] In 1904, according to a police estimate, it had 125. In 1909 a new bourgeois feminist organisation was founded — *Union francaise pour le Suffrage des Femmes* (French Union for Women's Suffrage). It claimed a membership of 10,000 in 1913, but the numbers covered a coalition of a number of societies and included temperance associations and trade unions of women clerks and post and telegraph workers. The branches of the Union itself were mainly composed of female students and, by its own admission, in more than one town of little more than isolated individuals.[24]

Puny Results

In the half century between the beginning of socialist parties in the late 1870s and the end of the First World War, the achievements in recruiting women into the socialist movement were negligible. C Millard, historian of the POF, the largest socialist party, counted 20 women members in the years 1890–1893 and 53 in the years 1894–1899, representing 3 and 2 per cent of the membership respectively. Half of these were wives and daughters of members.[25] There is no reason to believe that other socialist parties included a greater percentage of women. On the contrary, the POF was more attractive to women than the others.

The historian Boxer states that at the beginning of the twentieth century the total number of women socialists active in Paris would be no higher than one hundred, and no more than five hundred in the entire country, 'excluding wives and daughters whose names appear on membership lists or amid delegations to congresses.'[26] In 1912 'a young socialist woman' complained that there were no young socialist women in the provinces and so few in Paris that 'one would be ashamed to cite the number.'

By 1932, when the Socialist Party took its first formal count of women members, this had risen to only 2,800, 2.1 per cent of the total membership and the lowest in Europe.[27] The history of socialist women in France is largely a history of isolated individuals, who never managed to build large, stable organisations, let alone a mass movement.[28]

The odds against success in France were overwhelming: stacked against them were the extreme weakness of the trade union movement and the damaging burden of anti-feminist republicanism and Proudhonism. Women workers, being part of the working class — and a weaker part at that — cannot on their own overcome all the obstacles impeding the advance of the class as a whole — and one of the chief of these is the sexist division of the class itself. Women's separatism — a natural reaction to Proudhonist anti-feminism — was a sign of weakness and in no way helped to overcome the obstacles to organising women in the socialist movement.

9
Revolution and counter-revolution in Russia

'Revolutions are the festivals of the oppressed and the exploited. At no other time are the masses of the people in a position to come forward so actively as creators of a new social order.' (V I Lenin)

The international movement of working women, as well as of the working class as a whole, reached unprecedented heights in the Russian revolution of 1917. It was a milestone in the emancipation of women: the first occasion on which the complete economic, political and sexual equality of women was put on the historical agenda. With workers' control over production, the question of women workers' control over the conditions of reproduction entered the arena.

New political, civic, economic and family codes aimed to wipe away centuries-old inequalities at one stroke. The new government granted women the full right to vote, passed divorce and civil laws that made marriage a voluntary relationship, eliminated the distinction between legitimate and illegitimate children, enacted employment rights for women equal to those for men, gave women equal pay, and introduced universal paid maternity leave. Adultery, incest and homosexuality were dropped from the criminal code. In July 1919 Lenin could write, with justifiable pride:

> Take the position of women. In this field, not a single democratic party in the world, not even in the most advanced bourgeois republic, has done in decades so much as a hundredth part of what we did in our very first year in power. We really razed to the ground the infamous laws placing women in a position of inequality, restricting divorce and surrounding it with disgusting formalities, denying recognition to children born out of wedlock, enforcing a search for their fathers, etc,

> laws numerous survivals of which, to the shame of the bourgeoisie and of capitalism, are to be found in all civilised countries.[1]

On the second anniversary of the revolution Lenin proudly announced:

> In the course of two years of Soviet power in one of the most backward countries in Europe, more had been done to emancipate woman, to make her the equal of the 'strong sex', than has been done during the past 130 years by all the advanced, enlightened, 'democratic' republics of the world taken together.[2]

And nineteen years after the October revolution Trotsky, looking back, could write:

> The revolution made a heroic effort to destroy the so-called family hearth — that archaic, stuffy, and stagnant institution in which the woman of the toiling classes performs galley labour from childhood to death . . . The complete absorption of the housekeeping functions of the family by institutions of the socialist society, uniting all generations in solidarity and mutual aid, was to bring to woman, and thereby to the loving couple, a real liberation from the thousand-year-old fetters.[3]

Six weeks after the revolution civil marriage replaced the rule of the church, and before a year was out a marriage code was produced based on complete equality of rights between husband and wife, as well as between legitimate and 'illegitimate' children. The decree of 19 December 1917 made divorce very simple: if the divorce was by mutual consent, dissolution took place on the spot; if a single claimant requested it, there was a brief court hearing. No grounds were needed, no contest, no evidence or witnesses, and no bitter, painful recommendation in public. Thus Soviet Russia became the only country in the world with full freedom of divorce. As regards the name of the married couple, a Code of 17 October 1918 stated: 'Married persons use a common surname . . . On the registration of marriage they may choose whether they will adopt the husband's (bridegroom's) or wife's (bride's) surname or their joint surnames.'[4] Trotsky took the name of his wife, Natalia Sedov, for citizenship requirements, and their sons also received her name. The new code went on:

> Actual descent is regarded as the basis of the family, without any difference between relationships established by legal or religious marriage or outside marriage. Children descended from parents related by non-registered marriage have equal rights with those descended from parents whose marriage was registered.[5]

From the beginning the Bolsheviks thought that for women to be emancipated some limitation of the size of the family by birth control was necessary. Lenin had attacked laws against abortion or against the distribution of medical literature on methods of birth control as hypocrisy by the ruling classes. 'These laws do not cure the ailments of capitalism, but only serve to render them more harmful, more difficult for the oppressed masses.'[6] A Decree on the Legalisation of Abortions was issued in November 1920.[7] Soviet Russia thus became the first country in the world to legalise abortion. To protect the health of women the decree stipulated: '. . . such operations to be performed freely and without any charge in Soviet hospitals, where conditions are assured of minimising the harm of the operation.'[8]

But the laws alone were far from enough to gain women real equality. The economic foundation of the traditional family had to be assaulted. This was attempted in a set of decrees abolishing the right of inheritance and transferring the property of the deceased to the state, which was to take over 'women's work' through its communal institutions: maternity homes, nurseries, kindergartens, schools, communal dining rooms, communal laundries, mending centres and so on. Lenin explained:

> Notwithstanding all the laws emancipating woman, she continues to be a *domestic slave*, because *petty housework* crushes, strangles, stultifies and degrades her, chains her to the kitchen and the nursery, and she wastes her labour on barbarously unproductive, petty, nerve-racking, stultifying and crushing drudgery. The real *emancipation of women*, real communism, will begin only where and when an all-out struggle begins (led by the proletariat wielding the state power) against this petty housekeeping, or rather when its *wholesale transformation* into a large-scale socialist economy begins.[9]

Kollontai, in a book titled **Women's Labour in Economic Development**, published in 1923, stated:

> . . . communal feeding has established itself with the town populations as an inevitable element in life. In Petrograd during 1919–20 almost 90 per cent of the entire population was fed communally. In Moscow more than 60 per cent of the population are registered with the feeding-halls. In 1920 twelve million town-dwellers were served in one way or another by communal feeding centres.
>
> 'Separation of kitchen from marriage' is a reform no less important than the separation of Church and State, at any rate in the history of woman . . .
>
> The new housing conditions created by the Workers' Republic also played their part in the change in the living conditions of women. Hostels, communal quarters for families and especially for single people are multiplying. No other country has as many hostels as has the Workers' Republic. And it is to be noted that everyone is eager to join communal quarters . . . Communal houses are always superior in their fittings to private flats; they are supplied with light and heating; they often have constant hot water and a central kitchen; they are cleaned by

professional cleaners; some are provided with a central laundry, others with a creche or nursery . . .

Family households will inevitably die a natural death with the growth in number of communal houses of different types to suit different tastes . . . Once it has ceased to be a unit of consumption, the family will be unable to exist in its present form — it will fall asunder, be liquidated . . .

But . . . care of children and their upbringing was no less a burden, chaining her to the house, enslaving her in the family . . . Motherhood is looked at from a new angle: the Soviet government regards it as a social obligation. With this principle in mind the Soviet government outlines a number of reforms tending to lift the burden of motherhood from woman's shoulders and to place it on the state.[10]

The Zhenotdel

To communicate to women the new values embodied in the new legal and civil code, which proclaimed the equality of women in economic, political and family life, the Bolsheviks launched a major campaign for the political mobilisation of women. In September 1919 Lenin declared that 'the emancipation of working women is a matter for the working women themselves.'[11] In similar vein Inessa Armand wrote: 'If the emancipation of women is unthinkable without communism, then communism is unthinkable without the full emancipation of women.'[12]

Lenin expanded further on the theme in a talk with Clara Zetkin:

We cannot exercise the dictatorship of the proletariat without having millions of women on our side. Nor can we engage in communist construction without them. We must find a way to reach them. We must study and search in order to find this way . . .

We derive our organisational ideas from our ideological conceptions. We want no separate organisations of communist women! She who is a Communist belongs as a member to the Party, just as he who is a Communist. They have the same rights and duties. There can be no difference of opinion on that score. However, we must not shut our eyes to the facts. The Party must have organs — working groups, commissions, committees, sections or whatever else they may be called — with the specific purpose of rousing the broad masses of women, bringing them into contact with the Party and keeping them under its influence. This naturally requires that we carry on systematic work among women.[13]

The first conference of women convened by the Bolsheviks after the October revolution took place on 19 November 1917. Five hundred delegates representing 80,000 women from factories, workshops, trade unions and party organisations attended. The conference was called specifically for the purpose of mobilising support for the Bolsheviks in the elections to the Constituent Assembly.

A year later, on 16 November 1918, the Bolshevik Party convened the first all-Russian Congress of Working Women. It was organised by a commission which included Inessa Armand, Alexandra Kollontai, Klavdiia Nikolaeva and Yaakov Sverdlov (secretary of the Bolshevik Party), who sent agitators to the provinces to arrange for the local election of delegates.

In the Kremlin Hall of Unions there gathered 1,147 women, including workers and peasant women from distant regions of the country. The programme presented to the congress was impressive: to win the support of women for Soviet power; to involve women in the party, government and trade unions; to combat domestic slavery and a double standard of morality; to establish communal living accommodation in order to release women from household drudgery; to protect women's labour and maternity; to end prostitution; to refashion women as members of the future communist society. Nikolaeva chaired the congress. Sverdlov welcomed the delegates. The main speeches were delivered by Kollontai and Inessa Armand. Lenin addressed the congress on its fourth day. After outlining the measures already taken by the Soviet government to improve women's conditions, he called on women to play a more active political role. 'The experience of all liberation movements has shown that the success of a revolution depends on how much the women take part in it.'

The congress led to the creation of Commissions for Agitation and Propaganda among Working Women. Their special methods of political work were elaborated by Kollontai at the Eighth Congress of the party in March 1919. She explained that because women were politically backward, the party had really not had much success in trying to approach and recruit them on the basis of general political appeals. Furthermore, she argued that it was women's oppression which led to their lack of involvement in political life; the cares and concerns of the family and the household robbed the woman worker of her time and energy and prevented her from becoming involved in broader political and social pursuits. Kollontai proposed that the way to attract women to Bolshevism was to draw them into socially useful projects, such as day nurseries, public dining rooms and maternity homes, which would serve to liberate women in their everyday lives.

> We have to conduct a struggle with the conditions which are oppressing the woman, to emancipate her as a housewife, as a mother. And this is the best approach toward women — this is agitation not only by words, but also by the deed.[14]

This principle of political organisation, which became known as 'agitation by the deed', was the distinctive feature of the activities of the Bolshevik women's organisation in this early period.[15]

In September 1919 the Bolshevik central committee changed the Commission for Agitation and Propaganda among Working Women into the Women's Section or Department of the Party (*zhenski otdel*, or *zhenotdel*), part of the central committee secretariat, under the leadership of Inessa Armand. Local branches of the *Zhenotdel* were attached to the party committees at every level, staffed by volunteers recruited among party women, and charged with conducting activities among the unorganised women in factories and villages, drawing them into public affairs.

Inessa Armand drew up a list of guiding principles for the *Zhenotdel* which she submitted to the first International Conference of Women Communists which took place in Moscow in July 1920. The *Zhenotdely*, by aiming to involve women who were not members of the Bolshevik Party, attempted to overcome the shortage of women party members: the total number of women in the party in 1920 was only 45,297, or 7.4 per cent of all members.[16]

The basic organising unit was a Delegates' Conference of Worker and Peasant Women. The conference was modelled on the soviets. Elections were organised among women workers and peasants to select delegates — one for every five workers or twenty-five peasants — who would attend meetings and courses of instruction under party guidance and then be assigned to a variety of state, party, trade union and co-operative agencies. The delegates were involved in organising communal institutions for dining, hospitals, maternity homes, children's homes and schools. Delegates also served in the people's courts, sometimes in the capacity of judges. Delegates served for short terms — usually two to three months. The number of women actively involved was large. In the latter half of 1923 the *Zhenotdely* reported that the total number of delegates was about 58,000.[17]

In addition the *Zhenotdel* campaigned to mobilise women for support work in the civil war. Women performed medical services, served in the political departments of the Red Army, worked on communications, served in Saturday and Sunday work brigades, organised campaigns against desertion and epidemic diseases, and provided aid to the families of Red Army soldiers and to homeless children.[18]

One of the most important activities of each *Zhenotdel* was the spreading of literacy. 'An illiterate person,' declared Lenin, 'stands outside politics. He must first learn his ABC. Without that there can be no politics; without that there are rumours, gossip, fairy-tales and prejudices, but not politics.'[19] The literacy schools did not limit themselves to instruction in reading and writing, but became important vehicles for the dissemination of political, cultural and general educational work.

One of the leaders in the movement for women's literacy was Nadezhda Krupskaia. Before the revolution, she had taught workers in evening schools. Now she devoted even more attention to this activity.

The director of *Zhenotdel*, who was answerable to the party secretariat, supervised not only all the internal affairs of the *Zhenotdel* proper, but extended her influence into every corner of life where women were involved. Bolshevik women leaders with their own particular responsibilities and interests such as V P Lebedeva (maternity), Krupskaia (education) and Mariya Ulyanova (journalism) interlocked their activities with those of the *Zhenotdel*. The Bolshevik women's movement thus extended even beyond the national network of *Zhenotdely*.[20]

The *Zhenotdel* had a monthly paper of its own, **Kommunistka** (Woman Communist) with a print order in 1921 of 30,000. Its editorial group included Bukharin, Inessa Armand and Kollontai.

Inessa Armand drove herself to exhaustion, working sixteen hours a day or more. She was ordered by the party to the Caucasus for a rest. There, in October 1920, she caught cholera and died. Kollontai was chosen to succeed her. Her role ended after a year when she joined the Workers' Opposition. Then in 1922 she was assigned to a diplomatic post in Norway.

The harsh reality

It is clear that the traditional work of women — nursing, rearing children, cooking — continued to be the lot of women during the civil war. On the other hand, the central task of the time — the military struggle — was largely confined to men.

In the Red Army women served in medical capacities. They also took part in propaganda, espionage and police work. A small minority served as riflewomen, armoured train commanders, gunners. They performed police work in the towns, and combat duty in time of enemy siege. A few acted as partisans, the most well-known and colourful being Larissa Reissner. Women played an important part in the propaganda work of the army. Thus Kollontai, after a brief period serving the government, threw herself into the work of propaganda in the army with great energy. She roamed the front on a specially equipped agitational train. The political work in the Red Army was carried on through the political sections in each unit. These were centrally co-ordinated by Varya Kasparova.

But the total number of women fighting in the civil war was comparatively small. According to one account for 1920, it was 73,858, of whom 1,854 became casualties.[21] The total number of soldiers in the Red Army in 1920 was about three million, of whom probably two million were to be casualties.

The sexual division of labour, like the division between manual and mental labour, could not be overcome in the society emerging from the barbarism of Tsarist Russia, stamped with the hallmarks of centuries of backwardness. The harsh conditions of the civil war were certainly not conducive to overcoming this inheritance. As Marx said:

> Men do not build themselves a new world with 'earthly goods' as vulgar superstition believes, but with the historical achievements of the old world which is about to go under. In the course of evolution they must begin entirely by themselves to produce the material conditions for a new society, and no effort of the human mind or will can release them from this fate.[22]

The mighty sweep of idealism, the courage and soaring hopes of the Bolsheviks, crashed against the terrible backwardness of Russia. Cruel history brought about a sharp contradiction between the grand aspirations of the workers and their actual material and cultural poverty. This was much aggravated by the seven years of war and civil war. Russia emerged from the civil war in a state of economic collapse 'unparalleled in the history of mankind', as an economic historian of the period writes. Industrial production was about a fifth of the 1914 level and the city population had shrunk. Between the end of 1918 and the end of 1920 epidemics, hunger and cold killed nine million Russians. The world war as a whole had claimed four million victims of all nations.[23]

The industrial working class suffered a catastrophic decline in morale and political consciousness. The dream of women for emancipation, as embodied in the decrees of the government and the activities of *Zhenotdel*, ran into the sand. First it was necessary to survive.

During the period of War Communism (1918–1920) it was taken for granted that full employment would prevail. If unemployment did arise, it would be temporary and on a small scale. With these assumptions the fight for a woman's right to work was straightforward. And to start with, immediately after the October revolution, the unions dealt very equitably with women's right to work. In April 1918 the Petrograd Council of Trade Unions addressed the following appeal to all workers and factory committees:

> The question of how to combat unemployment has come sharply before the unions. In many factories and shops the question is being solved

> very simply . . . fire the women and put men in their places . . . The only effective measure against unemployment is the restoration of the productive powers of the country, reorganisation on a socialist basis . . . We must decide each case individually. There can be no question of whether the worker is a man or a woman, but simply of the degree of need.[24]

This attitude was upheld by the other unions and government organisations.

The New Economic Policy (1921–8), however, brought about widespread unemployment, rising from 175,000 in January 1922, to 625,000 in January 1923 and 1,240,000 in January 1925.[25] Since unskilled workers were the first to be laid off, and women were for the most part unskilled, they were the worst hit by unemployment.

> In March, 1923, women constituted 58.7 per cent of the unemployed in Petrograd and 63.3 per cent of the unemployed in the textile-producing centre of Ivanovo-Voznesensk. In the textile industry itself they constituted from 80 to 95 per cent of the unemployed in Moscow, Petrograd, and Ivanovo-Voznesensk. At the urging of the *Zhenotdel* the Commissariat of Labour decreed that in instances where men and women had the same level of skills, women should not be the first fired, but the *Zhenotdel* admitted that it was impossible to enforce quotas for the retention of women in the labour force. Even Communist Party members argued that it was unprofitable to employ women under the principle of equal pay for equal work, because the extensive laws protecting female labour made it more costly to hire women. (In early 1924 the *Zhenotdel* agreed to lift the ban on night work for women, in order to give employers as little excuse as possible to lay off women workers.)[26]

The principle of equal pay for equal work, and the laws protecting female labour, were not being observed even in state enterprises.

Unemployment delivered a severe blow to attempts at women's liberation, and the economic dependence of women on men got a boost. Oppressive, reactionary trends were strengthened, as the state sought to cut expenditure, and the extensive communal institutions of War Communism — communal kitchens, dining halls, children's homes and creches — were run down. It was estimated in November 1925 that 'public dinners' were served to only 20,000 workers in Moscow, 50,000 in Leningrad, and 67,000 in the provinces, a total of 137,000. Only three out of a hundred children were provided with places in creches. All the rest were reared entirely in individual families.

Women were pushed back into domestic slavery. The plight of children added to the woman's burden. Dislocation and poverty resulting from the war and civil war produced a massive army of abandoned children, the so-called *besprizorniki*, many of whom took to crime. In 1922 it was estimated tht the number of homeless children was as high as nine million.[27] The numbers were constantly increasing as parents failed to provide for their children. The pressure, on women above all, to preserve the family hearth as a haven for children was overwhelming. Because of the economic circumstances of the time, the freedom of divorce, when children were involved, meant 'the woman remains tied with chains to the . . . ruins of the family hearth. The man, happily whistling, can leave it.'[28]

Divorce therefore came to appear to women not only, or even mainly, as a harbinger of freedom, but of destitution. Men were far more willing to divorce their wives than wives their husbands. A sample of 500 questionnaires about broken homes which was discussed at a Viborg district conference showed that 70 per cent of separations were unilaterally initiated by men, and only 7 per cent by mutual agreement.[29]

The question of divorcees' entitlement to alimony, not even mentioned in the 1918 Family Code, became crucial for women in the 1920s. A long public discussion during 1925 convinced the government that a new Family Code was needed, to include the guarantee of alimony. If men could be forced to support their families, they might not abandon so many women or father so many unwanted children. The proposed law also entitled the spouse in common law marriages, those that had not been registered, to alimony. Furthermore, it asserted the right of the wife to share the property which the couple had acquired during their marriage.

The strongest pressure for the preservation of the traditional family came from the peasantry, who made up some four-fifths of the country's population. They looked to stability of the family to protect the farm. Thus in the debate on the newly suggested family code, one woman stated:

> There are many of these divorces, but consider: do they benefit us in any way? Every one of us, every man or woman, will agree, they do not. For example: a man and a woman get divorced. They own a little house, a cow, and they have three children. And here they are, splitting their little property in two. The mother of course will not leave the children with the father, for children are always dearer to the mother. What is the woman to do now, with her children? There is no danger for the husband. He will find another woman to live with. But for the wife life under such conditions is terribly difficult. The result of it all is poverty, and we have too much of that as it is.[30]

Another woman complained:

> Burdening the entire family with the payment of alimony is naturally liable to interfere with our agriculture. I consider it unfair, and I think it will lead to nothing but a campaign of ill-feeling against women. If, for

example, three brothers live together and possess one cow, and the court decides that alimony is to be paid by the whole family, is the cow to be divided into small pieces? No good will have come from such a decision, but the farm will have been ruined.[31]

In the harsh economic conditions of the 1920s the greater freedom of sex and marriage entailed the exploitation and abuse of women (and children). Taking the real circumstances into account, Trotsky supported the Family Code of 1926 as a necessary evil, a form of protection for women, although it was a great retreat from the 1918 Family Code.

The drastic deterioration of the position of women in the 1920s expressed itself also in a resurgence of prostitution. During the period of War Communism prostitution almost completely disappeared. In 1921 the number rose to 17,000 in Petrograd and 10,000 in Moscow, according to official statistics. In the next year the Petrograd figure climbed to 32,000, grimly signalling the fact that the problem was again reaching pre-revolutionary proportions. In the course of a single year, from April 1924 to April 1925, 2,228 procurers and proprietors of brothels were arrested for crimes connected with prostitution.

The Counter-revolution

The massive industrialisation and forced collectivisation of agriculture which was launched in 1928–9 was a turning point in the history of Russia, transforming the country into a state capitalist regime.[32] The regimentation of the working class brought about a number of radical changes in working women's conditions. Millions of women were rapidly mobilised into the labour force.

Female Workers and Employees 1922–1940[33]

Year	*Number of Female Workers and Employees*	*Per cent of Total*
1922	1,560,000	25
1928	2,795,000	24
1932	6,000,000	27
1940	13,190,000	39

The massive employment of women represents the *potential* for their liberation, but in itself is no liberation. it may indeed impose a *double* burden. The following facts in an article entitled 'Socialism and the Family', published in 1936 in a serious Soviet journal, deserve severe deprecation rather than congratulation:

Women play a very negligible role in capitalist mining industry. The proportion of women to the total numbers employed in the mining industries is, for France (1931), 2.7 per cent; for Italy (1931), 1.8 per cent; for Germany (1932), 1.0 per cent; USA (1930), 0.6 per cent; and in Great Britain, 0.6 per cent. In the USSR women represent 27.9 per cent of the total number of people working in the mining industry.[34]

The pattern of Stalinist industrialisation, with its extreme concentration of investment in heavy industry, led to the neglect of precisely those economic sectors of activity that might have lightened the burden of working women, such as housing, consumer goods and services.

The Stalinist regime also strengthened conservative attitudes. Now the authorities found the family useful, not only because it provided what the state did not — domestic work and child care — but also because it reinforced the bureaucracy's need for conservative supports throughout society. As Trotsky so aptly put it in 1936 in **Revolution Betrayed**: 'The most compelling motive of the present cult of the family is undoubtedly the need of the bureaucracy for a stable hierarchy of relations . . .'

In 1934 homosexuality was made a criminal offence, punishable with up to eight years' imprisonment, and an energetic nationwide campaign was launched against sexual promiscuity, quick and easy marriage, and adultery.

Motherhood became a central theme of propaganda. 'A woman without children merits our pity, for she does not know the full joy of life. Our Soviet women, full-blooded citizens of the freest country in the world, have been given the bliss of motherhood.'[35]

In 1936 legal abortion was abolished, except where life or health were endangered or a serious disease might be inherited.

The laws of 1935–6 also provided some sanctions against divorce: fees of 50, 150 and 300 rubles for the first, second and subsequent divorces. Probably more important, it required entry of the fact of divorce in the personal documents of those involved.[36] Sexual freedom was virulently attacked and puritanism extolled. A British observer who stayed in Russia for a long period wrote:

> Soviet sex morality today demands of young people continence until marriage and associates sex with children and family. Woe to the young factory worker or college student, man or woman, who is discovered to have had an affair outside marriage. The event is publicised and all the ignominy that stinging rebukes or Komsomol [Young Communist League] resolutions can evoke is levelled at the guilty one.[37]

He tells the sad tale of Galina, accused of 'immoral' conduct with a young married man. The factory Komsomol organiser, whose assistance she sought to get the rumour scotched, could only suggest that she 'go to a clinic, get a certificate of virginity, and show it around.'[38]

The regime trumpeted the sanctity of the family. 'Marriage

is . . . a lifelong union . . . Moreover, marriage receives its full value for the State only if there is progeny, and the consorts experience the highest happiness of parenthood.'[39] Scapegoats were found for sexual laxity and the instability of marriage:

> The enemies of the people, the vile fascist hirelings — Trotsky, Bukharin, Krylenko and their followers — covered the family in the USSR with filth, spreading the counter-revolutionary 'theory' of the dying out of the family, of disorderly sexual cohabitation in the USSR, in order to discredit the Soviet land.[40]

A further step in the sexual counter-revolution was the abolition of co-education in 1943. A Orlov, director of the Moscow Municipal Department of National Education, wrote on the subject on 10 August 1943:

> . . . the programme of education and the curriculum for boys' schools and girls' schools can be and must be differentiated. It is essential to introduce in girls' schols such additional subjects as pedagogics, needlework, courses in domestic science, personal hygiene and the care of children. In boys' schools, training in handicrafts must become a part of the curriculum.

Another Russian writer explained that co-education was harmful, as it led to 'covering up of masculine and feminine traits which are of social value.'

> . . . what we must have now is a system by which the school develops boys who will be good fathers and manly fighters for the socialist homeland, and girls who will be intelligent mothers competent to rear the new generation.[41]

Stalinist reaction as regards the family reached its climax with the law of 8 July 1944 which introduced heavy sanctions against divorce. A judicial process of divorce was instituted, and the fees raised to high levels — between 500 and 2,000 rubles. Such sums were prohibitive to all but the most affluent. In the judicial process the lower court was required to make every effort to effect reconciliation. If this proved impossible, the case was to be taken to a higher court, which could actually grant the divorce. A fundamental innovation was that the court could reject the suit. The law re-established the legal differences between a child born in wedlock and one born out of wedlock. The latter could not claim the surname (patronymic), the support or the inheritance of his or her father.[42]

A scale of cash payments was introduced to encourage mothers to have more children. Mothers with a large number were also awarded special decorations: 'Motherhood Medal, First Class and Second Class for those with five to six children; Motherhood Glory, First,

Second and Third Class, for those who produced seven, eight or nine children; Heroine Mother for those who bore and brought up ten children.' Bachelors, single citizens and citizens with small families were penalised by having to pay a special new tax.[43] The ideal of motherhood was associated with the newly triumphant Great Russian nationalism and the idea of the 'Motherland'.

With the transformation of Russia into a state capitalist regime, reference to the 'Woman Question' as a distinct subject of political and ideological concern ceased. An index of party resolutions and decrees over the yers 1917–1967 lists 301 entries on the subject 'Women' for the period 1917–1930, and only three for the next 37 years.[44]

Stalinist counter-revolution did not limit itself to the field of sexual relationships, but engulfed the whole of society. It established a massive, exploiting, highly-privileged state bureaucracy. In the 1940s the phenomenon of 'Soviet millionaires' was reported in the Russian press. Autocratic one-man management was established in the factories. Generals receiving fat salaries and entitled to large pensions commanded soldiers who earned a pittance. Millions of peasants were expropriated and forced into collective farms. Millions were incarcerated in slave labour camps. Mass purges culminated in the frame-ups of the Moscow Trials during 1935–8, which led to the murder of a whole generation of old Bolsheviks. The death sentence for theft was introduced for youths.[45]

The subjection of women was but one aspect of the Stalinist counter-revolution.

The Radical Feminist Interpretation

In complete contrast to the above analysis is the radical feminist interpretation of these events. Thus for instance Shulamith Firestone writes:

> *. . . the failure of the Russian Revolution to achieve the classless society is traceable to its half-hearted attempts to eliminate the family and sexual repression.* This failure, in turn, was due to the limitations of a male-biased revolutionary analysis based on economic class alone, one that failed to take the family fully into account even in its function as an economic unit.[46]

The well-known sexologist Wilhelm Reich had a different interpretation. He argued that if the Soviet Union had only not reversed its early plan to change family organisation and liberate sexuality, socialism would not have been defeated.

Here consciousness is endowed with more power than economic, social and military realities. For such writers Russia's backwardness, the industrial losses during the Civil War, the numerical weakness of the working class, the failure of the European revolution, these are nothing compared to the sexual policies of the rulers of Russia. But what are the roots of the sexual and family policies of the rulers of Russia? What shaped them? What made them change?

Into the desert . . .

The defeat of the Russian working class at the hands of the Stalinist bureaucracy led to catastrophic defeats of the international working class. For a whole historical period not only did the working-class movement as a whole retreat, but even more its women members. If social advance, as Marx pointed out, can be gauged by the advance of women, so also can retreat. The question of women's liberation was pushed right off the agenda for half a century.

At the same time, bourgeois feminism was dead. Once the bourgeois women achieved the vote, they stopped their agitation against male privilege. In the face of the general crisis of capitalism, they became a prop of reaction.

10
The failure of success: The women's liberation movement in the United States

Women's liberation returned to the agenda in the 1960s. There was now a growing challenge to Stalinism in Hungary, Czechoslovakia and Poland and, in the West, a slowly deepening crisis of world capitalism. Women were also now taking paid employment in greater numbers than ever before, aided by increased higher education on the one hand and more effective birth control on the other. In September 1978 the British women's liberation magazine **Spare Rib** wrote: 'The US women's movement is the mother of us all.' This is indeed so. It was the first on the scene and has maintained its international precedence — so our examination of the modern women's movement will start in the United States.

The Civil Rights Movement

The modern American Women's Liberation Movement (WLM) was born out of the civil rights movement. Once before, when working for justice for black slaves in the movement for the abolition of slavery in the 1830s–1870s, a handful of Southern white middle-class women had gained experience in organising collective action. They also gained a belief in human rights, which they used to justify the demand for equality for themselves. A similar process took place in the civil rights movement which reverberated through the 1960s, triggering the foundation of the WLM. The story of how the women's movement grew is told in an exciting way in Sara Evans's book, **Personal Politics: The Roots of Women's Liberation in the Civil Rights Movement and the New Left.**[1] My debt to her is great. Since

Sara Evans is not a Marxist, however, but a radical feminist, I cannot accord with her interpretation of events.

Students were crucial in organising the civil rights movement in the Southern states of America. Their main organisation was the Students' Non-violent Co-ordinating Committee (SNCC). This became involved in projects to register voters in the deep south and in mass sit-ins, involving hundreds of thousands of non-students, which aimed to end the racial segregation in such public places as restaurants, motels and bus stations. Sara Evans writes:

> War with white society seemed total. In such a context . . . by the winter of 1961 the SNCC staff had begun to walk, talk and dress like the poor black farmers and sharecroppers of rural Georgia and Mississippi . . . From the beginning a cluster of young white women committed their lives to the revolt of black youth.[2]
>
> Most white women who participated in the early years of the civil rights movement tended to be southerners, and virtually without exception white southern women who joined the civil rights movement came to it first through the Church.[3]

Between 1963 and 1965 hundreds of young white women from middle and upper-class backgrounds went south. However the deep differences of class, colour and sex prevented the white women who worked for the blacks from integrating with them. The SNCC acted *on behalf of* the blacks, and failed to build a mass movement. Without roots in a working class cemented by collective production, fissions were inevitable. The most natural was on colour lines, between blacks and whites. 'The presence of hundreds of young whites from middle and upper-class backgrounds in a movement primarily of poor, rural blacks exacerbated latent racial and sexual tensions beyond the breaking point,' writes Sara Evans. One black woman said:

> 'If white women had a problem in SNCC it was not just a male/woman problem . . . it was also a black woman/white woman problem. It was a race problem rather than a woman's problem.' And a white woman, asked whether she experienced any hostility from black women, responded, 'Oh! tons and tons . . .' Her sexual relationships with black men placed a barrier between herself and black women.[4]

The white women were deeply affected by their experience. A few fled immediately. Most, however, fulfilled their commitments and returned to the north seared by an experience that marked a turning point in their lives.[5]

But the conflict rending the SNCC was not only between black women and men and white women. It was also between white and black men as the latter became increasingly alienated from the concept of non-violence and of 'black and white together'. By 1965 the path to 'black power' was clearly signposted. 'Whites were less and less welcome in any part of the civil rights movement.'[6]

There was a corresponding movement among students in the northern states. When black students in the south began a wave of sit-ins in the spring of 1960, between 60,000 and 80,000 northern students responded in support.[7] Again they were predominantly 'from middle to upper-middle-class families.'[8] Students for a Democratic Society (SDS) was built in response to this movement. It began organising in northern cities between 1963 and 1965, using the SNCC as its model.

Few students in the SDS were prepared for the realities of day-to-day organising. They had chosen to organise among 'the Negro movement and the . . . unorganised poor', a section of society which, compared with the blacks of the south, showed no signs of self-organisation or collective consciousness. This was the section of society described by Marx as the 'lumpenproletariat'. As a result the SDS style of organising became tedious, frustrating and anxiety-ridden. It consisted of going into a neighbourhood and knocking on door after door hoping that whoever answered would be willing to talk to a stranger, then looking for openings for collective action, providing personal support, earning trust.[9]

But those who the students aimed to organise — 'persons whose economic role in society is marginal or insecure' — proved to be powerless and impossible to organise on a stable basis. Social revolution is not dependent merely on poverty. It also requires collective organisation, based on collective action in production, in the factories and workplaces. And this the poorest section of society, being unemployed or working in marginal jobs, lacks.

But the white, middle-class students, who belonged to the people by sentiment only, idealised the people, and above all the blacks. This idealisation showed particularly in the way the movement bowed to spontaneity. The closest thing to a theory that the movement had was the slogan on one of its badges: 'Let the people decide'. The organisers were not to give a lead, but only to reflect the wishes of the people; a clear plan was considered manipulative and not in the spirit of participatory democracy. Moreover poor people were unused to meetings and did not necessarily like them. Over and over again meetings were held at which the only people to show up were the organisers themselves.[10]

The women in the SDS were far more successful than the men. While the men tried, unsuccessfully, to organise the unemployed round the slogan of 'Job or Income Now', the women concentrated on 'women's issues' — recreation, day care, schools, street lights, housing and welfare. The women 'set about creating stable organisations of welfare mothers.'[11] They gained greatly in self-confidence. 'For the first time within SDS women had an independent ground from which to draw their self-respect and to command the respect of others.'[12]

The separation of the men and women of the SDS into two spheres of activity was accompanied by sharpening sexual tensions. The male members of the SDS were very much influenced by the milieu in which they worked. The poorest sections of society are so deprived that 'violence and physical aggression become a common way of life, particularly for young males.' One crucial form of this violence is *machismo* — sexual aggression.[13] This greatly affected the leadership of the black movement. Thus, for instance, Eldridge Cleaver, who was to become a Black Panther theoretician, describes in his autobiography **Soul on Ice** how in his youth he indulged in raping, first black women and then white, as a way of asserting himself. 'An insurrectionary act' he called it.[14] Another black leader, Stokeley Carmichael, was responsible for the infamous remark at the 1964 SNCC conference: 'The only position for women in SNCC is prone.'

At the University of Washington, an SDS organiser explained to a large meeting how white college youth established rapport with the poor whites with whom they were working:

> He noted that sometimes after analysing societal ills, the men shared leisure time by 'balling a chick together'. He pointed out that such activities did much to enhance the political consciousness of the poor white youth. A woman in the audience asked, 'And what did it do for the consciousness of the chick?'[15]

Many men in the SDS adopted this sexist attitude. Relations between women and men in the SDS came near to breaking point.

Women's Movement rises from disintegration of Civil Rights and Student Movements

The movement against the Vietnam War grew out of the civil rights movement and spread in spectacular fashion among students. 'Campuses suddenly ignited with protest' after President Johnson began to draft young men in large numbers to fight. On 17 April 1965 more than 20,000 protestors gathered in Washington to demonstrate against the war. Students saw themselves in opposition to the 'system', oppressed as students, potential cannon fodder. The SDS grew significantly, and sit-ins, learned from the civil rights movement, now broke out when recruiters for the armed forces appeared, or when universities refused to respond to demands concerning selective service ranking, tuition increases, wages for university workers, or curriculum reform.[16]

Women were very active in the mass student movement. But

after 1966 they felt pushed to the periphery. The central issue was now the draft.

> Men were drafted, women were not. Men could resist the draft; they burned draft cards; they risked jail. And women's role was to support them. 'Girls Say Yes to Guys Who Say No!' was a widespread slogan of the movement.[17]

Moving from the fight 'for other people' to the fight for their own liberation on the campuses, the students created a 'theory' that students, being trained for professional jobs in a highly technological society, were the key element in the modern working class. Students became the 'surrogate proletariat' and the universities must become 'Red bases'. Sara Evans writes:

> Students were becoming more introspective in general . . . These 'hippies' . . . glorified gentleness, love, community, and co-operation, and spurned competitiveness, polished professionalism in work, and materialism. Later on their trademarks became events like 'be-ins', 'love-ins', and phrases like 'getting your head together' and 'do your own thing'. Crucial ingredients for the future of women's liberation lay in this counterculture's rejection of middle-class standards and life-styles and its focus on personal issues. It called into question basic defining institutions for women like marriage and the family, asserting in fact that communal living was superior.[18]

Thus another strand in the future WLM came into being: concentration on one's own internal world — on lifestyle and what was later termed 'consciousness-raising'.

'The Movement' in 1967 was increasingly fragmented into a multitude of groups. In an effort to unite the fragments, the New Left convened a National Conference for New Politics (NCNP) in August 1967. Two thousand activists from 200 organisations turned up, most of them young veterans of civil rights and anti-war activities. 'Black power' was at its height and the hope for unity was faint.

Black delegates at the conference needed to unleash their fury at American racism on the whites, who for their part seemed desperate for black approval to validate their own activities. Black delegates shouted 'Kill Whitey!' and insisted that they should cast 50 per cent of the conference vote and occupy half the committee slots though they constituted about one-sixth of the delegates. Each time the conference gave in to black demands, the majority of whites applauded enthusiastically in apparent approval of their own denunciation.

The logic of black separatism dawned upon the women delegates to the NCNP. In extended discussions they devised a resolution requiring that women, who represent 51 per cent of the population, receive 51 per cent of the conference votes and committee representation.[19] The white men who capitulated to the black nationalists, however, were not ready to make any concessions to the women. Instead they ridiculed and patronised them and refused to allow time for the resolution. By threatening to tie up the conference with procedural motions, the women succeeded in having their statement tacked on to the end of the agenda. It was never discussed. The chair refused to recognise any of the women standing by the microphones, their hands straining upward. When instead he called on someone to speak on 'the forgotten American, the American Indian', five women rushed the podium to demand an explanation. But the chairman just patted one of the women on the head and told her, 'Cool down, little girl, we have more important things to talk about than women's problems.'

The 'little girl' was Shulamith Firestone, future author of **The Dialectic of Sex**[20] and she did not cool down.[21]

Ridicule pursued the infant women's movement. **Ramparts**, a successful would-be radical magazine, featured in January 1968 a woman's leotard-clad torso, cut off at the neck, with a Jeanette Rankin Brigade button dangling from one breast. 'Woman Power', **Ramparts** titled the picture: 'two tits, no head' was the general interpretation. A grossly patronising article accompanied it. **Ramparts** refused to publish a reply.[22]

At the January 1969 mass anti-war demonstration in Washington women had asked for and received time for two short speeches, after many objections from the men organising it. When they tried to speak they were hooted down with cries of 'Take her off the stage and fuck her!' Separation from men was inevitable.

The gross sexism of the men of the American New left was certainly one of the worst examples in history of sexism by men who claimed to be 'left'. It was much worse than women could expect to suffer in, say, a trade union meeting. The class origins of the New Left, plus their discounting of the organised working class as agents for change, led to all kinds of elitism, of which sexism was one form. Because they discounted the working class, their politics always pulled towards reformism, however radical their speeches might be. Their intervention in the civil rights movement was always *on behalf of* poor blacks, and the campaign against the draft was based on moral arguments and very individualist.

Some of the women who became feminists did so as a reaction to their treatment by the New Left. A few paid lip-service to the ideas of socialism, but because of this experience insisted on organising separately from men. Of course the whole period has become part of the mythology of the women's movement, to be regularly wheeled out as justification for separatism.

The middle-class origins of most of the women drawn towards the early women's movement also made it easy for them to see their problems in terms of the sexism of men. In the boom of the 1960s, with job opportunities opening up for women, the sexism of men competing for those jobs — particularly middle-class, professional jobs — could easily appear to be the main barrier for women.

These two factors created a situation where separatism was always on the cards. Both were the results of a particular historical situation, peculiar to the boom period of the 1960s and the development of a 'left' movement with no links to working-class organisation.

Thus did the women's movement grow out of the disintegration of the civil rights movement, the bankruptcy of the student movement, and in reaction to the gross sexism of the men in the New Left.

Before moving on to look at the women's movement itself, it is worth tracing what happened to the movements from which it grew. The black movement involved millions of people. Between 1964 and 1968 hundreds of riots shook US cities. The student movement, particularly when it turned into a movement against the Vietnam War, also mobilised masses of people. But neither undermined the capitalist system which they opposed. For neither the black revolutionaries nor the student radicals were able to build at the point where capitalism can be directly and collectively challenged — in the factories and workplaces where workers create capitalism's wealth. Both led their movements along separate paths, and both paths led downwards.

With the winding down of the Vietnam War in the early 1970s, the student movement declined and the students went back to their studies. With the collapse of the left generally, the black revolutionary left collapsed too. Many black activists, particularly those who advocated the seizure of Black Power, were assassinated by the government — but far more decided that revolution was a chimera and went into traditional politics. Out of the black movement rose a substantial layer of middle-class professionals mediating between the ghettos and the establishment: social workers, community organisers, Democratic Party politicians representing decayed urban areas, impotent representatives in Congress.[23]

In the history of the American women's movement — as of the black and student movements — one must distinguish between two periods: 1968–73, when the level of struggle was generally high, and the later period from 1974 onwards, when the level of struggle was in decline and the political scene moved rightwards.

Radical Feminist Theory

The central idea of the American Women's Liberation Movement is that the enemy is man. Thus the New York Radical Feminist

Manifesto declared:

> As radical feminists we recognize that we are engaged in a power struggle with men, and that the agent of our oppression is man in so far as he identifies with and carries out the supremacy privileges of the male role . . . We believe that the purpose of male chauvinism is primarily to obtain psychological ego satisfaction, and that only secondarily does this manifest itself in economic relationships . . . for this reason we do not believe that capitalism, or any other economic system, is the cause of female oppression, nor do we believe that female oppression will disappear as a result of a purely economic revolution. The political oppression of women has its own class dynamic. And that dynamic must be understood in terms previously called 'non-political' — namely the politics of the ego . . . the male ego identity [is] sustained through its ability to have power over the female ego.

Juliet Mitchell, who quotes this approvingly, concludes that an all-class unity is needed:

> . . . class differences are not what is important — it is for women to see how they are subjected as a whole that is crucial. In the home the social function and the psychic identity of women as a group is found . . . the position of women as women takes precedence: oppressed whatever their particular circumstances. Hence the importance of feminist consciousness in any revolution . . . Hence Women's Liberation.[24]

A 'theoretical' backing for the view that sexual oppression is the *base* and the economy the superstructure is supplied by Shulamith Firestone in **The Dialectics of Sex**. She writes first that the roots of the family structure, with the two 'classes' in it — man the oppressor and woman the oppressed, are in sexual reproduction. 'Unlike economic class, sex class sprang directly from a biological reality: men and women were created different, and not equal.'

> The sexual-reproductive organisation of society always furnishes the real basis, starting from which we can alone work out the ultimate explanation of the whole superstructure of economic, juridical and political institutions as well as of the religious, philosophical and other ideas of a given historical period.

The root cause of exploitation, she says, is psychosexual: 'The biological family is an inherently unequal power distribution. The need for power leading to development of classes arises from the psychosexual formation of each individual according to this basic imbalance.' And '*racism is sexism extended*.'[25]

Firestone's purely biological analysis makes sexual inequality inevitable. Many radical feminists draw the conclusion from Firestone's analysis that since all class and race antagonisms grow out of the initial inequality between men and women, a strike in the marriage bed would be a blow not only against sexism but also its by-products, class society and racism.

By the Middle Class, For the Middle Class

The social composition of the American Women's Movement and its supporters was and is overwhelmingly middle class. Thus Jo Freeman, one of the founders of the movement, describes its early composition as 'white, middle-class, college-educated, professionally employed women'. Among the members of the largest women's organisation, the National Organisation of Women (NOW), in 1974 66 per cent had degrees, and 30 per cent also had advanced degrees.[26] Maren Lockwood Carden found that 'almost 90 per cent of the Women's Rights groups' members interviewed had at least a BA degree; a third held PhDs, MDs or law degrees.'[27]

This is a far cry from the world of the majority of women. The abyss between these feminists and working-class women was highlighted at the International Women's Year Tribunal organised by the United Nations in Mexico in 1975. Here two worlds met. On the one side were the middle-class women led by Betty Friedan, the founder of NOW and one of the original inspirers of the women's movement in America. On the other were working-class women, among them Domitila Barrio, a Bolivian miner's wife and mother of seven. She had for fifteen years organised miners' wives in struggles to aid their husbands on strike. An indication of the miners' conditions was that their life expectancy was a mere 35 years. Domitila Barrio had organised a long hunger strike of women, and had gone to prison a number of times, on one occasion suffering a miscarriage while in custody. She bitterly attacked the rich feminists who turned up to the conference. To the president of the Mexican delegation she said:

> Senora, I've known you for a week. Every morning you show up in a different outfit and on the other hand I don't. Every day you show up all made up and combed like someone who had time to spend in an elegant beauty parlour and who can spend money on that, and yet I don't. I see that each afternoon you have a chauffeur in a car waiting at the door of this place to take you home, and yet I don't. And in order to show up here like you do, I'm sure you live in a really elegant home, in an elegant neighborhood, no? And yet we miners' wives only have a small house on loan to us, and when our husbands die or get sick or are fired from the company, we have ninety days to leave the house and then we're in the street. Now, senora, tell me: is your situation at all similar to mine? Is my situation at all similar to yours? So what equality are we going to speak of between the two of us? If you and I aren't alike, if you and I are so different?

The rich women, she claimed, were blind to the conditions of women like herself:

> They couldn't see the suffering of my people, they couldn't see how our *companeros* are vomiting their lungs bit by bit, in pools of blood. They didn't see how underfed our children are. And, of course, they didn't know, as we do, what it's like to get up at four in the morning and go to bed at eleven or twelve at night, just to be able to get all the housework done, because of the lousy conditions we live in.

She could not understand Betty Freidan's statement that she, Domitila, and her friends were 'manipulated by men'.

> I felt a bit lost. In other rooms, some women stood up and said: men are the enemy . . . men create wars, men create nuclear weapons, men beat women . . . and so what's the first battle to be carried out to get equal rights for women? First you have to declare war against men.[28]

She opposed both *machismo* and feminism.

> I think that *machismo* is a weapon of imperialism just like feminism is. Therefore, I think that the basic fight isn't between the sexes; it's a struggle of the couple. And when I say couple, I also include children and grandchildren, who have to join the struggle for liberation from a class position. I think that's fundamental now.[29]

The separatism of the women's movement, both in the US and elsewhere, weakened the chances that working-class women would join. So separatism ultimately became part of a vicious circle, condemning the women's movement to the ghetto of the young, educated middle class.

The milieu in which the white middle-class women active in the women's movement found themselves led many to slip into open racism. The black American writer Bell Hooks expressed her anger in her book **Ain't I a Woman? Black Women and Feminism**, writing: 'Every women's movement in America from its earliest origin to the present day has been built on a racist foundation . . . White middle and upper class women have dominated every women's movement in the US.'[30]

The black leader Angela Davis inveighed against Susan Brownmiller in the famous Emmett Till case of 1953, for putting the wolf whistle of a 14-year-old black boy at a white woman almost on the same level as his subsequent lynching by white racists.[31]

Escapism and Division

With the defeat of the black movement and the student movement the women were convinced that advances did not lie in politics or political parties, but in the development of human faculties, 'the emancipation of the person', as the Narodniks of Russia had said.[32] It took but a short time for the whole of the American WLM to turn into a collection of small groups, consisting of about eight women each, in which women talked to each other about their individual experiences and analysed them together. Jo Freeman writes that these groups 'have become mechanisms for social change in and of themselves. They are structures created specifically for the purpose of altering the participants' perceptions and conceptions of themselves and society at large. The means by which this is done is called "consciousness raising".'[33]

This trend for 'consciousness-raising' groups to become an end in themselves was by no means the only trend in the women's liberation movement in its early years. Many women, especially socialist feminists in Britain, argued that consciousness-raising was important not because it improved women's lives but because it gives women the confidence to take part in political activity. Alas, it doesn't. You don't build your confidence by separating yourself off from the struggle going on in the world around you. If you do, then just the opposite happens: you never get the chance to develop the skills and arguments necessary for political activity. As the experience showed, women tended to cling more and more to their small groups, and when these broke up, to drop out completely.

In a curious way, 'consciousness-raising' does not challenge the prevailing ideas that the family and personal relationships are separate from society at large, ruled by their own laws. 'Consciousness-raising', after all, aims to change the *ideas* of the individuals concerned — in the belief that with the 'right ideas' they could then go on to change their personal, sexual and family relationships. The logic of this is that personal relationships are moulded merely by the ideas which we carry in our heads, not by the real world in which we live. In contradiction to this, we will argue later that personal relationships arise from and are moulded by the total social relations of the society around us — and cannot ultimately be changed in isolation from that reality. But first let us see where 'consciousness-raising' led the women's movement.

At first the number of these women's consciousness-raising groups grew swiftly. But they had a short life. Jo Freeman wrote that they 'form and dissolve at such a rate that no one can keep track of them'.[34] Many disintegrated within a few weeks or months; some survived for two or more years; the typical groups lasted about nine months.

> However much or however little participants change their ideas as a consequence of participation, they generally reach a point at which the consciousness-raising group itself can contribute little more; it has

> 'served its purpose'. Members' realisation of this fact marks the group's second stage of development — one in which they try to redefine their common objectives . . . Only rarely do members agree on what they would like to do. Consequently, only rarely does the group continue through this second stage. Most commonly it disintegrates: 'Everyone went away for the summer and, when we came back, we couldn't seem to get started again'.[35]

Few of the women involved remained active. As early as 1973, Maren Carden wrote: 'Participants estimate that between 5 and 15 per cent remain active in Women's Liberation.'[36] Today probably less than one per cent of the members of the women's groups in the early 1970s are still active in the WLM.

The groups of socialist feminists suffered an even worse fate. These were never very numerous, not very strong and not clearly distinguishable from the radical feminists. Linda Gordon, author of **Women's Body, Women's Right**, writes that 'around 1974 there were a lot of attempts all over the country . . . to start organisations which explicitly identified themselves as socialist feminist. All of these organisations failed, there's not one left.'[37]

There was no co-ordination between the groups, no structure to keep them together or lead them. There was a 'conscious lack of hierarchy', as Jo Freeman says, with the result that 'the movement can neither be directed, controlled, nor even counted.' Out of this diffuseness elites naturally arise.

> . . . women who acquired any public notoriety for any reason were denounced as 'elitists' . . . The ideology of 'structurelessness' created the 'star system' and the backlash to it encouraged the very kind of individualistic nonresponsibility that it most condemned . . . The groups have no means of compelling responsibility from the elites that dominate them. They cannot even admit they exist.[38]

Such a situation leads naturally to squabbling, splits, expulsions and general tension. As early as the beginning of 1970 Marlene Dixon, one of the founders of WLM, could write: 'Hostility and misunderstandings have only grown more acute with time, and hostility and misunderstandings mean that women spend more energy fighting each other, or merely fighting male chauvinism, than they do organising the movement.'[39] Ti-Grace Atkinson, one of the founders of the movement, put it thus: 'Sisterhood is powerful: it kills sisters.'[40]

The end result of this fragmentation was the mushrooming of 'oppressions'. Black women were claiming that white feminists oppressed them on grounds of colour. Lesbians were claiming they were oppressed by heterosexual women . . . and so on. This was the result of believing, in the first place, that the source of oppression was one group of individuals: men. When women in the women's movement, now separated from men, still felt oppressed, they reacted by seeking out another group of individuals to blame. In this way you end up blaming those who agree with you and leaving the social system — the real source of oppression — untouched.

One of the bitterest conflicts within the WLM was between political lesbians and straight women. Lesbianism as a personal orientation has to be differentiated from *political* lesbianism. While it is fundamental to women's liberation that the oppression of lesbians (as of gay men) should be challenged, this does not signify that lesbian relationships are superior to heterosexual or that lesbianism is a necessary means towards women's liberation. Many in the WLM became political lesbians. Lesbianism

> developed into a world view which said that women should identify with, live with, and only associate with women. From this premise it was easy to argue that lesbianism was the vanguard of feminism: that a woman who actually slept with a man was obviously consorting with the enemy and could not be trusted . . . 'It is the primacy of women relating to women, of women creating a new consciousness of and with each other which is at the heart of women's liberation, and the basis for the cultural revolution.'[41]

Jill Johnson, in her book **Lesbian Nation: the Feminist Solution**, states: 'The sexual satisfaction of the woman independently of the man is the *sine qua non* of the feminist revolution . . . Until all women are lesbians there will be no true political revolution.'[42] Lesbian feminism had a strong appeal because it seemed to offer a personal means of action against men's oppression with immediate results. For the WLM at large 'it was also easier to spend one's energies on the essentially personal nature of the gay/straight conflict than deal with the harder political questions.'[43]

But someone had to pay for lesbian feminism, and Jo Freeman indicates who it was:

> Those women who remained straight but did not have any other political associations went through a good deal of personal trauma, including a couple of nervous breakdowns, and dropped out of the feminist movement entirely. They could not form or join another group because their identities as radical feminists had been destroyed.[44]

The Withering of the Women's Movement

With the general political weakness of the American left, even at its high point, and the growing economic recession of the 1970s — a reality no one could deny — the WLM, composed of tiny, fragmented groups and torn by intermittent squabbles, proved powerless. Women who were not content simply to contemplate their own consciousness, but wanted some action, turned towards the respectable, conservative Women's Rights organisations, of which the most prominent was NOW, the National Organisation of Women. In 1975 Jo Freeman wrote that 'NOW was often the only feminist *action* organisation available, even if its image was somewhat conservative.'[45] Since those words were written the collapse of the WLM has accelerated and NOW is in effect the only women's organisation. Its membership has grown from 1,000 in 1967 to 40,000 in 1974, to 60,000 in 1979, and 135,000 by the end of 1980.[46] The movement of women into NOW has been part of a general move rightwards urged on by the economic depression.

NOW's mode of operation is very traditional. It leans towards the Democratic Party, urges women to rely on the courts and Congress for reforms, and indulges in lobbying as a major activity.[47] Typically members of NOW have been very involved in the campaign for the ordination of women in the churches. In three years 'over 40 women have become episcopal priests'.[48] Some 15,000 women attended one of its conventions in November 1977, including three 'First Ladies'!

NOW has proved ineffective not only in failing to advance women's conditions, but even in blocking the attack on women's rights in recent years, especially since Reagan became President. Thus, the Equal Rights Amendment, which was declared by NOW to be the 'number one campaign' which it fought at the expense of all other women's issues, failed in 1982, as not enough states could be persuaded to ratify it.

Abortion rights also suffered a backlash. In 1973 abortion became legal, but in 1976 legislation stopped federal government funding of abortion for poor women unless the woman's life was in danger. This split the women's movement: '. . . middle-class women didn't come to the aid of their poorer sisters . . . All they knew was that you could still get an abortion if you could pay for one, and most of them had the money.' Another confusion resulted from the fact that a moral stand against racism within the women's movement involved a campaign against enforced fertility control for black women. From this viewpoint abortion came to be seen more as a method of population control than a woman's right, something to be opposed rather than demanded. The demand for the right to abortion therefore came to be seen as a 'white' (in other words privileged) women's issue.

Of course, the way out of this mess was to call for a woman's right *to choose*, the right to choose to have an abortion, or not to have an abortion. But by this time the WLM was so fragmented and moralistic that 'a woman's right to choose' became no more than an empty slogan and attempts to build a campaign in defence of the right to abortion were ditched in the process. In summer 1981 a sub-committee of the US Congress approved legislation which would make abortion (and even some forms of contraception) tantamount to murder.[49]

In 1981 NOW actively campaigned for the nomination of Sandra Day O'Connor to the Supreme Court, even though O'Connor is anti-abortion and pro-capital punishment.[50]

The best manifestation of NOW's further move to the right is the book by its founder, Betty Friedan, titled **The Second Stage**. In it she argues among other things for a coalition with 'Girl Scouts, Junior League, YWCA, women's clubs, to the religious sisterhoods, Catholic, Protestant, Jewish.'[51] When she visited West Point army academy, she waxed lyrical at seeing women training to become officers in the US army. This made her feel 'safer somehow because these powerful nuclear weapons that can destroy the world . . . will henceforward be in the hands of women and men who are, with agony, breaking through to a new strength.'[52]

In the field of wages women also suffered a setback. In 1955 the earnings of full-time women workers averaged 64 per cent of those of male workers; in 1970 the corresponding figure was 59 per cent, and in 1976 it went down to 57 per cent.

Some radical feminist groups have survived by devoting themselves to specific service projects, such as women's centres for support for rape victims, gynaecological care, psychological counselling or child care.

Feminism has also taken hold in the field of publishing. The most respectable and trendy publication is **Ms**, which started as a monthly in July 1972 and reached a circulation of 350,000 a year later. There are a few feminist publishing houses, and a number of women's bookstores around the country. The feminist publishers have largely concentrated on novels, which contributes to the preoccupation with individual experience and personal relations.[53]

Women's studies became respectable. Dockard reports that by the beginning of 1974 women's studies programs were functioning at 78 institutions, and about 2,000 courses were being offered at another 500 campuses. 'Now almost every college and university offers women's studies courses.'[54] Successful openings have thus been created for women authors and lecturers. Kathie Sarachild, one of the original leaders of WLM, complained: 'As soon as someone had a little bit of success, she would go off on her own and work in that very indirect way of being a feminist writer instead of maintaining contact with the troops.'[55]

So we can see a sharp contrast between the 'success' of some of the women in the movement, in making careers for themselves, and the failure of the movement itself to improve the lot of the mass of working women. The fate of the former activists of the WLM in the United States is similar to that of the majority of the Narodniks in Russia. Coming from well-off families, after a period of 'going to the people', they 'settled down to research, to literature, and even more often, to business and trade.'[56]

But the analogy between Russian Narodniks and American members of WLM should not be pushed too far. The former had to face the gallows, prison and exile in Siberia, while the latter largely spent their time 'consciousness-raising'.

11
The women's movement in Britain

It is worth comparing the general social and political conditions against whose background the women's movements of Britain and the USA grew, for these affected the differences and similarities between the two movements. This is particularly true where working-class women were concerned.

In Britain the trade unions, with more than half the working population in membership in 1978 (55 per cent),[1] are far stronger than those in the United States, where only one worker in five is a trade unionist (19 per cent). This difference applies even more among women workers, where 36.7 per cent are union members in Britain (1974) compared with only 11.6 per cent in the US (1978).

In the political field the differences between the US and Britain are even greater. In Britain there is a Labour Party with a mass vote among the working class, while in the US there are only openly bourgeois democratic parties. The revolutionary socialist organisations are also stronger in Britain, with greater influence in the working class.

Although there has never been a fusion of the women's and trade union movements in Britain, there have been a few noteworthy common actions.

The Struggle for Equal Pay

Equal pay was an important issue in the 1960s. By 1962, according to a TUC survey, 19 trade unions, representing 200,000 women, had equal pay agreements with employers. Thirty unions did not.

Many unions were pushing not only for equal pay but for maternity leave, equal job opportunities and equal terms and conditions of work. In 1963 the Trades Union Congress passed a resolution calling on the next Labour government — which was in fact to take office the following year — to make equal pay a requirement in law. The Women's Advisory Committee of the TUC followed this with an 'Industrial Charter for Women', demanding equal pay, equal opportunities for training, re-training facilities for women returning to industry, and special provisions for the health and welfare of women at work. They had very little immediate success.

But towards the end of the 1960s there was a general struggle for increased wages throughout the trade union movement. The demand for equal pay became one aspect of this. A crucial strike took place in 1968 by sewing machinists at Ford's Dagenham plant, followed by those in the company's Halewood plant on Merseyside. The women organised their own strike committee and brought Ford to a standstill. Their victory raised their pay to 92 per cent of the men's rates, although they failed to raise their grading from 'unskilled'.

The strike by the women at Ford inspired many other women workers. Out of it arose the National Joint Action Campaign for Women's Equal Rights (NJACWER), which adopted a five-point charter and called on the TUC to lead a campaign for equal pay and opportunity.[2] In May 1969 the campaign organised an equal pay demonstration which was supported by women trade unionists from all over the country.

Trade unions now made promises that they would fight for equal pay as part of their recruitment campaigns, and women streamed in as new members. In the ten years 1968–78, the women membership of the public employees' union (NUPE) more than trebled, that of the local government officers' union NALGO more than doubled, that of the health service union COHSE quadrupled and the white-collar workers' union ASTMS multiplied its women membership by *seven* times.[3]

1970–74 were years of mass working-class struggle, including two national miners' strikes, a national dockers' strike when five dockers — the 'Pentonville Five' — were jailed for picketing, and more than 200 factory occupations. These years also saw an impressive array of women's strikes. In 1970 London night cleaners fought for union recognition. The same year 20,000 Leeds clothing workers (85 per cent of them women) went on strike. Flying pickets closed clothing factories further afield in Yorkshire. Tens of thousands of teachers, three-quarters of them women, were also on strike over pay for the first time in half a century. 1971 saw a London telephonists' pay dispute, while at Brannan's, a small thermometer factory in Cumberland, women struck to defend trade union organisation. In 1972 women joined the occupations of Fisher-Bendix on Merseyside and Briant Colour Printing in London. The same year women at Goodman's, part of Thorn Electrical Industries, successfully struck for equal pay. In 1973 hundreds of thousands of hospital workers (the majority women) went on their first ever national strike. In the same year two hundred women in GEC, Coventry, struck for eight weeks over piece rates. Asian women at Mansfield Hosiery Mills struck over racial discrimination, and there was a national NALGO strike — mainly of women. There were many other women's strikes in this period of mass upsurge.

Parallel with this, there was progress in the women's movement. The groups which started in 1969 mushroomed. The first organisation to be set up was the London Women's Liberation Workshop, which followed the American example in being a network of small groups with information services. It stated:

> the men lead and dominate, the women follow and submit. We close our meetings to men to break through this pattern, to establish our own leaderless groups and to meet each other over our common experience as women . . . For this reason, groups small enough for all to take part in discussion and decisions are the basic units of our movement . . . to further our part in the struggle for social change and transformation of society.[4]

A different group produced the women's liberation magazine **Shrew** each month.

A few months later, in February 1970, the first National Women's Liberation Conference was held in Ruskin College, Oxford. Nearly 600 women turned up, mostly from the new women's liberation groups, some from NJACWER and some from Maoist and Trotskyist groups.[5] The conference adopted a structure of small women's groups based on localities, loosely co-ordinated through national meetings to which each group could send two delegates. The conference also set up a Women's National Co-ordinating Committee.

In November 1970 about a hundred feminists disrupted the Miss World Competition.

On 6 March 1971 International Women's Day was celebrated for the first time in London and Liverpool. The demonstrators carried on their banners four basic demands (worked out by the Women's National Co-ordinating Committee): for equal pay now, equal education and job opportunities, free contraception and abortion on demand, and free 24-hour nurseries.[6] The four demands clearly identified the aim of the women's movement as being to bring changes in the real world. They were *political* demands in that they were demands on the state, and they well suited the needs of working-class women.

Away from the Labour Movement

Unfortunately a number of factors pushed the growing women's movement away from the working class. The first was its middle-class composition. Sheila Rowbotham identified the social composition in 1979: 'Women's liberation has mobilised mainly women from a particular strata, teachers, social workers, librarians, journalists or clerical workers, as well as women working in the family.'[7]

This needs to be qualified: not all clerical workers, but only the upper ranks; not all housewives, but only those who could afford to indulge in changing their lifestyle. Sheila Rowbotham notes this phenomenon: 'Feminist politics can become preoccupied with living a liberated life rather than becoming a movement for the liberation of women.'[8] A feminist who had worked in a factory with other women commented:

> Experimenting with more 'open' relationships, or even trying to live communally takes up a lot of time, energy and discussion which simply are not at the disposal of women factory workers . . . other people's more exotic lives are not a possibility for them.
>
> Home and marriage was the most important thing for the women working on the line . . . For a start, you are so tired out by work and have so little time that you need to have a stable routine and reliable domestic set-up . . .[9]

Of course one may argue, and socialists should argue, that the values held by these working-class women — an acceptance of the traditional picture of home and family — are the *wrong* ones. It is still clear, however, that working-class women cannot come to terms with feminism. Working-class women do not have the time for 'consciousness-raising'.

> For most the only relaxation was watching telly and going out on Saturday night. Those with young children got up between five and six and went to bed at 9.30. After 10 was considered late — an early night meant seven or eight p.m.[10]

How far working-class women were out of place in the women's liberation movement is illustrated by the following letter to **Spare Rib** headed 'Intellectual Snobbery', by a working-class woman, Margaret King:

> I agree very much with the letter about intellectual snobbery shown by many women in the movement . . . I will not join women's liberation groups any more because of this . . . The last time I went to join a consciousness-raising group I was the only woman there who had started work straight from school, instead of going on to higher education. This made me feel inferior, which, as women of all people should understand, put me on the defensive. My reaction to this led one

> member to suggest that I contact a Women's Therapy Group! I left the meeting feeling really depressed, and determined never again to expose myself to such an experience from my so-called 'sisters'.[11]

A measure of how the women's movement distanced itself from the working class is the changes in its platform of demands. As we have seen, the original 1971 demands (equal pay now, equal education and job opportunities, free contraception and abortion on demand and free 24-hour nurseries) suited the needs of working-class women. In 1975, two new demands were added: 'Financial and legal independence' and 'an end to all discrimination against lesbians and a woman's right to define her own sexuality'. In 1978, at the last National Women's Conference, the following demand was added: 'Freedom from intimidation by threat or use of violence or sexual coercion, regardless of marital status; and an end to all laws, assumptions and institutions which perpetuate male dominance and men's aggression towards women.' The original four demands were clear, aimed at changes in the real world and directed towards the state; the added ones largely related to 'attitudes' and 'assumptions', to 'personal politics'.

The year 1974 was the peak of class struggle in Britain. That year a national strike by the miners forced the Tory government to call a general election, which it lost. The new Labour government, aided by the trade union leaders, quickly cooled down the working-class movement — including the militancy among women workers for equal pay and equal opportunity. But the arrival of a Labour government did not affect the growing economic crisis: inflation hit hardest for the lowest-paid (usually women) and rising unemployment saw the end of work for thousands of part-time workers (again usually women).

It was above all this general downturn which brought the inherent weakness in the women's movement to the fore. Until the mid-1970s it was possible to say that the women's movement had three strands. At one extreme were the radical feminists, for whom men were 'the enemy'. They were marginal, and their only practical option was to withdraw to build communes in Wales. At the other extreme were those bent simply on revising the present structures of society to make more space for women, the reformists and the career women.

In the middle were women who marched against the Vietnam War, and for the right to abortion, who probably supported the miners in their strike against the Tories, and who opposed sexism at work and in the media. They could loosely be called 'socialist feminists'. 'Equality' was for most of them a revolutionary demand — even if they did not always see it that way — since it was clear that the system could not accommodate such equality without drastic and fundamental change.

That 'socialist' strand of the women's movement has faded away as the downturn has deepened. We are left with the two extremes. The decline in the women's movement led it to turn away from the struggle of women in the workplaces and towards 'personal politics' and 'women against violence'. This decline was itself accelerated by divisions inside the movement which were largely responses to the worsening situation in the real world. It was not until this later period that the radical feminists' 'theory of patriarchy' elbowed aside ideas of class — and the 'feminist struggle' in the Labour Party is also a phenomenon of this later period.

Fragments

As in the United States, the structurelessness of the British women's movement accelerated its disintegration. After a couple of years, three of the founding members of the London Women's Liberation Workshop went to India to sit at the feet of Bhagwan Shree Rajneesh. Another four went back to America. **Spare Rib** describes the demoralisation:

> Our spirits sagged, and for weeks turning to months meetings were irregular, people coming late or never, and it was less than ever possible to redeem our lost group-confidence by organising energetic political pursuits when nobody was around anyway and whoever was felt despair at the desertions . . . In 1973 or '74 we started to meet about every two weeks for dinner in each other's houses. We were no longer politically active as a group . . . What we could provide for each other was a crucial network of affection and support.[12]

The same story is told by Lynne Segal, one of the authors of **Beyond the Fragments**, concerning the Essex Road Women's Centre in Islington, North London, which was opened in August 1972. This did not look towards women workers. In fact Lynne Segal commented: 'Our lack of structure perhaps made it difficult for working-class women who were outside of our friendship networks, to know how to get involved.'[13] The Centre oriented on the most marginal, oppressed, insecure people: 'prisoners, the homeless, claimants, etc. . . . But misery does not always equal militancy, and those most oppressed are sometimes so smashed that it's hard for them to fight back at all.'[14] The result of all the effort was therefore practically nothing. The Centre opened for two nights a week, and its adherents usually drifted off after about a year.[15]

A loose network of small groups does not aid the transfer of experience or continuity. Hence when a new Centre rose from the ashes of the old, Lynne Segal could comment: 'It is as though things are all starting again from scratch and I'm not sure that any lessons have been learned.'[16]

Lynne Segal drew further conclusions from the structurelessness of the women's movement, after years of panegyrics to 'participatory democracy' as an alternative to the supposed hierarchies of Leninism: 'I have found that sometimes it can be even harder to combat "leaderism" within the small group, and interactions are more likely to be seen in purely individual and personal terms, rather than as political manifestations.'[17] In similar vein Sheila Rowbotham writes:

> The problems about participatory democracy are evident. If you are not able to be present you can't participate. Whoever turns up next time can reverse the previous decision. If very few people turn up they are lumbered with the responsibility. It is a very open situation and anyone with a gift for either emotional blackmail or a conviction of the need to intervene can do so without being checked by any accepted procedure.[18]

Composed of middle-class women organised in unstructured groups open to arbitrary elites, the women's liberation movement was ripe for the activities of different sectarian groups. In 1868 Marx characterised a sect thus: 'The sect sees the justification for its existence and its "point of honour" not in what it has in *common* with the class movement but in the *particular shibboleth* which *distinguishes* it from it.'[19] In 1871 he added: 'The development of the system of Socialist sects and that of the real workers' movement always stand in reverse ratio to each other.'[20]

As early as 1971 the Women's National Co-ordinating Committee was dissolved because 'its meetings had become a sectarian battleground.'[21] The admission of men was an early casualty of the battle. Men were allowed into the first two national conferences of the Women's Liberation Movement but subsequently excluded, after a wrangle between two women over the microphone when the husband of one rushed to her aid. Men were also excluded from the London Liberation Workshop.

The British movement, like the American, was torn by a lesbian/straight feminist conflict. In April 1974 the first conference of lesbian feminists, 300 strong, declared lesbian politics to be central to feminism.[22] In September 1979 the Leeds Revolutionary Feminist Group issued a statement entitled: 'Political Lesbianism: The Case Against Heterosexuality'. It declared:

> We do not think that all feminists can and should be political lesbians . . . Penetration is an act of great symbolic significance by which the oppressor enters the body of the oppressed. But it is more than a symbol, its function and effect is the punishment and control of women . . . Giving up fucking for a feminist is about taking your politics

> seriously. Women who are socialists . . . will resist buying Cape apples because the profits go to South Africa. Obviously it is more difficult for some feminists to give up penetration . . .[23]

Another statement by the same group says that 'heterosexuality . . . has been created, maintained and enforced upon women by men, for their purposes, one of which is to oppress all women, everywhere, of whatever description.'[24]

The lesbian feminists drove many heterosexuals away from the women's movement. Anna Coote and Beatrix Campbell describe how many women

> felt they couldn't participate in the politics of the women's liberation movement, where the dominant question was whether one was for or against heterosexuality . . . There were ritual rows at one national conference after another, until the last one in Birmingham in 1978 — when the split was so bitter and painful that no one was prepared to organise another such gathering.[25]

One of the victims of the lesbian feminist offensive has been **Spare Rib**, the movement's only surviving journal.[26] At its beginning **Spare Rib** devoted much space to news and features relating to the work experience of working-class women. For instance, a five-page special feature was given over to descriptions by women strikers at SEI in Heywood, who were out for eleven weeks in the winter of 1975 for equal pay. A picture of one of the pickets appeared on the cover. After 1976, however, industrial issues practically disappeared. Instead, **Spare Rib** reflected all the problems within the women's liberation movement: the love-hate relationship with the 'male-dominated' labour movement; the quest for a 'feminist lifestyle'; finding niches of women's liberation within the prevailing social and political system.

The lesbian/straight split tore the editorial board of **Spare Rib** apart. An editorial in September 1980 admitted: 'It has been difficult to produce work and get along in a sisterly spirit. The seriousness of it all made us decide to hold a series of special meetings, with a group counsellor, to help us sort out structural and personal problems.' In a letter of resignation, Amanda Sebastyen, one of six who resigned from the editorial collective, stated: 'I was the sucker who said we should call in a counsellor — it's taken me six months of rage, misery and boredom to make me see I was wasting our time.'[27] **Spare Rib**, especially in its letter pages, became a battleground between lesbian and heterosexual feminists.[28] The collective has since split further. Black women have attacked white women. Arab women have attacked Jewish women. The magazine argued for months about the racism of white women, then produced a special 'black issue', followed by a four-month row about whether this was tokenism.

Another sect was the Wages for Housework Campai National Women's Conference in Manchester in March 19 James read a paper entitled 'Women, the Unions and W declared as a central task 'the struggle of the woman of the w class against the union [because] like the family, *it protects "the c ass"* at her expense.'[29]

The four demands of the women's liberation movement (equal pay, equal education and opportunity, 24-hour child care and free contraception and abortion on demand), Selma James argued, should be replaced by six different demands, the first two being:

> 1. We demand the right to work less.
> 2. We demand a guaranteed income for women and for men, working or not working, married or not . . . we demand wages for housework. All housekeepers are entitled to wages (men too).

Women at home, stated a pamphlet by Mariarosa Costa and Selma James in 1972, are producing, and hence are potentially '*social power*. If your production is vital for capitalism, refusing to produce, refusing to *work*, is a fundamental lever of social power.'[30]

> Hence we must refuse housework as women's work . . . We must get out of the house . . . to link ourselves to the struggles of all those who are in ghettos, whether that ghetto is a nursery, a school, a hospital, an old-age home, or a slum.[31]

The minimum demand for a housewife's wage, she says, should be equal to the average wage in society.

So housewives, isolated from each other by the four walls of their homes, with young children and perhaps older parents to look after, and carrying an even greater burden in caring for the young, the old and the sick as the state cuts back social services and the health service — housewives will suddenly organise and seize wages for housework! And this when women who *are* organised, in trade unions, have not yet achieved equal pay, and find it ever more difficult to defend the social benefits they *have* got.

Many women in the women's liberation movement have consistently focussed on the areas where men and women are at odds — rape, battered women, wages for housework — while ignoring or playing down the areas of struggle where women are more likely to win the support of men — such as opposition to the cuts in hospitals and schools, the right to abortion, and battles at work for equal pay or the right to join a trade union. Such women see themselves and others as *victims* of male supremacy, not as fighting members of the working class. Instead of concentrating on where women are strongest — where they are organised in the unions and in their workplaces — the women's liberation movement has come to concentrate on where women are weakest.

The first refuge for battered women was set up by Erin Pizzey in Chiswick in 1972. By 1980 there were 200 refuges, set up by feminists or by social workers not associated with women's liberation. National conferences were held in 1974 and 1975, the latter drawing representatives from 28 established and 83 potential refuges.[32]

The first rape centre was opened in North London in March 1976. Five years later there were sixteen similar centres in cities throughout Britain. Demonstrations to 'reclaim the night' took place in London, Leeds, Manchester, York, starting on 12 November 1977. Hundreds took part, singing and slapping stickers on windows of porn shops and strip joints.[33]

There is also a network of other centres: women's aid and women's study centres, women's collectives for writing and publishing, health, psychiatry, legal advice, child care, carpentry. To their participants these make up a 'complete alternative feminist culture'.

For socialists refuges for battered women and their children are an important social service, which needs to be defended like hospitals or schools. But in no way can they be seen as more than palliatives, of marginal impact on the human wreckage caused by capitalism.

On different rails . . .

While the women's movement has become more and more passive and powerless, engrossed in internal squabbles and splits, the women in the trade unions have not been inactive. We have told of the establishment in 1969 of the National Joint Action Campaign for Women's Equal Rights (NJACWER), with its four-point charter, also the mass movement of women into the unions and the exciting struggles of women in the years 1968–74.

The strikes involving women after 1974 were usually tough to carry through. A number went on for long periods: Trico, Grunwicks, Chix, Lee Jeans, the Liverpool typists, to mention but a few. On 22 January 1979, 80,000 workers, the majority women, came out on a demonstration in support of a National Day of Action for the low-paid, and shortly afterwards the unions in the public sector launched a programme of industrial action to protest at both low pay and government cuts. But women's strikes after 1974 were virtually completely ignored by the women's liberation movement — witness, for instance, the change in coverage in **Spare Rib**.

The Abortion Campaign: An Uneasy Alliance

In the campaign in defence of women's right to abortion, the trade unions and the women's movement to some extent worked together.

There were repeated attacks on the 1967 Abortion Act. In 1975 the National Abortion Campaign (NAC) was launched in reaction to the introduction of an Abortion Amendment Bill. In June 1975, 40,000 women and men participated in a demonstration called by the campaign. There were many banners from white-collar unions, and a sprinkling of banners from miners' branches and building workers. There were also many banners from socialist groups and women's organisations.

More and more unions passed resolutions at their annual conferences supporting the woman's right to abortion. The 1975 TUC Women's Conference carried by a large majority a resolution which pledged support for abortion 'on request'. Later that year the TUC Congress passed a similar resolution. The Abortion Amendment Bill never reached the statute book: it fell for lack of parliamentary time.

But in April 1976 the National Abortion Campaign had to call another mobilisation against another attempt at restriction. This second Bill, which came before parliament in 1977, aimed to reduce the time limit within which abortion was allowed, to impose higher fines for doctors who abused the law, and to require the signatures of two doctors for an abortion rather than one. Fifteen thousand people joined the demonstration and many more supported the campaign that followed. The Bill again fell for lack of parliamentary time.

When MP John Corrie introduced yet another restrictive Bill after the election of a new Tory government in 1979, the TUC carried into effect a TUC Congress resolution inspired by the TUC Women's Conference, and called for a mass demonstration. This was held on 31 October 1979, when some 80,000 women and men marched in London from Marble Arch to Trafalgar Square. It 'was the largest trade union demonstration ever held for a cause which lay beyond the traditional scope of collective bargaining; it was also the biggest ever pro-abortion march.'[34] A contingent of about 200 young radical feminists staged an angry protest, insisting that women should lead the march. The National Abortion Campaign steering committee sharply rebuked them. There are women, they said, who

> object to TUC involvement at all. The fact that the TUC organised the demo was not an accident, nor was it opportunism as some have suggested . . . We positively fought for a TUC demonstration because we believed that it was the best way of bringing together the widest number of people to oppose the Corrie Bill. Without the trade unions, there was no hope of reaching women outside the limited circle of the women's movement (and readers of **The Guardian**) . . .
>
> We started organising in 1975 at the TUC women workers' demo, shouting 'TUC take a stand, free abortion on demand'. We spent the

> next four years getting them to do just that . . .
>
> It was the women who had fought to get policy through the trade union branches who were in those trade union contingents at the front. The action of taking it over was an insult to them, an assumption that they had less right to be there than other women who had not been directly involved in the campaign at all.[35]

While the radical feminists were wrong to urge separatism, and the National Abortion Campaign on the other hand was too submissive to the union bureaucracy, the important thing throughout the abortion campaign was the crucial role played by trade unionists and socialists, both men and women.

The Women's Liberation Movement in the face of Tory attacks

All working people have suffered from the attacks of the Tory government under Margaret Thatcher on health, education and social services, and this is especially true of women. Unemployment and cuts in the value of child and maternity benefits also burden women more heavily. Maternity allowance, £25 in Britain, is many times lower than in most European countries. In France maternity allowance is £525 for the first child, £752 for the second, and a whopping £1,048 for the third.[36] The Equal Pay Act and the Sex Discrimination Act are practically dead letters. Women's average earnings for a full-time job, which in 1977 stood at 75.7 per cent of men's, had dropped to 73.9 per cent by 1982. In 1981 the number of cases brought for equal pay had dropped to 54, of which only six were won.[37]

In face of the Tories' and employers' offensive, any sectional response is futile. As I wrote in the autumn of 1979:

> The Tories are going to test out our working-class organisation. Hence it is necessary to see every attack in the context of the general offensive. This means it is crucial to rally the greatest possible support for every group of workers in struggle and to relate their struggle to the government's attack. The whole battle has to be given a clear, political — ie, general *class*, socialist, anti-government edge.[38]

In the heady years of 1968–74 things were easy, and even sectional actions could be effective. Then the women's movement grew. But when the going got tough, it closed in on itself despondently. In 1980 one feminist writer, Liz Heron, wrote that 'the waning of radical optimism . . . has prompted the retreat into the personal.'[39] Another, Rosalind Coward, said that there is 'a crisis of fragmentation, [which has] generated a gargantuan nostalgia for the days of "the women's movement".'[40] In a sad article in **Spare Rib**, entitled 'Where to Next?', Micheline Wandor looks at the bleak scene of the 1980s. It is no longer possible, she says, to talk of a women's liberation movement at all, but only of feminism. However, she argues, the past decade has not been a complete failure: 'Feminism has established some important professional niches.'

Micheline Wandor is right. A number of middle-class women have done well out of the women's liberation movement — in education, in journalism, in television. One of the best openings for some professional women was the establishment of Women's Studies. At present there are at least 30 universities with Women's Studies courses, besides those in adult education and WEA courses.[41]

Micheline Wandor concedes that for the mass of women, the fact that feminism has established some important professional niches is in no way good enough. Thatcherism, she admits, will make working-class and some displaced middle-class women move towards trade unionism, and towards general socialist parties.

This section may aptly be concluded by an 'Obituary' printed in the **Workers' Chronicle** (The Newcastle Trades Council paper) of January 1981:

> It is with great regret that we have to report the death of Newcastle Trades Council's Working Women's Charter Sub-Committee. After almost five years of activity, the Sub-Committee succumbed to failure of support and lack of active interest and passed away at the beginning of December . . .
>
> The main focus of the Sub-Committee's activities was education and publicity work. Among its many achievements in this field, worthy of mention, are a Video Film around the Ten Points of the Working Women's Charter; a similar Television Programme; a series of Ten Programmes on Local Radio; production of 'Women's Struggle' — a local newssheet; articles in the **Workers' Chronicle** and the local press — especially the **Evening Chronicle**; organising and participating in Day Schools; and leading discussions in Schools and Colleges . . .
>
> It is ironic that the Sub-Committee passed away at a time when women are most under attack.

Sharp Lessons from the Gay Liberation Movement

The oppression of gays and lesbians is a by-product of the oppression of women, for gays and lesbians break the role stereotyping of men and women which is imposed by capitalist society. The challenge to this stereotyping by the women's movement therefore spurred on a Gay Liberation Movement. But the gay movement was even less stable, even more wracked by internal contradications. A sketch of its development will throw further light on the nature of the women's movement.

In the autumn of 1970 the Gay Liberation Front (GLF) was

founded in London. It 'was the most typical and dynamic representative' of the new gay movement, writes Jeffrey Weeks, the historian of homosexual politics in Britain. On 28 August 1971 GLF organised an impressive Gay Pride demonstration of 2,000 men and women in London. In the first year of its existence it sold 8,000 badges, when wearing a gay badge was a courageous statement in itself.[42]

However, after a very short time the gay movement started to falter, then quickly fell to pieces. Since the roots of gay oppression are in capitalism itself, for any movement against gay oppression to succeed, it needs to be part of a general movement against capitalism. Without this, it suffers from the isolation of the gay ghetto itself, with all the limitations and powerlessness that goes with it. This is in fact what happened. Aubrey Walter writes that within only a few weeks, 'the expansive euphoria that had marked the whole of 1971 was dampened by the first of a series of bitter and damaging splits, and the collapse of the GLF had begun.'[43] Jeffrey Weeks summed up the situation six years later: GLF 'had been the last major product of the late 1960s euphoria; it collapsed as that euphoria died.'[44]

From the start the gay movement suffered deep internal conflicts. First there was conflict between men and women. Aubrey Walter writes:

> On top of the numerical presence of men, many of these still maintained very chauvinist and condescending attitudes towards women . . . As feminist consciousness developed, they understandably had decreasing patience dealing with the chauvinism of many gay men.

So in February 1972 the women left the GLF. Then, on the other side, 'many gays felt that in order to struggle against male privilege, they must do everything possible to show that they were prepared to give up this privilege in themselves.' These were the transvestites and transsexuals who 'insisted that they were doubly oppressed within the GLF, by the women as well as the men.'[45]

Another split was between socialists and those who advocated a new gay community style of living. Jeffrey Weeks writes:

> . . . gay communes . . . seemed to offer in embryo an alternative to the nuclear family. But they were also utopian . . . they came up against iron laws about property, about how to live together and work together harmoniously and uncompetitively within a hostile economic and social environment. They also conflicted severely with the emotional structuring of most members . . . the need for pair-bonding . . . Nevertheless communal experiments did emphasize an impotant dichotomy — that between 'personal' liberation on the one hand and political action on the other. Rarely did the two meet.[46]

The gay liberation movement believed that homosexuals constituted a potentially mass force for revolutionary change. But with only a tiny minority of homosexuals joining the movement — at most a couple of thousand out of a couple of million homosexuals in the country (drawn from the cautious estimate by Kinsey that homosexuals make up something like one in twenty of the population) — this proved to be an illusion. First of all homosexuals, unlike women or blacks, are not visible; they can 'pass' as straight. In fact the overwhelming majority of homosexual men manage to survive as husbands and fathers. Second, homosexuals are not bound by minority-group loyalty, like blacks, Jews and other ethnic groups. '. . . the homosexual is usually the only one in his family. He grows up keeping his deviance a guilty secret from almost everyone — especially from those closest to him . . . He lives in fear of exposure by other homosexuals.'[47] It is tragic but true that the great majority of homosexuals never overcome the internalised guilt they are condemned to in present society. Third, there are no economic-social bonds between homosexuals; they belong to all classes.

Thus the gay movement showed itself incapable of involving the mass of gay people, who are working class and live ostensibly heterosexual lives. The separatism of the gay movement added to the difficulties. It led to the exclusion not only of heterosexuals, but also of those gays who had not come out. As Lionel Starling, a member of the Socialist Workers Party, put it:

> . . . non-gays are systematically or indirectly excluded from gay struggle. At the same time, the involvement of gays, far from being maximised, is actually discouraged on two fronts; non-separatists are obviously put off and gays who have not yet come out socially as homosexuals are denied the opportunity to gain confidence by taking part in gay struggle *without at first identifying themselves as gay*. The politics of the gay movement are therefore self-limiting and condemn it to the downward spiral of an inward-looking clique.[48]

Homosexuals did not create their ghetto any more than the blacks created theirs. And in both cases the people inside the ghetto are unable to break its walls by their own action alone, without the mass action of the majority outside against the walls.

Various organisations have benefitted from the gay movement. There is the reformist parliamentary lobby of the Campaign for Homosexual Equality (CHE), which aims to achieve equality before the law for homosexuals. It became the largest gay organisation in the country, growing from 500 members in 15 groups in 1970 to about 5,000 members in 1976. It concentrates on social activities. The number of gay self-help groups, such as Gay Switchboard, also grew.[49]

> In each case they are committed to providing help and information so

> one individual with a problem may find an individual solution (with the marginal difference of Icebreakers forming small groups) . . . Gaysocs in universities and colleges performed the same function with the same limited and individualised influence.[50]

But far and away the greatest beneficiary was 'the pink economy'. The self-confident, affluent homosexual male lives in the pages of **Gay News**, **Him** and **Zipper**, which burst with advertising for gay books, films, cosmetics, videos and services. Advertising executives increasingly talk of a specific 'gay market'.

In conclusion we may say that organisations such as these, which have a narrow, immediate purpose, have remained stable. The more general radical gay groups have disappeared, and the college gay societies have declined in membership and militancy. While attitudes to homosexuality have changed a fair bit over the past ten years, and the potential for building support has grown, the organised pressure from homosexuals themselves has faded away.

The gay liberation movement, child of the women's movement, had an even weaker constitution than its mother. The activists of the women's movement, however, failed to draw the lessons from its failure.

Women and the Peace Movement

The women's movement received a new lease of life with the rise of the Peace Movement, centred around Greenham Common, the airbase in Berkshire used for Cruise nuclear missiles. The Peace Movement's philosophy is summed up in the words of veteran pacifist Dora Russell: 'That men must fight and women must weep is the implacable ruling of Fate . . . It has taken us centuries to discover that the voice which makes this arrogant assertion comes from only one half of the human race.' Another pacifist woman writes: 'Nuclear weapons are an expression of the twisted values of a male-dominated society . . . We see nuclear weapons and nuclear power as particularly horrendous results of male domination.'

Pacifism, which the Greenham Women profess, does not recognise that nuclear weapons are the fruit of a capitalist class society with its massive concentration of economic, political and military power. Hence the only way to get rid of the weapons is by overthrowing capitalism, by disarming the capitalist class and arming the working class. This is a far cry from the tokenism of the women's peace movement, as shown in this description of a web woven around the Pentagon by demonstrators: 'Generals minced their way through woman-made webs . . . At the end there was a braid around the Pentagon, and beautiful weavings at all the entrances. Women who were not arrested held a closing ritual circle.'

The women's peace movement also pays great attention to the internal life of its participants, a 'space' in which they can develop. As one participant writes:

> . . . in spite of the diversity, it is extraordinary to see how much all these groups have in common. They all emphasise the importance of considering the personal needs of their members, or providing emotional support . . . They constantly emphasise the positive: Women for Life on Earth, Children need Smiles. A feminist world will have healthy food, reproductive choice, etc. They emphasise the importance of imagination and use symbols . . . of subjective feelings as a guide to action.

The women involved, according to one of their members, are 'mostly middle-class'. Many have an 'alternative life-style', living in shared households, not having a 'straight' job, and so on.[51]

Believing that public opinion by itself can stop the slide into nuclear war, the logic of the Greenham Common women and the Campaign for Nuclear Disarmament is to adapt to public opinion. The Greenham Common women and the CND do not connect the struggle against Cruise and Trident missiles with the day-to-day struggles of working people for jobs, for better wages, better health care, education and housing. Hence they do not have roots in the life of the mass of people. If one cannot defend one's livelihood, how can one defend life? If we cannot stop the closure of a factory in our own town, how can we influence the actions of US President Reagan or Prime Minister Thatcher hundreds or thousands of miles away?

The Greenham Common women have retreated a long way from the early slogan of the women's liberation movement, 'women are angry', to an acceptance of 'intrinsic female characteristics' such as 'passivity' and 'domesticity', which the early women's movement rightly challenged.

Sliding Towards the Labour Party

In Britain, because of the strength of the labour movement, the same tendency towards incorporation into the establishment that pushes the US women's movement towards NOW, draws the British women's movement towards the Labour Party. Tony Benn made the overtures. At a meeting in Central Hall, Westminster, on 17 March 1980, which was misleadingly titled The Debate of the Decade, in which Tony Benn, Paul Foot, Tariq Ali, Hilary Wainwright, Stuart Holland and Audrey Wise took part, Benn went out of his way to praise Hilary Wainwright: 'Hilary Wainwright, in my opinion, put the most important question of all . . . I believe there is a very important relationship here between what Hilary Wainwright said and what I am saying . . . What Hilary said about the women's movement is very important.' The chairman of the meeting, Peter Hain, secretary of the Labour Co-ordinating Committee, introduced Hilary Wainwright as '. . . co-author of what many of us feel to be a seminal work on the Left, **Beyond the Fragments**.'[52]

In November 1980 Benn enthused over the *structure* of the women's movement:

> Structures *do* matter . . . the collectivity which is more common in the women's movement than in the male movement is very relevant. The idea that you rotate your chair, you're not just in the process of building a pedestal upon which spokespersons or spokeswomen operate, is very important too.[53]

A number of leading representatives of the women's movement reciprocated. Take for example the book written by Anna Coote and Beatrix Campbell, **Sweet Freedom: The Struggle for Women's Liberation**. This does not challenge the existing capitalist structure of society, but calls only for more participation by women in this structure — in parliament, local councils, political parties and trade unions. It does not call for a shift in the balance between the wages going to workers and the profits going to the employing class, but only in the balance between women's wages and men's wages. It endorses the Labour Party's 'Alternative Economic Policy', but adds to it the need for a feminist incomes policy, which would not seek to increase the share of the nation's wealth going to wages — and so to the majority of women — but would seek only to give women a greater proportion of the existing wages.

Yet experience has proved that the higher the wages of those workers who are in a strong position, let us say the miners, then the greater chance there is for workers in a weaker position to improve their wages too, whether they are women or men. This was clearly shown here in Britain in the years of the late 1960s and early 1970s, when workers in the stronger industries, particularly mining and engineering, forged ahead, and the rest of the working class — women and men — were able to improve their own wages in their wake.

Anna Coote and Beatrix Campbell sum up their strategy for equality in these words: 'The biggest obstacle, in our view, is not finding the necessary resources, but persuading men to relinquish their privileges.'[54] Not persuading the capitalist class to relinquish its considerable privileges over the working class, but 'men'! (In fact Beatrix Campbell, in an article in **The Guardian** on 9 August 1982 — in the middle of a hospital strike whose victory would have benefitted the wage packets of many thousands of women as well as men —

attacked trade unions as part of the 'patriarchal system' by which men oppress women, and strikes as an outdated 'dispute practice' inherited from the nineteenth century's male-dominated labour movement.)

Coote and Campbell call for 'redistribution of labour and wealth within the family' — thus ensuring the continuation of the individual family unit as the place for child care and housework.

They do not challenge the union bureaucracies, but call for positive discrimination — for women to hold full-time jobs on union executives and as full-time union officials. Positive discrimination also means more women MPs — completely irrelevant to the needs of working-class women — while women's strikes, through which thousands of women have battled to win their rights, are hardly mentioned.

Finally, they approvingly quote attempts to get more representation for women in the Labour Party. '. . . increasing numbers of women in their twenties and thirties were making the Labour party the main focus of their political activity as *feminists* as well as socialists.'[55]

Why do the remnants of the women's movement gravitate towards the Labour left? There is, in fact, an affinity between those who call themselves socialists in the two. First, the social composition is similar. The former is made up of white-collar and professional women, and so is the Labour left, though it also has more than a sprinkling of manual workers, and the support of many thousands of manual workers. Thirdly, for the socialist members of the women's liberation movement and the Labour left, ideas are not moulded by the collective class struggle of workers, but are seen simply as a debate between individuals. Fourthly, unlike the revolutionary socialist organisations, which would demand from anyone in the women's movement that she break with both the analysis of the movement and its style of work, the Labour Party, being a 'broad church', makes no demands. Fifth, even in terms of structure there is far more in common between the structurelessness and loose federalism of the women's movement and the bureaucratic swamp of labourism, than between either of them and the democratic centralism of a revolutionary socialist party. There is no party discipline, except where the bureaucratic right find it necessary.

Conclusion

The women's movement in Britain has wavered between two alternative paths: aligning with the labour movement — with workers' struggles, with the trade unions — or going its own separatist way. More and more it has turned in on itself, away from collective action and class politics, to life-style politics, 'consciousness-raising' and separatism; away from fighting for women's collective needs — equal pay, nurseries, abortion rights, women's strikes — to issues where women are individual victims of male oppression — rape, violence, pornography.

To the extent that members of the women's movement do try to relate to specific women workers' demands they fall into the reformist trap of proposing a feminist incomes policy. They aim to increase the share of women in existing resouces, when society is offering less and less to all working people. The other plank in their strategy — positive discrimination in favour of women in the trade unions and the Labour Party — is totally irrelevant to the real needs and aspirations of working-class women, who are alienated from the union bureaucracy, whether male or female, and from the MPs, who live a privileged and sheltered existence.

12

Class roots of the women's movement

As we have seen in Chapters Ten and Eleven, the Women's Liberation Movements in the United States and Britain were largely confined to graduates and students of universities and polytechnics. The majority of graduates of universities and polytechnics are destined to be white-collar workers. Many will be classroom teachers, only a few headteachers, or heads of departments. The latter are members of the new middle class. In Marxist terms they belong to the petty bourgeoisie, located between the basic classes of capitalist society, the bourgeoisie or ruling class, and the proletariat, the working class.

For Marx, the petty bourgeoisie was an anachronism, doomed to disappear. He wrote:

> Our epoch, the epoch of the bourgeoisie . . . has simplified the class antagonisms. Society as a whole is more and more splitting up into two great hostile camps, into two great classes directly facing each other: Bourgeoisie and Proletariat.[1]

But since the turn of the century it has become apparent that a new middle stratum of educated and salaried people has arisen and expanded rapidly. Often called the new middle class, this consists of such groups as small employers, managers and professional people of all sorts — such as supervisors, doctors, researchers, journalists, technicians, university teachers, high grade civil servants and local government employees. These have a degree of control over their own immediate labour process and probably over other workers too.[2]

Not all white-collar workers are part of the new middle class.[3] As Braverman shows in **Labour and Monopoly Capital**, the conditions of work and wages of the bulk of white-collar workers — most are women office workers — are comparable to those of manual workers. Their relationship to the means of production is the same as that of manual workers, and their employers have an identical interest with that of manual workers in lowering their wages and raising their productivity.[4] Most of those who go into white-collar jobs are young people whose parents are manual workers.

The size of the new middle class in the United States is, according to one estimate, 20–25 per cent of the population, while the working class are 65–70 per cent, the old middle class (such as shopkeepers, artisans and farmers) 8–10 per cent, and the ruling class 1–2 per cent.[5]

The new middle class, like the old, finds itself subordinated to capital, but above the working class, from whom it is separated by an abyss. For instance, only a tiny proportion of workers' children manage to enter the professions — 1.8 per cent of the sons of workers in the United States, and only 0.8 per cent of men from the working class become self-employed professionals.[6]

The new middle class is also culturally differentiated from the working class. Its members share educational background, consumption and life-style patterns. Also marriage 'down' to the working class or 'up' to the ruling class is comparatively infrequent.[7]

The new middle class lacks homogeneity. Different sections of it will be driven in different directions, towards or away from capital or labour, depending on the pressures upon them. A double pressure, for instance, pushes many groups in the new middle class towards organisation in professional organisations or trade unions: pressure may come from above — such as that on university and polytechnic lecturers for increased workloads; or it may come from below — such as when lower-paid workers relatively increase their wages at the expense of managers.[8]

The new middle class is resented by workers who often suffer harassment and humiliation at the hands of its members, rather than at the hands of the ruling class with whom they have little contact.

At the same time the new middle class, even those members of it who are distant from the working class, feel increasing alienation from capitalism. As Al Szymanksi put it:

> Scientists are not really able to determine what kind of research they will do or how their work will be used because of corporate funding and direction of their work; university teachers are under great pressure to mass produce students without raising fundamental criticisms of the way things are; social workers are forced to act like policemen; architects are made to design monstrosities which fall apart and factories that pollute . . .[9]

Both men and women of the new middle class suffer from this sense of alienation, but the women doubly so, because of consistent discrimination in job promotion, which blocks their moves up the social ladder compared with men. Thus 19 per cent of all women college graduates and 7 per cent of those with some post-graduate education are employed as clerical, sales, factory or service workers.[10] The prestigious and remunerative positions in the professions and business are overwhelmingly held by men.

The college and its campus, besides giving women the expectation of professional equality with men, also provide an opportunity for new personal relationships away from the control of the family, which later lead many to question their roles within the traditional family structure. Such women no longer go from the house of their father to that of their husband. They go to college first, where more equal relationships abound.

In general, college women have greater expectations than other women and less opportunity for realising them. If they are professionally trained, particularly in one of the male-dominated professions, their 'relative deprivation' is as tangible as their comparatively lower pay packets. US vice-president Adlai Stevenson said in 1955 of college-educated housewives: 'Once they wrote poetry. Now it's the laundry list.' Middle-class women, he said, could bewail the lost female 'Einsteins, Schweitzers, Roosevelts, Edisons, Fords, Fernis and Frosts'.

Working-class experience is very different. Both women and men suffer from the choking of intellectual advance, from routine and boredom. The idea of equality with men has a completely different meaning for a working-class woman. The shorthand typist, shop assistant, charlady and other women employed in jobs of a similar routine nature, with little prospect of advancement, cannot relate to the professional woman's desire for equality with men in job satisfaction — which presupposes the 'intrinsic value of work'. Working-class women work by and large for one reason only: to earn money. Their jobs offer them little else. For the professional woman domestic routine, where she cannot use her acquired skills, is frustrating. The working-class woman does not notice much difference between the routine work in or outside the home. Nor can she envy the man's position outside the house. She would not opt for the monotony and stress of a job on the conveyor belt of a car factory. Women's diseases associated with housework run parallel with men's diseases associated with their work.

When feminists say they want equality with men they often gloss over the fact that men are unequal in capitalist society. Too often the equality they see is within the present class structure, that is, equality for the more fortunate.

Like the new middle class, the women's movement is not homogeneous. By and large it can be divided into two groups, a Women's Rights movement and a Women's Liberation movement. Women's rights members, as Joan Cassell, who made a study of the American women's movement, describes, are more likely to have professions themselves or upper-middle-class husbands and families, and have a stake in 'the system'. Women's liberation participants, on the other hand, tend to be women in transition — students, recent graduates, political lesbians, women holding low-paying jobs while dreaming of highly-paid prestigious professions, or divorcees seeking new identities and ways of life.[11]

The women's rights members 'make no attempt to do away with status and hierarchy'. They do not seek to transform themselves or their world; they wish to improve their situation so that it will more closely resemble the situation of the men they perceive as their equals; they advocate 'a higher position for women in the structure of power and control', instead of its being mediated through men only. They want to move women up the ladder.[12] Many of these elite women earn good salaries, like their husbands, so they are able to buy the services of other people, predominantly women, to do their housework and mind their children. Thus Cynthia Epstein, in her book **Woman's Place**, quotes a study showing that about half the full-time professional and business women interviewed had two or more full-time servants to look after the house and mind the children.[13]

The Women's Liberation Movement seeks different ends:

> The women with fewest alternatives in the outside world wished to turn their feminist group into a way of life. Rather than attempting to change institutions within the larger society, which meant entering that society and engaging with it, the group was to be an 'alternative' . . . the group must be a family, a haven, a way of life, a mechanism for earning a living. The feminist group, in short, must replace the traditional role of husband and nuclear family. Rather than helping to change a participant's outside life, the group is to *become* that life.[14]

A prominent German feminist at the turn of the century said that 'the women's movement is the product of an individualistic, liberal historical current . . . It is the belief . . . in the blessings of individual freedom, which . . . has let women strive to free themselves from intellectual, economic and legal bonds.'[15]

Thus do feminists emphasise the individual. As against this, Marx defined 'human nature' as 'the ensemble of social relations'.[16]

> The more deeply we go back into history, the more does the individual, and hence also the producing individual, appear as dependent, as

> belonging to a greater whole . . . The human being is in the most literal sense a *zoon politikon*, not merely a gregarious animal, but an animal which can individuate itself only in the midst of society. Production by an isolated individual outside society . . . is as much of an absurdity as is the development of language without individuals living *together* and talking to each other.[17]

'My *analytic* method,' Marx wrote towards the end of his life, 'does not start from *Man* but from the economically given period of society.'

The old petty bourgeois individualism was rooted in the aspiration to continue to be one's own boss; that of the new petty bourgeoisie is rooted in careerism. When there is the possibility of upward mobility, the hopes of the underprivileged focus on individual advancement rather than collective action. Hence in the new middle class the dominant idea is that an individual's achievement depends on education, will and effort.

Working-class attitudes emphasise the opposite. They stress uniformity — the pre-determination of one's place by tradition, by the class into which one is born. A worker joins organisations — trade unions — to improve his or her position through the collective to which he or she belongs. New middle class men and women join groups — professional associations and elite clubs — in order to enhance their individual status and as a means of acquiring improved professional contacts. Even when they join proper unions — such as in Britain the National Union of Teachers or the local government officers' union NALGO, many higher-ranking members are torn between collective aspirations towards improving the conditions for everyone, and individualistic aspirations to climb up the career ladder.

Even the most radical members of the women's liberation movement, who consider themselves socialists, emphasise individualism rather than collective advancement as a precondition for individual freedom. This is what Marx called 'petty-bourgeois socialism'. In the **Communist Manifesto** he praised the ability of 'petty-bourgeois socialism' to criticise capitalism, but showed that its positive contribution was weak; because of its individualism it 'ended in a cowardly fit of the blues'.[18]

The radical feminists today seek to detach the bourgeois ideal of individual freedom from the unfree reality of bourgeois society: they seek to withdraw the individual from the social. This is encapsulated in the women's liberation movement slogan 'the personal is political'. This turns politics into a personal matter, redefining it and negating collective action aimed at political change.

The argument prevailing in the women's movement is that women have to free themselves from repressive patriarchal attitudes — as for example Germaine Greer's 'revolution in the bedroom'.

Marxists argue that it is not attitudes which control our lives but social conditions, the real power of capitalism, and the capitalist state, from which women, as well as men and children, must free themselves.

Another integral part of 'personal politics' is 'consciousness-raising'. To the extent that membership of the new middle class 'begets no community, no national bond and no political organisation' (to use Marx's words on the individualistic peasantry),[19] 'consciousness-raising' is a useful cement for amorphous or cross-class groups. Joan Cassell explains:

> . . . the term 'consciousness' is ambiguous, referring to a personal, subjective experience. This ambiguity may be a source of strength in the women's movement, where co-participants are able to agree that the consciousness is ascending, without the necessity to examine the possibly divergent contents of such individual consciousness. In a movement where participants may hold widely differing views, it is more unifying to discuss raised consciousness than to investigate the content of that consciousness.[20]

'Consciousness-raising' is foreign to working-class men and women. They do not come into politics to try and understand themselves and raise their consciousness. They join an organisation because they seek *collective* power to change their conditions, to change the world.

A further expression of 'personal politics' is the emphasis on changing lifestylcs: refusing to marry, setting up 'liberated communes', experimenting with free love. This *separates* these women from most working-class women. For most working-class women a 'liberating lifestyle' is determined by the size of the pay packet, the cost of necessities, the housing conditions.

To the extent that 'personal politics' separates the individual woman from the social, the lesbian feminists reach the pinnacle — they create enclaves where men do not exist.

The women's liberation movement, lacking an anchor in the organised working class and in the absence of a mass struggle by workers, slides on a downward spiral, taking refuge in personal relations, or for a few lucky ones, in literary creation or academic work, and abandoning any attempt to change the crisis-ridden world. The two trends in feminism — separatism and reformism — converge. The separatists opt out of the existing structure of society, seeking to create a liberated oasis inside the system; the reformists adapt to it, seeking to alter the capitalist system so that there are places at the top for a few.

A worker who comes to socialism identifies with his or her class. For a member of the middle class to come to socialism, that man or woman has to break the connection with the social milieu of the middle class, and join the proletariat in spirit and body. This is a very difficult task, and only a few manage it.

Even those sections of the women's movement who speak about the working class generally relegate it to the role of an accessory of their own movement. The class struggle is demoted to being a sideshow outside the broad arena of the women's movement, the black movement, or whatever. The working class is never for them the *subject* of history; at best it is one element in a motley variety of left groupings. The **Communist Manifesto**'s conclusion of its analysis of 'petty-bourgeois socialism' — that it is the enemy of proletarian socialism — applies today to the whole feminist movement, even its most radical elements. The recourse to moral posing only increases general helplessness and desperation in face of the increasingly authoritarian capitalist state.

13
The survival of the family

Friedrich Engels and Karl Marx argued again and again that under capitalism the working-class family would wither away. This has not happened. The institution of the family has been preserved, and not against the wishes of working people, including women.

Engels and Marx put forward two reasons why they expected the family to disappear. First, they said, private property and its associated inheritance rights are irrelevant to the working class of the towns and cities — who have no property. Secondly, the mass employment of women and children in the factories would abolish the economic dependence of women on men. In **The German Ideology** (1845) Marx wrote: 'the family is *actually* abolished . . . with the proletariat . . . There the concept of the family does not exist at all.'[1] In the **Communist Manifesto**, published in 1848, Engels wrote of the impact of industrial capitalism on the family:

> On what foundation is the present family, the bourgeois family, based? On capital, on private gain . . . But this state of things finds its complement in the practical absence of the family among the proletarians . . . The bourgeois claptrap about the family and education, about the hallowed co-relation of parent and child, becomes all the more disgusting, the more by the action of Modern Industry all family ties among the proletarians are torn asunder, and their children transformed into simple articles of commerce and instruments of labour.[2]

Some four decades later, in 1884, in **The Origin of the Family, Private Property and the State**, Engels repeated the argument:

> . . . since large-scale industry has transferred the woman from the

house to the labour market and the factory, and makes her, often enough, the breadwinner of the family, the last remnants of male domination in the proletarian home have lost all foundation.[3]

In the early years, when industry was growing on a massive scale, this did seem likely to be the case. Women — and children — were employed in huge numbers in the textile mills. Employers, indeed, were eager to take on women:

> . . . men were more 'difficult to manage', and more likely to cause trouble by their combinations. These disadvantages were not compensated for by extra production, since the steam loom placed all workers on the same level. Hence . . . women's work was accounted for by the fact that the master, 'finding that the child or woman was a more obedient servant to himself, and an equally efficient slave to his machinery — was disposed to displace the male adult labourer . . .[4]

In 1856 in Britain, which is where the patterns of industrial development were first set down, 57 per cent of all textile workers were women, with children a further 17.2 per cent, and men only 25.8 per cent.[5]

But after the middle of the nineteenth century this trend was reversed. The relative importance of the textile industry declined drastically, while iron and steel production, the manufacture of heavy machinery and the development of the railways became the dominant elements in the British economy. These employed practically only men. By 1907 women were only 3 per cent of the workforce in the leading industry, engineering.[6] In 1911 only 9.6 per cent of married women worked outside their own homes.[7]

Why did this happen? Practically all radical feminists[8] argue that it was the result of antagonism by male workers to the employment of women. There is an element of truth in this where skilled craft workers are concerned, for they used their trade unions to exclude women from some trades — as they excluded many men too, namely unskilled and immigrant workers. But that is not the full explanation. After all, only a tiny proportion of workers were in trade unions in those years — 11.2 per cent in 1892, for instance.

Reaction to the horrors of the Industrial Revolution

The main reason lies in the reaction of workers — both men *and* women — to the horrors and misery associated with the industrial revolution.[9] This is a description of women's work in the coal mines:

> Quite often women did the lifting and heavy part of the work, and endured conditions which men would not tolerate. 'Females submit to work in places where no man, or even lad, could be got to labour in,' said one mining foreman; 'they work in bad roads, up to their knees in

water, in a posture nearly double.' The natural result of this compliance was that women's labour was most frequently to be found in the worst mines, where they endured the most arduous toil in a foul atmosphere, dragging their loads along low, slushy roads in water-laden pits . . .

'Chained, belted, harnessed, like dogs in a go-cart,' said a Commissioner in describing 'hurrying' or 'putting', the task that employed the greatest number of women and young people of both sexes, 'black, saturated with wet, and more than half naked, crawling upon their hands and feet, and dragging their heavy loads behind them — they present an appearance indescribably disgusting and unnatural.'[10]

Here is a description of the results of working conditions in Oldham textile mills:

In the early 1850s deaths in Oldham from tuberculosis, the characteristic disease of overwork, were more than double the national average. The group worst affected, with treble the national rate, was women aged between twenty-five and thirty-four — the same group that also supplied the greatest share of millworkers. One in eight of Oldham's women died while in this age group, and over one-third worked in the mills.[11]

In the 1850s William Acton, a doctor, commented:

If we compare the prostitute at thirty-five with her sister, who perhaps is the married mother of a family, or has been the toiling slave for years in the overheated laboratories of fashion, we shall seldom find that the constitutional ravages often thought to be the necessary consequence of prostitution exceed those attributable to the cares of a family and the heartwearing struggles of virtuous labour.[12]

Above all working people's heads hung the terrible threat of the Poor House. In 1834 a new Poor Law was passed, abolishing 'outdoor relief', forcing those who fell destitute to enter workhouses, or, as the only alternative, to take extremely low-paid jobs, if they could get them. The workhouse separated man and wife and mother and child. Michael Anderson records that in Lancashire the mass of the population 'almost invariably speak of the workhouse as the "Bastille", and to be taunted as a "pauper" would be by many regarded as the most opprobious of epithets.'[13] A contemporary witness writes in 1857:

Misery is running riot through the greatest part of this district . . . The poor here have resolved to die rather than go into the union houses, and I have not the least doubt that numbers would have starved sooner than go there; certainly they would have resisted hunger until the feebler bodies of their children perished, or been so reduced as never to recover their health.[14]

Misery enhanced family loyalties. In the absence of state-supported social services, members of the family had to depend on one another. Barbara Taylor, in her brilliant study **Eve and the New**

Jerusalem, shows how, in contrast to the dreams of the early nineteenth-century utopian socialists for women's liberation, women turned towards the family as a refuge in a cruel world, and many looked to the husband as a provider. From the widespread common-law marriage among working-class people of the early nineteenth century, working-class women from about the middle of the century onwards started looking for security in legal marriage:

> The combined effect of pressure from above and a changed social environment from below was to narrow women's options and increase their sexual vulnerability. Under these circumstances, women were usually more interested in enforcing the obligations of marriage than in abolishing them. Safer relationships, rather than freer ones, were a common goal. It was at least partly for this reason that many women turned to the church, in the hope of imposing its conjugal code on men . . .
>
> In a period when women's prospects outside marriage were worsening and the burden of family support falling on many women inside marriage was intolerably heavy, it is not surprising that women themselves tended to look towards a home-centred existence, supported by a reliable male breadwinner, as a desirable goal. Or perhaps more accurately, they found it almost impossible to imagine any real alternative, except in the current reality of economic insecurity and overwork.[15]

The scene which shows up most sharply how defence of the worker's family served the interests of all its members — man, woman and child — is the fate of black slave families in the United States. Legal marriage was denied to slaves, and relationships were impossible to sustain. It was common for a woman slave to be sold away from her man and/or children, or vice versa. Numerous slave narratives provide dramatic accounts of the events surrounding the forced separation of couples, or parents and children.

Slavery dehumanised the black man and the black woman equally, atrocities being meted out to men and women with equal ferocity. Angela Davis sums up:

> The sheer force of things rendered her equal to the man . . . Though the ruling class was male and rabidly chauvinistic, the slave system could not confer upon the Black man the appearance of a privileged position vis-a-vis the Black woman. The man-slave could not be the unquestioned superior within the 'family' or community, for there was no such thing as the 'family provider' among slaves. The attainment of slavery's intrinsic goals was contingent upon the fullest and most brutal utilisation of the productive capacities of every man, woman and child. They all had to 'provide' for the master. The Black woman was totally integrated into the productive force.[16]

> . . . the slave system also discouraged male supremacy in Black men. Because husbands and wives, fathers and daughters were equally subjected to the slavemasters' absolute authority, the promotion of male supremacy among the slaves might have prompted a dangerous rupture in the chain of command.[17]

The slavemasters smashed the slave's 'family', so as 'to crush every symbol of humanity, affection, and compassion within slaves'.[18]

Against this, the slaves fought hard to defend the 'family'. Joyce Ladner tells of 'numerous historical accounts of black men lashing out against slavery because of its inhuman effects upon their families'. Although 'countless slave families were forcibly disrupted' through 'indiscriminate sales of husbands, wives and children', she says that 'the bonds of love and affection, the cultural norms governing family relations, and the overpowering desire to remain together survived the devastating onslaught of slavery.'[19] 'The family's vitality,' argues Angela Davis, 'proved stronger than the dehumanising rigors of slavery.' There is 'fascinating evidence of a thriving and developing family during slavery'.[20]

Thus in the case of the slaves also, the defence of the 'family' played a crucial part in their class struggle.

Rebuilding the Worker's Family

Marx clearly recognised that the structure of employment of the working-class family was central in determining the value of any industrial worker's labour power. The employment of men, women and children spread the value of labour-power over the whole working-class family, and so reduced the value of the labour-power of each. In addition, competition for jobs became sharper. Thus John Foster's book **The Class Struggle and the Industrial Revolution** shows that in the Nottingham footwear industry wages fell so radically after the 1820s as a result of the drawing of women and children into work in the factories, that the *total* wages of all members of the family was below the wages earned by the man alone before women and children were employed.[21]

Working-class recognition that the employment of women and children cut living standards and raised the degree of exploitation, and that this trend could be fought through a campaign for a 'family wage' — a wage sufficient to support the man and his wife and children without their working — is reflected in the following extract from the **Trades Newspaper** of 16 October 1825:

> Wages can never sink below the sum necessary to rear up the number of labourers the capitalists want. The weaver, his wife and children, all labour to obtain this sum; the blacksmith and the carpenter obtain it by

> their single exertions . . .
>
> The labouring *men* of this country, of all classes, should return to the good old plan, of subsisting their wives and children on the wages of their *own* labour, and they should demand wages high enough for this purpose . . . By doing this, the capitalists will be obliged to give the same wages to men alone which they now give to men, women and children . . . I recommend my fellow labourers, in preference to every other means of limiting the number of those who work for wages, to prevent their wives and children from competing with them in the market, and beating down the price of labour.[22]

Jane Humphries also argues, correctly, that women's domestic labour could, by producing things of value in the home, raise the family income to levels higher than when they were all working.

Tilley and Scott in their book **Women, Work and the Family**, provide ample evidence of the gains made by women from the achievement of the 'family wage':

> A factor which influenced married women's employment rates was related to improvements in real wages. The increased standard of living improved the diet, the health, and the life span of working-class adults. The decline of incidences of illness and death of a husband thus drove fewer married women into the labour force. In the course of her lifetime, a wife faced fewer emergencies which compelled her to become the family breadwinner.[23]

The 'family wage' and the retreat of women from employment, were of course blows to women's sexual equality, constituting an important factor in women's oppression. The cash nexus, plus the economic dependence of women on men, inevitably meant the devaluation of work at home, and women's social inferiority. As Margaret Benston points out, 'in a society in which money determines value, women are a group which works outside the money economy. Their work is not worth money, is therefore valueless, is therefore not real work.'

Women became restricted to marriage — to becoming wives and mothers. With this vocation came all the accepted attributes of femininity: submissiveness, passivity, emotionalism, caring. Women also became passive objects to be won or taken by the virile men.

These changes were the inevitable results of women's massive withdrawal from gainful employment. But under the conditions of the nineteenth century there was no other way of defending the elementary physical and moral needs of women, children and men of the industrial working class.

In the abstract, of course, there could have been a fight for adequate childcare facilities, maternity leave and equal pay. Heidi Hartmann argues:

> Instead of fighting for equal wages for men and women, male workers sought the 'family wage', wanting to retain their wives' services at home. In the absence of patriarchy a unified class might have confronted capitalism, but patriarchal social relations divided the working class, allowing one part (men) to be bought off at the expense of the other (women).[24]

This is nonsense. The labour movement at the time was far from having the knout to achieve any part of such a utopian scheme. Jane Humphries answers the supporters of the theory of patriarchy very well:

> . . . any analysis that treats working women as mere passive victims in the face of the imperatives of capital and the attitudes of man characterises them as sheep-like creatures incapable of perceiving, defending or acting upon even their most basic interests.

This would deny working-class women 'any semblance of self-determination and dignity'.[25]

The working-class family of the second half of the nineteenth century was created and recreated jointly, though not usually amicably, by men and women, the woman both resisting and accommodating to her own oppression. While the family provided the man with privileges, it gave the woman, while removing her from productive labour, a sense of dignity and security, especially in her function as mother. Linda Gordon gives an excellent description of this:

> In the nineteenth century women needed marriage far more than men. Lacking economic independence, women needed husbands to support them, or at least to free them from a usually more humiliating economic dependence on fathers. Especially in the cities, where women were often isolated from communities, deprived of the economic and psychological support of networks of relatives, friends and neighbours, the prospect of dissolving the cement of nuclear families was frightening. In many cases children, and the prospect of children, provided that cement . . . Women . . . were also dependent on their children to provide them with meaningful work. The belief that motherhood was a woman's fulfilment had a material basis: parenthood was often the only creative and challenging activity in a woman's life, a key part of her self-esteem.[26]

It is true that the *idea* of the family in which the wife does not work outside the home was initially established by the capitalist class itself. The influx of workers into the new cities of the Industrial Revolution brought about the virtual collapse of the old peasant family.

> In addition to alienation and exploitation at work, the proletariat had to contend with fragmentation and alienation, as the old rural forms of

> collective life were threatened in the cities . . . Proletarian children, it was often said, were raised by the street, not by the family.[27]

The nineteenth-century philanthropists concerned themselves with the increasing cost to the state of maintaining abandoned children, and with the problems of disease, 'vice' and 'disorder' arising in the vast concentrations of working-class men and women in cities such as Manchester.

The solution was to turn the working-class woman into a housewife performing the labour of caring for man and children in the home. Jacques Donzelot explains:

> This solution offered three advantages. First, it would allow a social expense to be replaced by an additional quantity of unpaid labour. It would also allow elements of hygiene to be introduced into working-class life in the areas of child-rearing and nutrition, and would make possible a regularisation of behaviour, the lack of which explained the frequency of premature deaths, illness and insubordination . . . Finally, this would make it possible to have the man controlled by the woman, since she would provide him with the benefits of her domestic activity only to the extent that he deserved them . . . [For the philanthropists] woman, the housewife and attentive mother, was man's salvation, the privileged instrument for civilising the working class.[28]

Various techniques were used by the capitalist class to encourage workers to adopt this solution, through schooling, religion, entertainment, and many other channels. For example, state-provided housing began to be built, small enough for only a nuclear family of man, woman and children to live in, with separate bedrooms for parents and children of different sexes. Since the development of the welfare state, many new methods have been devised — taxation, social security benefits, the intervention of social workers in the home — all these encourage working-class men and women to adopt the nuclear model of the family as their own.

A variety of different pressures, both from above and from below, thus led to the creation of the modern working-class family. But workers *adapted* the values and standards imposed from without to their own needs. For working-class women motherhood, however tough, was in fact the most important and significant part of their oppressive lives, which they preferred to its only possible alternative.

The assumption of many present-day feminists that working-class women were anxious in the past for work outside their homes, but prevented from it by their husbands' opposition, has been shattered completely by the massive entry of women, including married women, into employment since the Second World War, on a scale comparable to the absorption of agricultural labour into the early factories.

If the crucial factor in the workers' class struggle for a century — from the middle of the nineteenth to the middle of the twentieth centuries — was the striving of men and women workers to defend the family, keeping practically all married women at home, now it is the withering away of the 'family wage' by the involvement of women workers in work outside their homes which is the crucial factor in women's struggles.

The feminists explain the rise of the 'family wage' in the nineteenth century mistakenly, and they are no less mistaken in seeing *all* women today as mainly housewives, rather than wage-earners — which is how it is first and foremost for working-class women. Paid employment is the key for working-class women in gaining strength and confidence and thus in winning women's liberation.

14
The family: Haven in a heartless world?

Under capitalism women's oppression is unique in being rooted in the family where child-rearing, food preparation, and reproduction take place in a private world, separated from social production. As the family is part of the superstructure of society, shaping the ideas and emotions of men and women, children and adults, we should look at the impact of the contemporary family on the emotional side of people's lives.

In the previous chapter we saw how in the second half of the nineteenth century working men and women protected the family as a solace and refuge from the horrors with which industrial society threatened women, children and men, symbolised by the Poor House. The rehabilitation of the working-class family was buttressed by bourgeois ideas percolating down into the working class. The cliche, 'The Englishman's Home is his Castle' was born. 'Home Sweet Home', first heard in the 1870s, became 'almost a second national anthem'. Few walls in lower working-class houses lacked 'mottoes'— coloured strips of paper, about nine inches wide and eighteen inches in length, attesting to domestic joys: 'East, West, Home's Best'; 'Bless Our Home'; 'God is Master of this House'; 'Home is the Nest where All is Best'.[1] 'Home', wrote John Ruskin, '. . . is the place of peace; the shelter, not only from all injury, but from all terror, doubt, and division . . . so far as the anxieties of outer life penetrate into it . . . it ceases to be a home'.

Marx, in his **Economic and Philosophic Manuscripts** (1844), noted the schism in the male worker's feelings between home and work outside it:

> The worker . . . only feels himself outside his work, and in his work feels outside himself. He feels at home when he is not working, and when he is working he does not feel at home . . . Man (the worker) only feels himself freely active in his animal functions — eating, drinking, procreating, or at most in his dwelling and in dressing up, etc.[2]

For the housewife, even the latter possibility does not exist, for 'home' is itself the focus of her alienated situation. She is expected to provide nurture for others, with no place or scope for herself.

Concentrating on the working-class family, the present chapter will try to show that the family is both protective and oppressive, both a haven from an alienating world, and a prison. We shall show first how the family is oppressive; secondly, that it is oppressive for both men and women; thirdly, that it is more oppressive for working-class people than for other classes; fourthly, that nevertheless it is accepted because it still does provide some sort of haven in a capitalist world; and finally, that the institution of the family imposes the harshest oppression on people such as gays and lesbians who do not fit it.

The prevailing view of the family as an unchanging, eternal institution leads most writers to abstract it from the class structure of society. Of course there are major similarities of form between working-class and middle-class families — the nuclear household composed of father, mother and children facing issues of work, child-rearing, personal relations, leisure. But beneath the form lie sharp differences of content which are rooted in the class position of each family. The outside world impinges on the working-class family in a radically different way from the middle-class family.

Most studies of the family today are of middle-class, white families. The only two notable exceptions are **Blue-Collar Marriage** by Mirra Komarovsky, whose detailed examination of the American white working-class family was completed in 1959, and Lillian Rubin's brilliant book, **World of Pain: Life in the Working Class Family**.[3] Nothing like these works has been undertaken in Britain. Their insights, however, are of general importance in understanding workers' families in advanced capitalist societies, including Britain, and such studies as do exist in Britain confirm the main perceptions of the American writers, despite differences of place and time. I have borrowed from them extensively.

In both books the working-class women interviewed talk of themselves as wives and mothers — as housewives and not wage workers. The fact that women's own conception of themselves is in contradiction to the *actual* situation, in which they are both earners and housewives, results from two main factors: first, ideas lag behind reality; secondly, so long as the private family remains, men think of themselves not as fathers but as earners, and women by and large think of themselves as mothers, even if they do earn. Even at work the great majority of working-class women, unlike women with interesting jobs and career prospects, think and worry about their homes. And of course there are periods in the lives of the majority of working-class wives — when they have infants to look after — when they *are* totally dependent on their husbands financially, and therefore look upon themselves as 'merely housewives'. Even of the women who do have a paid job, two-fifths in Britain at present work part-time, hence in their concept of themselves housewifery plays a predominant role. And again, the education system also conditions girls to see their future function as housewives — wives and mothers — and not as workers.

Shattered Dreams

Working-class girls accept the traditional feminine role. Sue Sharpe, in **Just Like a Girl: How Girls Learn to be Women**, a study of schoolgirls in Ealing, West London, most of them from working-class families, writes:

> In a College of Further Education in London, a teacher noted that the girls who were taking hairdressing, commercial and typing courses . . . 'dress according to **Girl**, **Petticoat**, and 'Brook Street Bureau' ads. They are totally immersed in self-image; nails, eyelashes, platforms and accoutrements.' The girls taking O-levels however . . . which might eventually lead them to Teachers' Training College or University . . . Often their whole attitude is different . . . And this is reflected in their dress which is correspondingly more relaxed; jeans, T-shirts and not so much make-up.[4]

Middle-class girls, Sue Sharpe says, 'have . . . developed individual ambitions in which marriage and children figure as desirable but also intrusive events and ones to which they would reluctantly commit the whole of their lives.[5] Working-class girls, on the other hand, look to 'Marriage as Liberation', and in a chapter with this title, Mirra Komarovsky writes: 'The greater control which the family exercises over the adolescent daughter in comparison with the son no doubt largely explains the greater frequency with which women listed escape from home as one of the benefits of marriage.'[6] Marriage entices the young women also because it is an escape from boring, dreary jobs. Sue Sharpe writes:

> They see many of their relatives and friends doing jobs from which they seem to gain minimal enjoyment. It therefore makes sense to make their priorities love, marriage, husbands, children, jobs and careers, more or less in that order . . . Work is then not seen as attractive but as an unfortunate necessity of life and therefore the apparent opportunity to

> avoid it seems one of the advantages of being a woman.
>
> In addition to this there are other inducements. For instance children are more worth spending time and energy on than many boring and alienating jobs, since they actually respond and grow. The apparent choice of whether to work or not after marriage and after children, and the ability to organise life in the home without supervision gives an illusion of freedom and greater choice of action.[7]

Alas, the dreams are shattered quickly after the wedding. Thus Lillian Rubin writes:

> The economic realities that so quickly confronted the young working-class couples of this study ricocheted through the marriage, dominating every aspect of experience, coloring every facet of their early adjustment. The women, finding their dreams disappointed, felt somehow that their men had betrayed the promise implicit in their union. They were both angry and frightened.

She quotes one young working-class mother:

> 'The first thing that hit us was all those financial problems. *We were dirt poor*. Here I'd gotten married with all those dreams and then I got stuck right away trying to manage on $1.50 an hour — and a lot of days he didn't work very many hours. It felt like there was nothing to life but scrimping and saving; only there wasn't any saving, just scrimping.'

Another woman, 26 years old, mother of two, married seven years, expressed her fear and anger with her husband when he was laid off: 'I could hardly ever forgive him for getting fired from his job. We never stopped arguing about that. I felt so frightened. I almost couldn't stand it. I was scared we'd just get into deeper trouble.'

The men, disappointed in themselves and equally frightened as they looked toward an uncertain future, responded defensively and uncomprehendingly to their wives' angry concerns. A 30-year-old postal clerk, father of three, married nine years, told the interviewer:

> I couldn't figure out what the hell she wanted from me. I was trying, and I didn't like how things were coming out any better than she did.
>
> *Did you tell her that?*
>
> Tell her? Who could tell her anything? She was too busy running off at the mouth — you know, nagging — to listen to anything. I just got mad and I'd take off — go out with the guys and have a few beers or something. When I'd get back, things would be even worse. Sometimes I'd feel like hitting her just to shut her up. I never could figure out why the hell she did that. Did she think I didn't care about not making enough money to take care of my family?

Instead of marriage as an escape to freedom, home has become a prison. No longer is the young couple free to run around with the old crowd, to prowl the favoured haunts, to go to a movie or party whenever the mood struck. Both wives and husbands were shaken as it quickly became clear that the freedom they had sought in marriage was a mirage, that they had exchanged one set of constraints for another perhaps more powerful. A 28-year-old clerk in a cleaning store, mother of three, married eleven years, sums up those feelings: 'One day I woke up and there I was, married and with a baby. And I thought, "I can't stand it! I can't stand to have my life over when I'm so young." Her 31-year-old husband recalls:

> I had just turned twenty and, all of a sudden, I had a wife and kid. You couldn't just go out anymore when you felt like it . . . I'd get so mad at her, at my whole life, that I'd cut out on work a lot, and that would make things worse because then we had more money problems. Even when I worked steady, my paycheck wasn't big enough, then when I missed days, we were really in trouble.
>
> But you know, a guy's got to have some freedom. He's got to feel like he doesn't have to go to that same lousy place every day of his life, like a slave.

The man's self-esteem was on the line every time he brought home a pay packet that was inadequate to meet the bills, or, worse still, failed to bring one home at all. For the woman, whose self-esteem and status, if she was kept at home bringing up young children, was intimately tied to her husband's accomplishments, the issue became one of 'husband-esteem'. A woman of 35, mother of four, married eighteen years, said: 'A man who can't take care of his family hasn't got the right to come in and order people around. A man's got to deserve it to have people listen to him when he talks. As long as he wasn't supporting us very good, he didn't deserve it.' Lillian Rubin comments:

> Whether overtly or covertly, these feelings were communicated to the man and, quite naturally, heightened the marital conflict. The men began to act out their anger and frustration — sometimes by drinking and staying out late, sometimes by violence, and almost always by assuming a very authoritarian stance within the family. How else could they assert their manliness? How else could they establish their position as head of the household? The women resisted.[8]

Capitalist society forces men to translate social position into terms of personal worth. Spending money and acquiring property (a house, furniture and so on) are weapons for defending workers' dignity. A feeling of powerlessness at work leads to a sense of individual guilt and corrodes the male worker's self-respect in a world based on social inequality. Financial worries affect the most intimate part of the marriage; they invade the marriage bed. Mirra Komarovsky writes:

. . . some poor providers felt 'beat' and . . . the husband himself or his wife traced the decline in the husband's potency to his sense of economic failure. In other cases it is the wife whose sexual response is affected by her disappointment in her husband as a provider. Some wives are quite explicit in making this connection.[9]

Inequality in the Family

There is little, even formal, egalitarianism in the working-class family, as exists in professional middle-class families. Lillian Rubin writes:

. . . the professional middle-class man is more secure, has more status and prestige than the working-class man — factors which enable him to assume a less *overtly* authoritarian role within the family. There are, after all, other places, other situations where his authority and power are tested and accorded legitimacy. At the same time, the demands of his work role for a satellite wife require that he risk the consequences of the more egalitarian family ideology. In contrast, for the working-class man, there are few such rewards in the world outside the home; the family usually is the only place where he can exercise his power, demand obedience to his authority. Since his work role makes no demands for wifely participation, he is under fewer and less immediate external pressures to accept the egalitarian ideology.

The worker's wife usually shows sympathy for her husband, she understands his psychological needs and tries to accommodate to them. Lillian Rubin writes:

. . . on the surface, working-class women generally seem to accept and grant legitimacy to their husbands' authority, largely because they understand his need for it. If not at home, where is a man who works on an assembly line, in a warehouse, or a refinery to experience himself as a person whose words have weight, who is 'worth' listening to? But just below the surface, there lies a well of ambivalence; for the cost of her compliance is high. In muting her own needs to be responsive to his, she is left dissatisfied — a dissatisfaction that makes her so uncomfortable, she often has difficulty articulating it even to herself.

Sadly, probably no one is more aware than they are that the person who must insist upon respect for his status already has lost it.

This understanding and sympathy of the wife for the husband's predicament is seldom reciprocated by the husband understanding the wife's predicament!

Often the pressure on the worker in the outside world is so great that he sees his own family as a trap which has forced him to hunt and be hunted out there.

In fact, any five-year-old child knows when 'daddy has had a bad day' at

> work . . . When *every* working day is a 'bad day', the family may even feel like the enemy at times. But for them, he may well think, he could leave the hated job, do something where he could feel human again instead of like a robot.[10]

Professional middle-class families lead far more active social lives than working-class families. Mirra Komarovsky writes:

> In Glenton[11] joint social life with friends is far from being the important leisure-time pursuit that it is in higher socio-economic classes. This applies to exchanges of home visits as well as to joint visits to public recreational places. About one-fifth of the couples never visit with another couple apart from relatives. An additional 16 per cent do so only very infrequently, a few times a year. And these social occasions may include so impersonal an event as a Sunday school picnic or a company Christmas party.
>
> Even those who maintain social relations with other couples have a very small circle of friends. For one-half of them this circle consists of only one or two couples. Only 17 per cent see as many as four or more different couples in the course of a year (included in this count are couples seen at least a few times a year).[12]

Why the meagre social life? First, there is a lack of money. Secondly there is a lack of common interests between men and women. Also some husbands feel awkward on social occasions. Hence it is a common occurrence for husband and wife to clash when they have to decide how to spend their leisure hours. The men, after monotonous, boring work at the factory, want to stay at home and relax. Women who have been forced to stay at home have different needs.

> They're more often bored and restless, feeling locked in by the walls of their houses, ready to get out — any place, just so long as it's out of the house . . . he, out at work, is . . . happy to get back into the peace and quiet of the house, while she's desperate to leave it. For him, the house is a haven; for her, a prison.[13]

Lillian Rubin writes:

> The professional middle class families . . . have more active leisure lives on every count. They do more, go more, read more, have more friends, see more people.

This is partly due to financial differences, which mean that for middle-class families a baby-sitter, a movie, a dinner out, a family vacation, a weekend without children, do not feel like major investments.[14]

For working people work and home are worlds apart. Hence there is little husband and wife can talk about. Mirra Komarovsky writes: 'Generally, having neither competence nor interest in the mate's topic of conversation, each complains that the other "goes on and on about boring things" in unnecessary detail . . .'[15] About his own job a 36-year-old steeplejack said: 'There is nothing to elaborate about my job. I just mix paint all day and put it on. It's monotonous.' Mirra Komarovsky comments: 'Talk about the job carries the connotation, for the husband, of "griping", which is thought to be unmanly.'[16]

Life contains little beyond the immediate daily tasks. It leaves little space for common cultural activities that might broaden the narrow overlap of interests and crushing spiritual poverty.

> Thus are both women and men stuck in a painful bind, each blaming the other for failures to meet cultural fantasies — fantasies that have little relation to their needs, their experiences, or the socio-economic realities of the world they live in . . . [the] burdens . . . are especially difficult to bear in a highly competitive economic system that doesn't grant every man and woman the right to work at a self-supporting and self-respecting wage as a matter of course.[17]

In addition there is little social contact between the wife and her husband's mates: 'The great majority of the wives, some 80 per cent, have no social contact with their husbands' work-mates. The friendships husbands may form on the job do not include their wives.' Things are radically different among middle-class spouses. Lillian Rubin writes:

> For the professional . . . there is not the separation between working and living that so often characterises the working-class experience. Work and life — which also means play — are part and parcel of each other. Their friends are often colleagues or other professionals in similar or related fields. Evenings spent with them mean that the ideas that engage them at work also involve them at play. Social life is almost always a coupled affair, a shared experience of husband and wife.[18]

Housework

Housework makes women's lives extremely narrow and oppressive. Not because the working-class woman abhors housework, like the woman of the professional middle class. As Mirra Komarovsky writes:

> Unlike some college-educated housewives who detest housework, our respondents never say that they are too good for it, that housework is unchallenging manual labor . . . They accept housewifery. There is hardly a trace in the interviews of the low prestige that educated housewives sometimes attach to their role, as reflected in the familiar phrase, 'I am just a housewife.'[19]

Because working-class men as well as women accept the traditional segregation of masculine and feminine tasks, the 'wives do not normally expect assistance from their husbands'.

> When the wives were asked to rank qualities which characterise a good husband, 'willing to help wife with housework' was low on the list, the 18th among the 21 qualities presented for rating. Only 4 per cent of women considered 'helps with the housework' as 'very important'. Even 'helps with care of babies' was evaluated as 'very important' by only 12 per cent of the women.

As against this,

> The high school men help their wives with shopping and with infant care more than do the less-educated . . . Forty per cent of the less-educated 'never or hardly ever help with the babies', against only 10 per cent of the high school graduates.

One reason why middle-class professional husbands are more helpful to their wives, Mirra Komarovsky argues, is:

> The marriages of the high school graduates tend to be happier, and the warmer the relationship, the more likely the husband is to help with the infants. A happily married man tends to be less calculating about the balance of services.

The fact that the working-class woman accepts, in principle, her sex-typed function of housekeeping, does not mean that she is satisfied with carrying this burden. Actually working-class housewives are generally frustrated and depressed. Mirra Komarovsky writes:

> The homemaker herself attributes her major problem to the lack of sufficient money for necessities of life, for pleasanter living arrangements, for babysitters and fun. But the sharp segregation of the roles of the sex, despite her acceptance of it, adds to her sense of restriction and isolation . . . Unrelieved responsibility for young children and a feeling of being tied down creates discontent.[20]

Parents and Children

Poverty and insecurity quite often push the parents, especially the fathers, to complete withdrawal. Thus one 31-year-old steelworker told Lillian Rubin:

> My father was a very quiet man. he almost never talked, even when you asked him a question. He'd sit there like he didn't hear you. Sometimes, an hour later (it was like he'd come out of a spell), he'd look at you and say, 'Did you want something?' Most of the time, he just didn't know you were there.

A 25-year-old woman, the elder in a family of two, recalls:

> My father never seemed to talk or be a part of the family. The only thing I can remember that he enjoyed was working in his garden. He'd come

home, eat, and go out in the yard almost every night of the year, even when it was raining. Otherwise, he'd just sit quiet for hours, like he wasn't there or something.

Lillian Rubin's comment on these statements is:

It's true that fathers in the professional middle-class homes may also be recalled as silent, as not 'part of the family'. But none of the adults who grew up in those homes recall the kind of brooding, withdrawn quality that so often describes the experience in a working-class home. The child of a professional father may recall that he was 'always working even when he was at home'; that he was 'preoccupied a lot'; or that he 'always seemed to have something on his mind'. But that same person also is much more likely than his working-class counterpart to remember some ways in which fathers participated in family life, even if only to recall the dinner hour as a time for family conversation. Preoccupation, then, would seem to be the most remembered quality about fathers in professional families; withdrawal, the most vivid memory in working-class families.

Many working-class fathers feel inadequate; they know they haven't 'made it'. In a society where money is a source of self-esteem and power, workers lack both. They are not accorded respect. They feel unsure of themselves, of their work. Their children perceive it clearly.

They know when their teachers are contemptuous of their family background, of the values they have been taught at home. They know that there are no factory workers, no truck drivers, no construction workers who are the heroes of the television shows they watch. They know that their parents are not among those who 'count' . . . And perhaps most devastating of all, they know that their parents know these things as well. Why else would they urge their children on to do 'better', to be 'more' than they are? Why else would they carry within them so much generalised and free-floating anger — anger that lashes out irritationally at home, anger that is displaced from the world outside where its expression is potentially dangerous?[21]

Failing, inadequate working-class parents tend to impose authoritarian rule over their children. Komarovsky writes:

. . . working-class parents emphasised what was termed the 'traditional' values of obedience, neatness and respect for adults. The middle-class parents . . . on the other hand, wanted their children to be happy, to confide in them and to be eager to learn . . . Working-class parents do not speak of emotional security or capacity to relate to others. Such concepts are not in their frame of reference.[22]

Economic and cultural deprivation, together with the heavy hand of the father, crush the development and realisation of personality in the children.

> For the child — especially the boy — born into a professional middle-class home, the sky's the limit; his dreams are relatively unfettered by constraints. In his earliest conscious moments, he becomes aware of his future and of plans being made for it — plans that are not just wishful fantasies, but plans that are backed by the resources to make them come true. All around him as he grows, he sees men who do important work at prestigious jobs. At home, at school, in the neighborhood, he is encouraged to test the limits of his ability, to reach for the stars.
>
> For most working-class boys, the experience is just the reverse. Born into a family where daily survival is problematic, he sees only the frantic scramble to meet today's needs, to pay tomorrow's rent. Beyond that it's hard for parents to see. In such circumstances, of what can children dream?

What about the girls?

> Among the women, a few recall girlhood dreams of being a model or an actress, but most remember wanting only to marry and live happily ever after . . . It's not that the girls from middle-class homes dreamed such different dreams. But along with the marriage fantasy, there was for them some sense of striving for their own development . . . for those middle-class women, marriage came much later since it was deferred until after college. Moreover, once these girls left home for college, they had at least some of the freedom and autonomy young people so deeply desire while, at the same time, they were engaged in an activity that brings status and respect from both family and peers.

For working-class people childhood is not a rosy memory. Lillian Rubin writes:

> . . . few adults from working-class families look back over those early years with the 'Oh-to-be-a-child-again' fantasy so often heard among middle-class adults. Small wonder, too, that the working-class young grow up so fast while an extended adolescence — often until the mid-twenties and later — is the developing norm in much of the professional middle class. Such a moratorium on assuming adult responsibilities is a luxury that only the affluent sector of society can afford.
>
> Were there no tales of happy childhoods? The answer: very few. There are always a few good memories, some families less troubled, more loving than others; but happy childhoods: no . . . I recalled my own impoverished background. Yes, there were happy moments — an ice cream cone, a small toy, an infrequent and unexpected family outing, a rare approving remark from a harassed, frightened, and overburdened mother, a few cents occasionally to spend as I would and the exquisite agony of making a choice. But those were isolated moments, not descriptive of the warp and woof of my life. The dominant memories of

childhood for me, as for the people I met, are of pain and deprivation — both material and emotional, for one follows the other almost as certainly as night follows day.[23]

Violence in the Family

That the ideal picture of the family as a source of love, understanding and unlimited support is far from the reality, becomes clear when one looks behind the veneer of the family to the physical assaults quite common in it.

In the nature of things there are no reliable statistics on violence in the family. But it is now accepted that violence inside the family is far more common than was previously thought. Suzan Steinmetz and Murray Straus in their book **Violence in the Family** write: '. . . it would be hard to find a group or institution in American society in which violence is more of an everyday occurrence than it is within the family.'[24] In extreme cases the physical violence becomes murder. An official report in 1977 came 'to the conclusion that over 300 children are killed every year in England and Wales alone, and 3,000 seriously injured. Four hundred receive injuries which result in chronic brain damage, while a further 40,000 children suffer mild or moderate damage.'[25]

The more exploited and deprived people are, the greater the violence. Richard Gelles writes in his book, **The Violent Home**:

> . . . while violence occurs in families at all socio-economic levels, it is most common in families occupying positions at the bottom of the social structure . . . the bulk of conjugal violence and violence towards children occurs in families with low income, low educational achievement, and where the husband has low occupational status.[26]

Similarly Mirra Komarovsky finds a clear association between low education and high family violence. While 33 per cent of wives who had less than 12 years' education mentioned a physically violent quarrel with spouses, among those with 12 years or more the figure was only 4 per cent.[27] Another researcher found that nearly half of the fathers of battered children were unemployed during the year preceding the decisive act, while 12 per cent were unemployed at the time the battering took place.[28]

A study of severely ill-treated young children in North and East Wiltshire in the seven years 1965–71 showed that 48 per cent of the fathers (or men who were in the role of father) were unemployed, 71 per cent of them were unskilled labourers, and 98 per cent did not own their own home.[29] Another research project conducted in the Strathclyde Region into non-accidental injury to children in 1980 shows that only 10 per cent of their mothers were in full or part employment, and two-thirds of the fathers were unemployed.

While women are largely the victims of men's violence in the family, the woman is often the main perpetrator of violence on the children. As Richard Gelles writes: 'The most physically aggressive parent is the mother . . . it is the mother who usually explodes into violence when she runs out of patience.'[30] Two American researchers reported that out of the 57 cases of child-battering they dealt with, the mother was the abuser 50 times.[31]

One form of child abuse in which power and sexual oppression are enmeshed is incest. Incest is rare, but not all that rare. One comprehensive three-year study estimated the number of cases annually in New York at 3,000. Other researchers thought this conservative. 'The most frequently-named abuser was the father, male relative or mother's boyfriend, all of whom had easy access to the home. The victims' ages ranged from one or two months old to seventeen or eighteen years.' Incest, like physical violence, 'is more likely to occur where poverty brings loss of privacy together with other handicaps.'[32]

It is precisely because the family is a 'heart in a heartless world', because people in an alienated environment demand of the family more than it can deliver, because in it husband and wife become more and more dependent upon each other for the satisfaction of emotional needs, that it becomes the cauldron of pressures, frustrations and hate. As Richard Gelles writes:

> . . . prolonged interaction, intimacy, and emotional closeness of family life expose the vulnerability of both partners and strip away the facades that might have been created to shield personal weaknesses of both husband and wife. As a result, couples become experts at attacking each other's weaknesses and are able to hurt each other effectively with attacks and counter-attacks . . . [Both spouses] become experts as to their partner's vulnerability. Each soon learns what upsets the other. In the course of family squabbles, arguments or confrontations, one or both of the spouses will 'go for the jugular' by attacking weak spots.[33]

The stereotype of husband as provider, and dependent, nurturing wife, survives despite the fact that in Britain in 1979 the 'typical worker' — a married man with a non-working wife and children — represented a mere 8 per cent of the male labour force and 5 per cent of the total labour force.[34]

The Family as Incubus of Mental Illness

Mental illness is no less injurious than physical illness. An important piece of research by George Brown and Tirril Harris into depression among women shows the interrelation between the class to which women belong and the frequency of psychological disorders.

The women interviewed live in Camberwell, South London. It was found that severe events in life such as a dangerous illness of someone close, the loss of a job, an unwanted pregnancy, failure to obtain a house, or an eviction, caused working-class women greater psychiatric distress than they did middle-class women. This was particularly marked among women with children: 39 per cent of working-class mothers developed a psychiatric disorder after a severe event as against 6 per cent of middle-class mothers.

Working-class women whose youngest child is less than six years old have a particularly high rate of disturbance — some 42 per cent (as against 5 per cent among middle-class women whose youngest child is less than six). Also,

> we found that if a woman does not have an intimate tie, someone she can trust and confide in, particularly a husband or boy-friend, she is much more likely to break down in the presence of a severe event or major difficulty.

Brown and Harris, like Rubin and Komarovsky, found that class sharply affected this sort of intimate support. In working-class families, husbands are psychologically less supportive of their wives than in professional middle-class families. Only 37 per cent of working-class women with a child under six at home had a high level of intimacy with their husbands or boyfriends — half the proportion of the corresponding middle-class group.

The middle-class woman has greater material and psychological reserves to meet severe events in life than the working-class woman. She can move into new areas of activity or make new contacts on which she can build. Brown and Harris write:

> The middle-class woman can more often travel, visit friends at some distance, or buy a new dress; she has perhaps greater confidence and skills in seeking out pleasurable experience; and also a stronger belief that she will eventually achieve certain goals of importance. Adjustment in adversity may prove to be largely a matter of how to sustain hope for better things.

The most important factor detrimentally affecting the working-class woman's psychiatric state is her feeling of being 'cooped in' — the restriction imposed by not going to work. The importance of a job for women's mental health becomes clear from the following figures: of non-employed women with a child at home, but without intimate ties with their husbands, 79 per cent were disturbed when a serious life event occurred to them; the corresponding figure for women who were in similar circumstances but who held a job was only 14 per cent.

In the conclusion to their book Brown and Harris write:

In summary: some of the social class difference in risk of depression is due to the fact that working-class women experience more severe life-events and major difficulties, especially when they have children; problems concerning housing, finance, husband, and child (excluding those involving health) are particularly important. Incidents of this kind are the only kind of severe event to occur more commonly among working-class women and are the most obvious candidates for the 'inner city' stresses which are the focus of much current social commentary.

One of the most important contributions made by the research of Brown and Harris is the light it throws on the intersection of *class and family* as it affects women's mental health. Belonging to the working class does not make a woman liable to a high rate of psychiatric disorder — if she is single. On the other hand a married woman would not be liable to a high rate of psychiatric disorder — if she belonged to the middle class. The dangerous combination is being working class and married.

. . . single women have a particularly low rate of psychiatric disorder (one in twenty is a case) and those widowed, divorced, and separated a particularly high rate (one in three is a case), but in neither group is there an association with class. Class differences are restricted to married women.[35]

In conclusion, the high level of mental illness among married working-class women looking after young children and not holding a job is a reflection of both capitalist exploitation and of sexual oppression intertwined with it.

How do women compare with men as regards the incidence of mental illness? Many researchers have dealt with this question. An important summary of the research is an article called 'The Relationship between Sex Roles, Marital Status, and Mental Illness' by W R Gove. Gove says that research in all countries has

shown that married women have noticeably higher rates of mental illness than married men. In contrast, it is shown that when single women are compared with single men, divorced women with divorced men, and widowed women with widowed men, these women do not have rates of mental illness that are higher than their male counterparts. In fact, if there is a difference within these marital categories, it is that women have lower rates of mental illness.

Gove estimates from the statistics that women are damaged twice as much by marriage as men. He argues that the reason for this is that 'men have two major roles, jobholder and household head, while the women tend to have only one, housewife.' (The large-scale employment of women contradicts this, but — and this is the important point — women, and men, do still conceive their roles in this way.) In support of Gove's contention that the differences between the job roles of men and women largely explain the differences between the rates of mental illness, he looks into what happens when men reach pensionable age and retire, and finds that 'there is at least tentative evidence that the rates of mental illness of married men and women are more similar after the age of retirement.'[36]

The Family is not an Impregnable Sanctuary

The family does not serve as a safe haven insulated from the world of work. Work intrudes into every aspect of the worker's life. Lasch writes:

> The same historical developments that have made it necessary to set up private life — the family in particular — as a refuge from the cruel world of politics and work, an emotional sanctuary, have invaded this sanctuary and subjected it to outside control. A retreat into 'privatism' no longer serves to shore up values elsewhere threatened with extinction.[37]

A Ford worker describes his situation:

> I never thought I'd survive. I used to come home from work and fall straight asleep. My legs and arms used to be burning. And I know hard work. I'd been on the buildings but this place was a bastard then. I didn't have any relations with my wife for months. Now that's not right is it? No work should be that hard.[38]

A study of the effect of the 'Continental' shift system shows that the men cannot sleep properly, their appetite is affected, they feel permanently tired, get constipation, ulcers, rheumatoid arthritis, headaches and rectal complaints. In addition:

> The most frequently mentioned difficulties in husband-wife relationships concern the absence of the worker from the home in the evening, sexual relations, and difficulties encountered by the wife in carrying out her household duties . . . Another area of family life that seems to be adversely affected by certain kinds of shift work is the father-child relationship . . .[39]

Capitalism has also transformed sex itself into a major commodity, serving a huge market in fashion goods which claim to increase the sexual attraction of women and potency of men, and in pornography. Sexuality becomes a set of physical sensations alienated from the *person*. As George Frankl, in **The Failure of the Sexual Revolution**, puts it: '. . . the mass manufacturers of dreams . . . concentrate entirely on sexual performances and sexual situations, and do not allow the personality of their subjects to obtrude.'[40] Long ago, in 1921, Alexandra Kollontai denounced this concept of sex:

> The bourgeois attitude to sexual relations as simply a matter of sex must be criticised and replaced by an understanding of the whole gamut of joyful love-experience that enriches life and makes for greater happiness. The greater the intellectual and emotional development of the individual the less place will there be in his or her relationship for the bare physiological side of love, and the brighter will be the love experience.[41]

A mechanical approach to sex increases anxieties among both women and men. The woman asks herself, 'Am I as attractive, as successful in bed as the women portrayed in magazines, on films and TV?' The man asks himself, 'Am I a potent stud?'

Sexual permissiveness has not challenged the idea that a woman's place is in the home; it has simply added 'and in the bed'.

Capitalism distorts all human beings in society, depriving men, women and children of the capacity to develop their potentialities in every area of life. The family, that part of this society to which people look for love and comfort, reproduces the external relationships, and this turns it into a cauldron of personal conflicts — of anger, jealousy, fear and guilt. Both men and women fail to live up to the impossible ideal stereotype which society gives them of one another.

Why, if the family is less and less effective in securing the emotional, personal needs of people, do people still cling to it? Why, of all institutions, does this one show the greatest ability to survive?

While it is true that the harsher the world, the less effective is the family in protecting the emotional and material needs of its members, at the same time the greater is the need for just such a sanctuary. The satisfaction of almost all personal needs is to be found nowhere else. To be outside the nuclear family, an orphan, widow or widower with no close relatives, or a middle-aged or old single man or woman, is lonelier and worse. Mutual aid is a basic necessity for men and women. Out of loneliness the nuclear family gains strength. The institution of the family oppresses the woman. She, on her part, participates in creating the chains that bind her, decking them with flowers of love.

The family is an opaque wall preventing people from seeing and questioning the harsh, competitive society outside. It makes a person's inhumanity to another more bearable. The horrors of the outside world explain the extreme tensions in the family, but also explain its perseverance. The contemporary family is the product of capitalism and one of its main supports.

The 'Deviant' Homosexuals

Sex roles are enforced by our society on everyone. Because of the crucial role of the family, any adult who does not marry and raise a family is marked out as deviant. Homosexuals challenge both the *material* base of the present-day family — privatised reproduction — and its ideological superstructure — the stereotypes and ideas which define the sex roles of women and men. And this is notwithstanding the fact that homosexuality is far more common than is usually assumed. Kinsey's research found that 37 per cent of his male, and 13 per cent of his female, respondents had experienced homosexual relations to orgasm by the age of 45.[42]

Homosexuals are stereotyped as deviants despite the fact that the monogamous family has not been the historical norm. Of 554 societies listed by George Murdock, in only 135 was monogamy the norm.[43] Nor has homosexuality always been viewed as deviant. C S Ford and F Beach found in their study of 190 societies, that for 76 for which data was available concerning homosexuality, 49 perceived it as normal.[44]

In our society homosexuals are forced into the closet. When gay people manage to get out of their isolation by meeting other gays, they are forced into a social ghetto away from work, the family and the mainstream of social life. The gay ghetto breaks the isolation for individual gays, but maintains the isolation of gays from mainstream society.

Even relations between gays themselves are not free from the *diktat* of the traditional roles of men and women. However hard they try, gays cannot escape the pressures and conditioning of capitalist society. Hence the heterosexual world in which man oppresses woman imposes its own divisions on gays too. One writer explains the male role played by gays:

> Playing roles in a society which demands gender definitions, sexual role-playing, masculine versus feminine — what can we do, those whom society dismisses and condemns as half-men? Too often we react by over-playing. The absurd parodies of straight sexuality we see in the bars, ultra-butch, camp bitch, are cold and brittle. Their eyes betray fear and loathing as they compete viciously, to allay the panic of loneliness at the end of the night.[45]

The division between 'butch' and 'femme' is usually used in relation to women homosexuals. Thus Sidney Abbot and Barbara Love, in their thoughtful book, **Sappho was a Right-on Woman**, write:

> Some lesbians use terminology like 'marriage', 'husband', or 'wife', but there is a profound reason for this. These are the only words in our culture that convey love, trust, permanence, and responsibility in a relationship . . . Presumably role-playing among Lesbians exists because Lesbians are raised in a role-playing society . . . Lesbians have spent all their time in a culture that forcefully sells a way of life based on

male and female dominance and submissiveness, independence and dependence, aggressiveness and passivity.[46]

In fact the notion of 'male' and 'female' partners in homosexual relationships is inaccurate. As Arno Karlen, in his massive **Sexuality and Homosexuality**, quotes one psychologist as saying: 'A small percentage always take the female role; another small percentage are muscle men, homosexual pin-ups, who always take the active role. But for the most part, they often switch roles.'[47] But however forcefully the contemporary gay movement and the lesbian groupings in the women's movement reject the gender-related roles, they cannot win. Although the **Gay Liberation Front Manifesto** denounces marriage and speaks of the death of the family, gays, in seeking emotional security in a harsh world, imitate the institution their own sexuality denies. However, as Kinsey showed, lasting couples are rare among homosexuals, although many lesbian pairs live together for five, ten or fifteen years. Arno Karlen writes: 'Many homosexuals say they are looking for a lasting affair and are quick to shack up, but in fact have a series of brittle, stormy, short-lived relationships.'[48]

Homosexuals do not demand less emotional commitment from their partners than heterosexuals, despite the superficially more liberal attitude to 'extra-marital' sex. Living under terrible pressure in a hostile world, they feel their sexuality far more intensively than most heterosexuals, hence the pervading possessiveness — because possession of things, as of people, gives a modicum of security. As Abbott and Love write: 'In Lesbian society, where there is no marriage, no social or legal sanctions to help sustain relationships beyond the initial period of romantic love, insecurity and jealousy have a field day.'[49]

The homosexual world, which appears to undermine capitalist notions, is also completely invaded by capitalism.

> The gay subculture is riven with clashes and illusions. The women tend to be split off from the men, butch men from fem, leather queens from drag queens, and so on. Many of these attitudes are themselves reflections of heterosexual values; others of the pervasive cash nexus. In this gay world it is all too easy for people to lose their individualities, sex becomes the aim of life; individuals become things.[50]

In conclusion, capitalism has turned homosexuality into a 'problem'. So long as the traditional family is an economic unit, for rearing children and satisfying the consumption needs of the adults, homosexuals are bound to be considered deviant: the homosexual male is not seen to fit the man's role as provider for wife and children, and the homosexual female is not seen to act the role of mother and wife. The contemporary family is not only a prison for those in it, but also enslaves those who do not fit into the sex-role stereotypes connected with it.

15
The struggle for socialism and women's liberation

The Class Roots of Women's Oppression

Throughout this book we have taken the relations of class exploitation as our starting point in analysing women's place in society. In doing so we have followed Friedrich Engels' **The Origin of the Family, Private Property and the State** (first published in 1884). This work laid the basis for a materialist analysis of women's conditions by locating sexual oppression and the family within the economic structure of society. Engels argued that changes in the mode of production — the way society organises to produce the things needed for life — affected the whole mode of human existence, including the form of relations between men and women.

Engels wrote in **The Origin of the Family**:

> The determining factor in history is, in the last resort, the production and reproduction of immediate life. But this itself is of a twofold character. On the one hand, the production of the means of subsistence, of food, clothing, and shelter and the tools requisite therefor; on the other, the propagation of the species.[1]

Production and reproduction are not independent of one another; the first is decisive in shaping the second, and the more society develops the more is this the case. What ensues is 'a society in which the family system is entirely dominated by the property system.'

Following the American anthropologist Lewis Morgan, Engels argued that women enjoyed a status equal to that of men in the primitive communist societies which preceded the emergence of classes. The division of labour reflected men's and women's different natural strengths; sexual relations were based on the free choice of the partners; under the rule of 'mother right', descent passed through the mother and not the father. But, with increases in the productivity of labour, social relations changed. Herds of animals came to be wealth and it was the men who reared the cattle. Gradually women, who had been supreme within the home, found their position eroded. As the new cattle-wealth increased, men wanted to be able to pass it on to their own male children. Mother-right stood in their way, and so was overthrown. In its place was set the monogamous family, in which one woman was bound to one man for life, and subject to his will.

> The overthrow of mother right was the *world-historic defeat of the female sex*. The man seized the reins in the house also, the woman was degraded, enthralled, the slave of the man's lust, a mere instrument for breeding children.[2]

This defeat, Engels argued, was part of the same process as that through which society was divided into exploited and exploiting classes, with the exploiters monopolising the means of violence through their control of the state:

> The first class antagonism which appears in history coincides with the development of the antagonism between man and woman in monogamian marriage, and the first class oppression with that of the female sex by the male.[3]

Consequently, the struggle for women's emancipation could not be separated from the struggle against class society itself.

Since the writings of Morgan and Engels in the late nineteenth century, modern social anthropology has poured scorn on their claim that there was a matriarchal primitive communism. So much mud has been thrown at the theory that, while the revolutionary ideas of Marx and Darwin have been kept alive, those of Morgan have been buried under a mountain of criticism.

It is clear that Morgan and Engels did make errors in their interpretations of the evidence. There is no factual evidence for a primal promiscuous co-habiting horde of brothers and sisters, as Morgan claimed. On the contrary, the more 'primitive' the tribe the more strict the sexual prohibition between 'brothers' and 'sisters'. Nor is it true, as Engels claimed, that pairing marriage evolved from the women's desire to be free from the sexual claims of a group of men. Considering the evidence against this that he had from Morgan alone, this was an absurd concession to Victorian morality.

Morgan's and Engels' view of matriarchy as symmetrical to patriarchy is probably incorrect. For lack of enough data it is difficult to know what, in different periods and places, the relative weight of gathering (women's work) was *vis-à-vis* hunting (men's work), as the material base of matriarchy. For obvious reasons anthropology is bound to be far more speculative than, say, history, not to speak of the exact sciences.

But the critics of Morgan and Engels concentrated, not on such factual errors, but on their historical and materialist method of interpretation. Since there are no primitive tribes remaining from the earliest periods in human society, argue the anthropologists, the historical method cannot be used. The conclusions of Morgan and Engels, they say, are therefore mere 'conjecture'. So modern anthropology provides a welter of factual detail concerning life in primitive societies, but without linking these facts to primitive social institutions such as the family. Where they *do* attempt to explain the origin of primitive marriage laws, however, they are not slow to make conjectures themselves, based upon psychological and economic principles which they claim to be 'universal' but which in fact do no more than betray their own class prejudices.

By and large the same anthropologists who reject the method used by Morgan and Engels also deny that there ever existed a period of equality between the sexes, and likewise assert that private property has been a feature of all societies, even the most primitive.

A few writers have used more recent evidence to re-assert the thesis put forward by Engels and Morgan. Robert Briffault,[4] in 1927, used a study of the social life of animals to reject claims that there had been a primordial 'nuclear family'. He argued that prolonged maternal care among the higher apes had spurred the females to push forward the development of social life, thereby taking the first step towards humanity. More recently Evelyn Reed[5] has argued that co-operative labour between men and women was established through a taboo against cannibalism and sexual relations within the matriarchal horde. Freedom and equality between the sexes in a hunting and gathering economy, she says, was an essential precondition for women to give the lead from animality to humanity. Much of Evelyn Reed's work is based on the evidence of orthodox anthropology itself, which may be too speculative a method.

The arguments put forward by Briffault and Reed need detailed evaluation, but it is clear that, whatever errors have been made by Marxists in the study of our earliest beginnings, they do not include either the evolutionary and materialist method, nor the concept of a primitive communism with basic equality between men and women. For Marxists the position of women in society and the structure of the family can be understood only in the context of the prevailing mode of production.

Far from women being the victims of an unchanging 'patriarchy', their position in society and the structure of the family have undergone enormous changes even in the past two hundred years. The peasant household in which most people lived before the Industrial Revolution was very different from the modern nuclear family. It was a unit of production as well as consumption. Women and children worked together under the supervision of the male head of the household, producing goods not only for their own consumption, but for exchange with the outside world. The peasant family was not 'privatised', closed off from outside society. As Mark Poster puts it,

> the basic unit of early modern peasant life was not the conjugal family at all but the village. The village was the peasant's 'family' . . . Women's work was vital to the survival of the family and the community, and women worked hard and long. Peasant women cooked, cared for children, tended domestic animals and gardens and joined the village in the fields at crucial times, like the harvest. Women regulated births and supervised courtship at evening gatherings.[6]

Only since the development of industrial capitalism has the role of women tended towards isolation in the home. The family has ceased to be a unit of production, while childcare, cooking and washing have become 'domestic labour', the task of the housewife in the confines of her own home. The 'privatised' family has thus emerged, which Tory ideologues such as Margaret Thatcher's speechwriter, Ferdinand Mount, regard as a 'natural' feature of all societies.[7]

Yet women's labour in the home, though excluded from social production, is essential to the way capitalism organises this production, essential to the capitalist mode of production. For the labour performed inside the family household provides capitalism with its workforce. From generation to generation, it is the labour of women that reproduces the workforce itself, both physically through childbirth and culturally through the raising of children, and on a day-to-day basis, women's labour also 'reproduces' the workers in the family, making them fit for work the following day. As Marx put it:

> This incessant reproduction, this perpetuation of the labourer, is the *sine qua non* of capitalist production . . . The maintenance and reproduction of the working class is, and must ever be, a necessary condition to the reproduction of capital.[8]

The dialectical unity between production and reproduction is, however, concealed by the fact that the domestic labour involved in reproduction is 'privatised'; it is an individual task performed *outside* society. But if women did not perform this unpaid labour inside the working-class family, then, in order to ensure the reproduction of its workforce, capitalism would either have to pay higher wages or provide considerably more welfare services to replace the services now provided by housewives.

The institution of the family itself is not only part of the economic base of society but also part of its superstructure. We have already shown how women's oppression, located in the family, permeates every aspect of life, and recreates the distortions of sex stereotyping in the next generation. As Engels argued, the way women's oppression serves the capitalist mode of production means that it affects women of different classes differently. In capitalist class society, the role of bourgeois women is to produce legitimate heirs, who will be able to carry the accumulated wealth of the ruling class into the next generation. The role of working-class women is to reproduce this and the next generation of workers. And women of the ruling class *do* benefit from the oppression of working-class women, for they benefit from the employment of cheap female labour.

It is true that bourgeois women are discriminated against *vis-à-vis* men of the same class. But the divide between the two is nothing compared to the abyss which separates bourgeois women from working-class women. Evidence from two key areas for capitalist society, property and education, shouts loud and clear. In 1970 women, who make up half the population, owned approximately 40 per cent of the privately-owned wealth in Britain[9] — yet of this, millions of working-class women have nothing or a minute share. In education there is discrimination by sex, for only one third of the university students in Britain are women, but discrimination by class is far sharper. In 1975–6 only 2.9 per cent of girls from comprehensive schools went to university, as against 16.9 per cent from grammar schools and 30.1 per cent from direct grant schools.[10] The impact of *class* on a girl's chances of going to university is *decisive*.

In these two key areas, bourgeois women have far more in common with men of their own class than with women of the working class. These so-called 'sisters' are worlds apart.[11]

Who are the beneficiaries of women's oppression? Radical feminists, as well as many who describe themselves as socialist feminists and even Marxist feminists, answer: men. Our answer to this is an emphatic *no*.

To be a working-class woman, financially dependent on husband, carrying the double burden of housework and holding down a boring, low-paid job, is very oppressive. However, to be a working man, to have the role of breadwinner in a harsh and threatening world, with unemployment hanging like the sword of Damocles over your head, is no privilege. The working man is as dehumanised as the woman. As Lindsey German put it in her excellent article, 'Theories of Patriarchy':

> . . . the family wage did not materially benefit *men*. It did not cover

> more than the minimum costs of reproduction: the amount needed to keep the whole family . . .
>
> Under the family wage system, the married woman suffers insofar as she is excluded from direct capitalist production and thus, like the unemployed, is denied even the appearance of being a sovereign consumer. This is an important part of what we mean when we say housewives are *oppressed* while workers are exploited. But it does not signify that male workers benefit from women's oppression . . .
>
> Housework, by definition, is work that is not subject to the tempo imposed by capitalist exploitation in the factory or the office. It does not involve intensive effort for a certain number of hours, followed by a period of recuperation in order to allow application of another fixed spell of intensive effort. Therefore there is no way the amount of labour that goes into it can be measured against the amount of labour that goes into factory work. All that can be said with certainty is that both factory work and housework are debilitating — one leading to occupational diseases (which is why symptoms such as chronic bronchitis are much higher among male workers than among housewives), horrific accidents, acute fatigue and often, an early death; the other to demoralisation, atomisation, insecurity, and a variety of ailments that are normally ignored by doctors.[12]

But, many feminists argue, the actual oppression of women is carried out by men. Men are rapists, pornographers, wife-beaters and so on, they say. But while feminists correctly point to individual men as the agents of these forms of oppression, they are wrong to identify these as the main ways in which women are oppressed. Not all — or even most — men are rapists, pornographers and wife-beaters. Moreover these are the actions of individuals and are small compared to the way the capitalist system structures and perpetuates women's oppression through its institutions. Low pay, sections of the economy effectively barred to women, lack of childcare provision, and the institution of the family itself are the means by which reproduction remains privatised and whereby women are ensured a double burden. These structures are at the root of women's oppression. They are built into the class society in which we live, and controlled as it is controlled, not by individual men and certainly not by individual working-class men.

This is not to deny, however, that men behave in certain ways which are oppressive to women. To pretend otherwise is to fall into the idealist error of denying that social relations are *always* relations between real people. But the blame should be placed squarely on class society, not on its individual agents. Women's oppression damages the interests of both working women and men. It is a situation from which only the ruling class benefits.

Women in Paid Employment

If working-class women were only housewives, their oppression would make them powerless. The woman as a housewife is isolated and weak. As Margery Spring Rice, in her unique record of working-class women's domestic labour in the 1930s, states:

> She eats, sleeps, 'rests', on the scene of her labour, and her labour is entirely solitary . . . whatever the emotional compensations, whatever her devotion, her family creates her labour, and tightens the bonds that tie her to the lonely and narrow sphere of 'home'.[13]

The housewife's isolation leads to a sense of powerlessness. She is prone to extreme fatalism, defined incisively by Emile Durkheim as 'an excess of regulation found in persons whose future is relentlessly blocked, whose passions are violently repressed by an oppressive discipline, by the unavoidable and inflexible character of a role over which one is powerless.'

Working-class mothers who have no alternative to housework bolster their self-esteem through their stereotyped role. As Sue Sharpe put it: 'Intense concern with domestic tasks is rational if there seems to be no alternative, and many women draw much of their self-esteem from their indispensibility to the family. To deny this seems to remove the whole purpose of their existence.'[14] Linda Gordon, in her brilliant book, **Woman's Body, Woman's Right**, emphasises the aspect of self-preservation:

> . . . mystique is used by women in their own interests . . . it is a rational ideology for women's survival and for maximising the creative and enjoyable aspects of their lives. Full-time motherhood, when it is possible, is for most women preferable to the other job alternatives they have.[15]

In similar vein, a black American mother explained the value of pregnancy in this way: 'To me having a baby inside me is the only time I'm really alive. I know I can make something, do something, no matter what color my skin is and what names people call me.' And Linda Gordon comments: 'Child care, for all its difficulty, is inherently less alienated and more creative than most other work; it offers a mother at least a semblance of control over her working conditions and goals.'[16]

A woman may well claim to be 'happy' to be 'only' a wife and mother, while she suppresses the thought of associated consequences — being cooped up in a flat in a high-rise building, frantically worried about money, working unlimited hours at drudgery. But she claims this because she is caught in a trap she does not know how to get out of, and because it is expected of her to be happy. If she admitted to herself that she was *unhappy* she would have failed as a person, and that would mean even greater unhappiness.

The traditional image of woman as wife and mother is still held strongly by millions. One crude expression of this prejudice worth quoting is the remark of Patrick Jenkin, Secretary of State for Social Services in the first Thatcher government: 'If God had meant women to go out to work, he would not have created two sexes.' Practically all bourgeois sociologists and feminists place women firmly within the family structure, while ignoring, or at least very much downplaying, their role in the labour force. Even many so-called 'Marxist feminists' concentrate their attention on domestic labour. Studies which do deal with women as wage-earners by and large concern themselves with the way women's participation in the labour market is affected by their position in the family.

And this approach is inevitable unless one uses the Marxist method to show the synthesis — both the unity and the contradictions — between the two realms of women's work. *Appearances* alone would give domestic labour greater weight than wage labour: after all, women *do spend* far more time on domestic labour — as Ann Oakley found in an interview with a number of housewives, on average 77 hours a week.[17]

Again, in terms of their own feelings, women make domestic labour take precedence over wage labour — and are conditioned to do so. If asked which they prefer of their exhausting double burden, they naturally say they prefer domestic labour. What alternatives do they visualise? To neglect the children, to employ a servant, to live in a hotel? Hence full-time motherhood, when it is possible, is for most working-class women preferable to other job alternatives.

But when it comes to the reality, most women for most of their lives are engaged in paid labour. The 1971 census showed that 87 per cent of all British women had worked some time in their lives. At present women make up 41 per cent of the labour force in Britain. As noted previously, in 1979 the so-called 'typical worker' — a married man with a non-working wife and children — represented a mere 8 per cent of the male labour force and 5 per cent of the total labour force.[18]

In the United States in 1979, 14.6 per cent of all families were provided for by women alone.[19] There too, only one family in ten fits the conventional pattern of the nuclear family.

Since the Second World War, women have entered massively into paid employment. Firstly, the spread of contraception and increasing longevity means that married women are more able to seek work. Secondly there are more jobs available for married women. This table shows the change:

Employment in Great Britain (millions)[20]

	1951	*1961*	*1971*	*1976*
Men	15.6	16.1	15.9	15.9
Married women	2.7	3.9	5.8	6.7
Other women	4.3	3.9	3.4	3.2
TOTAL (women)	7.0	7.7	9.2	10.0
TOTAL (men and women)	22.6	23.8	25.1	25.9

Thus between 1951 and 1976 Britain's working population increased by 3.3 million. Of this increase three million were women. In 1951 they formed 31 per cent of the labour force; today they form over 40 per cent, and this is probably a considerable underestimate as many of the statistics do not include those workers — part-time or on low incomes — who do not enter the tax bracket.

A similar movement of women into paid jobs took place in other countries of Western Europe and the United States. In the United States the number of women in the labour force rose from 13,840,000 in 1940 to 43,693,000 in 1980, an increase of 215 per cent. Even more impressive was the rise in the number of married women in paid employment: from 5,040,000 to 26,347,000, or 422.8 per cent.[21]

This change has brought a radically different reaction to the double burden carried by working-class women when compared with the reaction a century ago. Being at work, their expectations and aspirations are altered and raised, and they acquire the financial ability at least partially to fulfil these. The family side of the burden can also be limited today by more effective contraception. Women today therefore rebel against the traditional sex roles, both of the wife and her husband.

This is brought into sharp relief in an extensive survey carried out in Norway by the sociologist Harriet Holter.[22] This showed that the attitude of women to traditional sex roles depended enormously on whether they were gainfully employed or not:

		(Percentages)	
	Least traditional	*Intermediate*	*Most traditional*
Housewives not gainfully employed	8	36	52
Housewives gainfully employed part-time	20	64	14
Housewives gainfully employed full-time	45	43	9

Holter comments: 'Wives who work outside the home have more egalitarian attitudes than other women.' She shows, in another table, that 'men with occupationally active wives are more egalitarian than men whose wives stay home.'

	(Percentages)		
	Least traditional	*Intermediate*	*Most traditional*
Husbands with wives not gainfully employed	4	31	63
Husbands with wives gainfully employed	30	60	10

Thus, instead of the pat norm accepted by bourgeois sociologists and feminists, which sees women's attitudes as being formed outside and brought into the workplace, where they help reinforce the irrationalities of degraded women's labour, we see how the habits and ideas created in the workplace in fact invade the home. While the two realms of production and reproduction are dialectically united, production is the primary of the two. Women's wage labour is more decisive in affecting domestic labour and attitudes towards it than vice versa.

Marx was right when he wrote of the effect which the drawing of women (and children) into social production would have on relations within the family and relations between the sexes:

> However terrible and disgusting the dissolution, under the capitalist system, of the old family ties may appear, nevertheless, modern industry, by assigning as it does the important part in the process of production, outside the domestic sphere, to women, to young persons, and to children of both sexes, creates a new economic foundation for a higher form of the family and of the relations between the sexes . . . Moreover, it is obvious that the fact of the collective working group being composed of individuals of both sexes and all ages, must necessarily, under suitable conditions, become a source of human development.[23]

The path to the liberation of working-class women from exploitation and oppression is not in their isolated homes, but in their collective relationship as wage-earners where they can unite with fellow workers, men and women.

The change in women's attitudes at home is especially great when they are engaged in far-reaching industrial struggles. For instance the ideas of the women who occupied the Lee Jeans factory in Scotland for seven months in 1982 changed radically in the struggle, and they challenged the assumptions of men — including their husbands and boyfriends — regarding the relations between the sexes. 'I'm busy. You go and make the tea and look after the children,' was a frequent attitude among the women.

Only in the struggle to transform social relations do people change. It is the workplace that opens up to women the widest opportunities to struggle to organise and hence to change themselves. It is through involvement in social production that women, like men, are anchored as workers into the relations of production which are the pivot of class society. Marxism is about *class power*, and in the workplace this comes into sharpest focus.

Extensive efforts are made by the employing class to divide the working class. The uneven development of different countries, of different regions in the same country, of different branches of the economy, of different enterprises, fragments the working class. Racial, ethnic and sex discords add to the disunity. Disparities of skill, often exacerbated by craft unionism, widen these fissures, as does the employers' divide-and-rule practice of using women as cheap labour to weaken the bargaining position of men, and using the craftism and sexual prejudices of men to weaken the position of working women.

The ideas of the ruling class prevail in society — and the family home is one of the most effective institutions for ensuring this. The home, where we are isolated into the smallest of groups, is fertile ground for the media to spread the ruling ideas of society. Television in particular is powerful in moulding the ideas of the mass of isolated people, including women.

The domestic division of labour increases a woman's financial dependence on her husband and this weakens her bargaining position in the labour market. This makes her even more dependent on her husband, and so closes the vicious circle. In another way too, a woman's role in the family affects her role in paid employment. Domestic labour, with its range of relatively unchanging skills, prepares women for only unskilled work. The break in employment when women leave to rear children, and their treatment on return as new entrants, does not serve to enhance their skills. Thus marriage and motherhood effectively 'deskill' women.

The tendency for women to take part-time jobs is also directly related to their domestic responsibilities. The main growth in women's employment since the Second World War has been in the field of part-time work. In 1951, 12 per cent of women in Britain worked part-time; in 1976, 40 per cent. In 1975 two out of every three married working women with two or more children worked part-time.[24] Part-time work is associated with jobs which need little training, are dead-end, boring and low-paid. Women who take part-time jobs are forced to accept wages and conditions which would be unacceptable to full-time workers. Many do not get paid holidays, pensions, or protection by redundancy payments schemes.

The sexual division of labour in the workplace, largely influenced by women's place in the household, is very much alive.

Despite these difficulties, however, the general sweep of history, with pauses and retreats, has been to narrow the divide between the male and female sections of the industrial working class, to advance the homogeneity of the class. The great expansion of women's employment, with most women concentrated in large workplaces such as offices, hospitals and department stores, leads to a narrowing of the differences in working conditions for men and women workers. The gap between manual and white-collar workers is also closing.

One clear measure of this is the rapid narrowing of the gap between the unionisation of men and women. The recruitment of women into trade unions took giant steps after the Second World War:

Trade union membership in Britain[25]

Year	*Women*	*Total*	*Women as percentage of total membership*
1886	37,000	636,000	5.8
1896	118,000	1,608,000	7.3
1906	167,000	2,210,000	7.6
1939	553,000	4,669,000	11.4
1958	1,387,000	8,337,000	16.6
1968	1,767,000	8,726,000	20.2
1978	3,411,000	11,865,000	28.7

Women are still less unionised than men: 36.7 per cent of women workers were in trade unions in 1974, compared with 56.9 per cent of men. The gap is slightly wider among manual workers — women 42.1 per cent, men 64.7 per cent — and narrower among white-collar workers — women 32.6 per cent, men 44.5 per cent.[26]

We have already seen how the attitudes of women towards stereotyped roles in the family are affected according to whether they go out to work or not. The workplace, and the fight by working women to improve their circumstances there, is the key to changing ideas, 'raising consciousness' — for collective action increases your confidence in yourself, your workmates, and your class. It is in fact the only way to break the ideology of oppression which is internalised by women. Working-class women, whose main concern is survival, cannot afford the luxury of purely intellectual 'consciousness-raising'.

This does not mean that women workers ought only to organise at the workplace, or only around workplace issues, but that all other dimensions of the struggle are rooted there. Marxism rejects the idea that only at the point where problems arise are the solutions to be found. Women's oppression cannot be overcome by women simply fighting oppression any more than old age pensioners can free themselves from poverty simply by their own efforts. In the struggle against oppression, the decisive factor is not the wretchedness of the contestants, but their strength. So the starting point for a struggle against women's oppression is not that of oppression itself, but the point where working-class women are strong, where, with the men of their own class, they can fight to change society.

The need for a workers' party

Marx and Engels stated that 'with the development of industry the working class not only increases in number; it becomes concentrated in greater masses, its strength grows, and it feels that strength more.' The independent artisan, the tradesman, the peasants, all disappear because of the development of capitalism, but the working class gains in strength.

> In proportion as the bourgeoisie, i.e. capital, is developed, in the same proportion is the proletariat, the modern working class, developed . . . Of all the classes that stand face to face with the bourgeois today, the proletariat alone is a really revolutionary class. The other classes decay and finally disappear in the race of Modern Industry, the proletariat is its special and essential product.[27]

The power of the working class to change society lies in its collective nature. Workers have no ownership over the industrial wealth of society, and cannot obtain it as individuals, since industry cannot be parcelled out into small pieces. Workers are organised collectively by capitalist industry and must act collectively to defend themselves and their working conditions. This collective strength gives the working class the power ultimately to emancipate the whole of human society.

But Marx was clear that while the working class has the potential for united action, *actually* it is often split, as we have seen. For the majority of workers do not recognise their collective strength and potential, because the *prevailing* ideas in society are the ideas of the ruling class. It is the ruling class which controls the means for the propagation of ideas: the media, education and — in many societies — the church.

The vast majority of people therefore carry a whole host of conflicting ideas in their heads. Some ideas are the result of what we have been taught to believe by the capitalist society around us; other, contradictory, ideas are the result of struggles in which workers, perhaps we ourselves, have played an active role. As the Italian Marxist Antonio Gramsci pointed out:

> The active man-in-the-mass has a practical activity, but has no clear theoretical consciousness of his practical activity, which nonetheless involves understanding the world in so far as it transforms it. His theoretical consciousness can indeed be historically in opposition to his activity. One might almost say that he has two theoretical consciousnesses (or one contradictory consciousness): one which is implicit in his activity and which in reality unites him with all his fellow-workers in the practical transformation of the real world; and one, superficially explicit or verbal, which he has inherited from the past and uncritically absorbed.

> The personality is strangely composite: it contains Stone Age elements and principles of a more advanced science, prejudices from all past phases of history at the local level and intuitions of a future philosophy which will be that of a human race united the world over.[28]

Individuals, when isolated, are vulnerable to ruling-class ideas; in the workplace, where workers are able to organise and act collectively, they can resist them.

Because of the lack of homogeneity in the working class and the contradictions in the ideas of workers there is an imperative need for a revolutionary socialist party. The party can help workers to change their ideas in struggle, to free themselves from the influence of bourgeois ideas. The decisive role of the party is in giving a lead, an organisation and a focus to raise the self-activity and consciousness of the workers, so that one day they will take power for themselves.

The revolutionary workers' party is also crucial for forging unity between *all* those who are oppressed, in fighting for liberation. In the same way that capitalism divides worker from worker, so it divides one section of the oppressed from another. Black people and women are both oppressed — but blacks do not *automatically* support women, nor vice versa (as, indeed, the history of the women's movement has shown).

In fact the opposite is frequently the result. If people see no escape from their oppression, they may turn to oppress someone else in order to overcome their own feeling of powerlessness. For example, the Nazis sent thousands of gays to concentration camps. But gays did not therefore automatically become anti-Nazi. Tens of thousands of gays supported Hitler in his rise to power. For an oppressed gay, putting on a Nazi leather jacket and boots gave a sense of power — and he could then oppress Jews, women and anyone else.

For any oppressed group to fight back there is need for *hope*. And that is to be found, not in the isolation of oppression — the housewife trapped in the home, the gay in the closet, the Jews in the ghetto — but in the collective strength of the working class. For Marxists the notion that the working class, by liberating itself, will liberate the whole of humanity, is central. Which is why the revolutionary socialist party must support struggles against *all* forms of oppression, not only of the working class but of any downtrodden section of society, and unite these with the working-class struggle. As Lenin wrote:

> Working-class consciousness cannot be genuine political consciousness unless the workers are trained to respond to *all* cases of tyranny, oppression, violence, and abuse, no matter *what class* is affected — unless they are trained, moreover, to respond from [a revolutionary socialist] point of view and no other . . .

If these tyrannies are exposed, he continues,

> the most backward worker will understand, *or will feel*, that the students and religious sects, the peasants and the authors are being abused and outraged by those same dark forces that are oppressing and crushing him at every step of his life. Feeling that, he himself will be filled with an irresistable desire to react, and he will know how to hoot the censors one day, on another day to demonstrate outside the house of a governor who has brutally suppressed a peasant uprising, on still another day to teach a lesson to the gendarmes in surplices who are doing the work of the Holy Inquisition.[29]

While the working class is divided by prejudices such as sexism and racism, the revolutionary socialist party, which can see beyond these divisions to the potential of the working class for self-emancipation, must not concede to any pressure from backward workers influenced by the bourgeois prejudices of the society around them. The party must struggle relentlessly against all those divisions in the working class — of race, of nationality, between men and women, skilled and unskilled, employed and unemployed — which are systematically fostered by the ruling class. Hence for Lenin the struggle against anti-Semitism was the task of the revolutionary socialist party as a whole, and not only of its Jewish members. Likewise for us today, the struggle against women's oppression is the task of the whole party, not just of women.

Because of the specific situations in which working women find themselves, many special demands need to be fought for, such as for equal pay, for free abortion on demand, for the free availability of birth control information and facilities, for improvements in training for women and the up-grading of women's jobs, for better-paid maternity leave without loss of seniority, for the same rights for part-time as for full-time workers, for free nurseries and so on. These are *class issues*, and would benefit the working class as a whole, women, men and children.

The importance of struggling for reforms specially tailored to the needs of women workers, like that of the struggle for reforms in general, lies not so much in the intrinsic value of the reforms themselves. Under capitalism any achievable reforms are bound to be small and open to assault, especially during the economic crisis of the system. Their main value is that they raise the confidence, consciousness and organisation of the workers involved. They are class issues in this sense also: that the struggle for them and success in achieving them depend upon the overall balance of class forces. While fighting for such reforms, women workers, and men workers, have to be won to the total politics of revolutionary socialism. For women's oppression will only fully be ended with the self-emancipation of the working class as a whole, and the final abolition of the class society which benefits from it.

Communism and the Liberation of Women

For Marx and Engels the emancipation of women demanded not only the entry of women into social production, but also the socialisation of the care of children, the old, invalids and others. The present sexual division of labour is hierarchical, placing men in superior and women in subordinate positions. The hierarchical principle has to be eradicated, together with the division of labour between the sexes. This is a prerequisite for women to attain social equality.

The abolition of the sexual division of labour under communism will be an integral part of the ending of *all* divisions of labour. In **The German Ideology** Marx and Engels wrote that

> in communist society, where nobody has one exclusive sphere of activity but each can become accomplished in any branch he wishes, society regulates the general production and thus makes it possible for me to do one thing today and another tomorrow, to hunt in the morning, fish in the afternoon, rear cattle in the evening, criticise after dinner, just as I have a mind, without ever becoming hunter, fisherman, shepherd or critic.[30]

Only after the division of labour has been abolished will men and women attain the full development of their human personality. Communism will therefore bring real freedom to the individual. Communist society, declares **The Communist Manifesto**, will be 'an association in which the free development of each is the condition for the free development of all.'[31]

What will be the impact of communism on personal relations?

Marx and Engels never tried to guess what the nature of the family in the future communist society would be before the material conditions for its creation existed. They dealt only in the broadest terms with the likely developments. They believed that individual sexual love would reach much fuller expression under communism, because the old pressures of economic necessity and the alienation of all social relations would disappear. Engels in his draft for **The Communist Manifesto** wrote that communist society

> will make the relation between the sexes a purely private relation which concerns only the persons involved, and in which society has no call to interfere. It is able to do this because it abolishes private property and educates children communally, thus destroying the twin foundation of hitherto existing marriage — the dependence through private property of the wife upon the husband and of the children upon the parents.[32]

Both Engels and Marx took it for granted that under communism equality between the sexes would mean there would be complete freedom to leave a dead union and form a new one. There would be 'serial monogamy'. In **The Origin of the Family, Private Property and the State**, Engels wrote that communism would bring about *real* monogamy:

> Since sex love is by its very nature exclusive — although this exclusiveness is fully realised today only in the woman — then marriage based on sex love is by its very nature monogamy . . . monogamy, instead of declining, finally becomes a reality — for the man as well.[33]

Similar conclusions about sex relations under communism were reached by Trotsky when he wrote in 1933:

> A long and permanent marriage, based on mutual love and cooperation — that is the ideal standard . . . Freed from the chains of police and clergy, later also from those of economic necessity, the tie between men and women will find its own way, determined by physiology, psychology, and care for the welfare of the human race.[34]

Similar views were expressed by Lenin and Rosa Luxemburg.

A very different view, assuming the *withering away* of all forms of monogamy, was put forward by the French Marxist Jules Guesde (1845–1922) when he wrote about the family:

> . . . a day would come when it will no longer have any *raison d'être* . . . It might be that . . . the warm atmosphere of benevolence and affection developed in the bosom of the collectivity by the equality of well-being of each member, will render unnecessary that second special matrix which the family constitutes, and will permit the reduction of the family in space to the mother and child, and in time to the period of lactation. On the other hand, sexual relations between men and women, founded on love and mutual concern, can become free, as variable and as multiple as intellectual or moral relations between individuals of the same or opposite sex.[35]

It would be foolish to speculate whether Marx and Engels or Guesde will prove right. We simply do not know. There is no crystal ball to tell us how people will feel and act in their personal relations under communism.

We can, however, be sure of a few points regarding personal relations. In present society the relations between men and women in marriage are held up as the most intimate human relations. But the intimacy is poisoned at its roots by capitalism: women are unequal to men, and real intimacy cannot be achieved except among equals. Real intimacy, emotional fulfilment, sexual satisfaction, will be possible for the first time under communism.

At present the family is seen as a refuge in a hostile world, and the expectations demanded of it are far too high. Under communism caring and loving will be more widespread; the family will not be able to claim them narrowly for its own. Children will be far freer. Today, many a mother and father have a high emotional stake in their children: their own lives have been so frustrating and disappointing that they seek in their children a greater achievement. The child is being used. Such parental expectations are usually cruelly dashed, with both parents and children paying the price. The possessive relationship between parents and children — part of the ethos of competitive individualism engendered by capitalist society — will be replaced under communism by social solidarity.

Human beings will then be living under completely new circumstances, which will affect their lives, including the relations between men and women, men and men, and women and women. The crucial point is that under communism the stereotyped polarisation of sex roles will not exist. Men and women will carry out all necessary tasks communally — child-rearing, cooking, cleaning, these will be tasks of both sexes equally, not one. All sexual relationships will have the same validity. Heterosexuality and homosexuality will both be accepted as valid and normal, in the same way that left-handed people or red-headed people do not stand out as abnormal today. Only under communism can real sexual love between men and women, men and men, and women and women, be possible without twists and distortions. Only under communism can respect for the identity of the individual be achieved, and thc use of a person of either sex only as an object for another person's pleasure be obliterated. The essential humanity of every individual will be recognised when sexual prejudices are endcd.

Above all, communism is about freedom. Certainly many lifestyles will co-exist, and it will be up to individuals to choose, again and again.

Notes

★Introduction

1. In this book I avoid using the words 'feminism' or 'feminists' without the addition of adjectives. These words have gone through several meanings. For the great Utopian socialist Charles Fourier feminism was a crucial aspect of socialism. For Alexandra Kollontai (as well as Clara Zetkin, Inessa Armand, Rosa Luxemburg and others of the same generation) it was a word of abuse for the bourgeois women's movement. A similar transformation of meaning has occurred with other words, such as 'radical'. Radical was used to describe the popular movement in Britain in the period between the French revolution and the end of Chartism, but later it became associated with the Radical Whigs and Radical Tories, or members of the Radical wing of the Liberal Party, and as such became anathema for socialists. Then, once the idea of an independent Labour Party took hold, radicalism appeared vague and regressive.
2. Kate Millett, **Sexual Politics** (London 1977).
3. Frederick Engels, **The Origin of the Family, Private Property and the State** (New York 1979).
4. For example, in the revolutionary wave which swept Europe in the years 1915–20 working women often played a leading role, despite being the least organised section of the working class. They were also the worst paid. Yet in the First World War they were expected to feed their families from dwindling food stocks, as well as labour long hours in the munitions industries. On a number of occasions women provided the spark that detonated mass outbursts of militancy. In the Glasgow rent strike women, backed by threats of strike action in the shipyards, won a limitation of rent rises. Hunger riots led by working women in Leipzig in 1917 generated the first German workers' council, while women both as protestors and strikers created the Turin insurrection of the same year. Probably the

most dramatic example of their activity was the February 1917 revolution in Russia.
5. Frederick Engels, **The Condition of the Working Class in England** (London 1973).

★Chapter One: Birth of a Dream

1. K Thomas, 'Another Digger Broadcast', in **Past and Present,** no 42, February 1969.
2. A collection of Winstanley's writings is available edited by Christopher Hill, **Winstanley: The Law of Freedom and Other Writings** (London 1973).
3. A L Morton, **The World of the Ranters** (London 1970) page 78.
4. Morton, page 71.
5. Winstanley, page 388.
6. Quoted in Christopher Hill, **The World Turned Upside Down** (London 1975) page 319.
7. Hill, page 257.
8. Similar arguments were used by Eleanor Marx and Edward Aveling in their pamphlet, **The Woman Question** (1886): 'Many advanced thinkers plead for greater facility of divorce now . . . and most important of all, that the conditions of divorce should be the same for the two sexes. All this is excellent, and would be not only feasible but just, if — but mark the if — the economic positions of the two sexes were the same. They are not the same. Hence, while agreeing with every one of these ideas theoretically, we believe that they would, practically applied under our present system, result, in the majority of cases, in yet further injustice to women. The man would be able to take advantage of them, the woman would not, except in the rare instances where she had private property or some means of livelihood. The annulling of the union would be to him freedom; to her, starvation for herself and her children.' (E Marx and E Aveling, **The Woman Question** (London 1886) page 10.)
9. Quoted in Hill, pages 314–5.
10. Quoted in Hill, page 318.
11. Hill, pages 319–20.
12. Hill, page 340.
13. Engels, 'The Book of Revelation', in **Progress**, vol 2, 1883.

★Chapter Two: The French Revolution

1. Simone de Beauvoir, **Le Deuxieme Sexe**, vol 1, pages 107 and 182–3.
2. E Racz, 'The Women's Rights Movement in the French Revolution' in **Science and Society**, Spring 1952.
3. Racz.
4. W Stephens, **Women in the French Revolution** (London 1922) pages 165–7, 177 and 247–8.
5. J Abray, 'Feminism in the French Revolution' in **American Historical Review**, February 1975.

6. Racz.
7. G Rudé, 'Prices, wages and popular movements in Paris in the French Revolution' in **Economic History Review**, no 3, 1954.
8. G Rudé, **The Crowd in the French Revolution** (London 1959) pages 19–20.
9. For records of these strikes, see G Rudé, 'The Motives of popular insurrection in Paris during the French Revolution' in **Bulletin of the Institute of Historical Research**, 1953, pages 71–3.
10. O Hufton, 'Women in Revolution 1789–96' in **Past and Present**, no 53, 1971. Germinal and Prairial were months in the new calendar introduced by the revolution, which measured dates from the Fall of the Bastille in 1789. So Year III was 1792.
11. Rudé, **The Crowd in the French Revolution**, pages 73–5. The *faubourgs* were districts of Paris, of which the Faubourg Saint-Antoinc was strongly working-class.
12. Rudé, page 78.
13. Rudé, pages 86–7.
14. Hufton.
15. D Guerin, **Class struggle in the First French Revolution: Bourgeois and Bras Nus 1793–95** (London 1977).
16. Quoted in Guerin, page 59.
17. Hufton.
18. M Cerati, **Le Club des Citoyennes Republicaines Revolutionnaires** (Paris 1966) pages 23–4.
19. Abray.
20. S H Lytle, 'The Second Sex (September 1793)' in **The Journal of Modern History**, March 1955.
21. Lytle.
22. Guerin, page 131.
23. Guerin, pages 142–3, 145 and 174.
24. G Lefebvre, **The Thermidoreans** (London 1965) page 104.
25. Hufton.
26. Hufton.

★ Chapter Three: The Paris Commune

1. Karl Marx and Friedrich Engels, **Writings on the Paris Commune** edited by Hal Draper (New York 1971) page 76.
2. **Writings on the Paris Commune**, pages 27–8.
3. S Edwards, **The Communards of Paris 1871** (London 1973) page 15.
4. Quoted in E Hyams, **Pierre-Joseph Proudhon** (London 1979) page 274.
5. M J Boxer, **Socialism faces Feminism in France 1879–1913** (PhD thesis, University of California) page 33.
6. Hyams, page 246.
7. **Minutes of the General Council of the First International** (Moscow, no date given) vol 1, pages 92–241.
8. Boxer, pages 33–4.
9. Quotes from P Lissagray, **History of the Paris Commune** (London 1976)

page 419.
10. Edith Thomas, **The Women Incendiaries** (London 1966) page 45–6.
11. Thomas, pages 62–4.
12. Thomas, pages 55–6.
13. E Shulkind, **The Paris Commune of 1871** (London 1971) pages 33–4.
14. See Thomas, chapter 6.
15. Thomas, pages 66–7.
16. Thomas, page 70.
17. Edwards, pages 117–20.
18. Thomas, page 89.
19. Thomas, page 90.
20. Thomas, page 202.
21. Edwards, **The Paris Commune of 1871** (London 1971) page 290.
22. Thomas, page 53. It is astonishing that Marx writes that the Commune gave 'universal suffrage' (in 'The Civil War in France', **Writings on the Paris Commune**, page 74), not noticing that half the adult population — women — were excluded. Lenin, writing on the Commune in **State and Revolution**, makes the same mistake.
23. Edwards, **The Paris Commune 1871**, pages 317–8.
24. Lissagray, page 307.
25. Lissagray, pages 277–8.
26. Thomas, pages 201–3.
27. Edwards, **The Paris Commune 1871**, page 330.
28. Thomas, pages 167–70.
29. Lissagray, page 305.
30. Lissagray, page 316.
31. Edwards, **The Paris Commune 1871**, page 201.

★Chapter Four: The nineteenth-century American Women's Movement

1. E Flexner, **Century of Struggle: The Women's Rights Movement in the United States** (Cambridge Massachusetts 1976) page 41.
2. Quoted in Flexner, page 75.
3. Flexner, page 77.
4. Flexner, page 147.
5. A Kraditor, **The Ideas of the Woman Suffrage Movement 1890–1920** (New York and London 1965) pages 84–5.
6. Kraditor, page 165.
7. Kraditor, page 137.
8. Kraditor, page 7.
9. P S Foner, **History of the Labor Movement in the United States** (New York 1955) vol 1, pages 207–9.
10. Foner, vol 1, page 431.
11. One incident sheds light on the attitude of the feminist leaders to trade unionism. In January 1869 the National Typographical Union (the second national trade union to admit women into membership) declared a strike in the book and job printing section of the industry, to bring wages there up to the union scale. Women compositors and male unionists co-operated,

many women joining the union in the process. Susan B Anthony saw in the strike an occasion for women to improve their job opportunities . . . by volunteering to break the strike. Anthony went to a meeting of the employers' association to suggest that they organise a special training school to teach women to set type. The employers adopted her suggestion enthusiastically. In retaliation the National Labor Congress expelled Anthony from its midst. (E C Du Bois, **Feminism and Suffrage: The Emergence of an Independent Women's Movement in America. 1848–1869** (Ithaca 1980) pages 153–60).

12. Foner, vol 1, page 440.
13. Foner, vol 1, page 507.
14. Foner, vol 2, page 56.
15. Foner, vol 2, page 58.
16. Foner, vol 2, page 509.
17. Foner, vol 2, page 66.
18. Foner, vol 2, pages 67 and 71.
19. Foner, vol 2, page 70.
20. Foner, vol 2, pages 62–3.
21. Foner, vol 2, page 61.
22. Foner, vol 2, page 66.
23. Foner, vol 2, page 83.
24. Foner, vol 2, pages 157, 166 and 168.
25. Foner, vol 2, page 277.
26. Foner, vol 2, pages 359–60.
27. Foner, vol 2, pages 364–5.
28. Foner, vol 2, page 190.
29. Foner, vol 3, page 202.
30. Foner, vol 3, pages 139–46.
31. Foner, vol 4, page 36.
32. I Kipnis, **The American Socialist Movement: 1897–1912** (New York 1972) pages 320–1.
33. Kipnis, page 415.
34. Foner, vol 4, pages 115–7.
35. Foner, vol 4, pages 149.
36. Foner, vol 4, pages 126–7.
37. M Tax, **The Rising of the Women** (New York 1980) page 127.
38. P S Foner, **Women and the American Labor Movement** (New York 1979) page 421.
39. Quoted in Tax, pages 180–2.
40. Foner, **Women**, page 405.
41. Quoted in Tax, pages 255–6.
42. Quoted in Tax, page 155.
43. Quoted in Tax, page 141.
44. E Gurley Flynn, **The Rebel Girl: An Autobiography** (New York 1976) pages 88–9.
45. Quoted in P Renshaw, **The Wobblies** (London 1967) page 65.
46. Foner, **Women**, page 281.
47. **The Autobiography of Mother Jones**, edited by M F Parton (Chicago 1976).

48. Foner, **Women**, page 382.
49. **Autobiography of Mother Jones**, pages 202–3.
50. Foner, **History**, vol 4, page 320.
51. Foner, vol 4, page 323.
52. Foner, vol 4, pages 321–2.
53. Foner, vol 4, pages 348–9.
54. Gurley Flynn, page 150.
55. Foner, vol 4, page 462.
56. Tax, page 12.
57. Tax, page 99.
58. G Boone, **The Women's Trade Union Leagues in Great Britain and the United States of America** (New York 1942) page 166–8.
59. Foner, vol 4, page 128.
60. Tax, pages 229–30.
61. W L O'Neill, **Everyone was brave** (Chicago 1969) page 220.
62. Boone, page 242.
63. Foner, vol 3, page 372.
64. Quoted in Foner, vol 3, page 381.
65. P S Foner, **American Socialism and Black Americans** (Westport Connecticut 1977) pages 222 and 225–6.
66. Kipnis, page 397.
67. Quoted in Kipnis, pages 169–70.
68. Foner, **History**, vol 4, page 413.
69. Kipnis, page 266.
70. In telling the story of women in the American Socialist Party, I have borrowed heavily from M J Buhle, **Feminism and Socialism in the United States 1820–1920** (PhD thesis, University of Winsconsin 1974).
71. Buhle, pages 132–3.
72. Buhle, page 114.
73. Buhle, pages 116–7.
74. Buhle, pages 119–20.
75. Tax, pages 187–8.
76. Kipnis, pages 211 and 215.
77. Quoted in Buhle, page 202.
78. Quoted in Buhle, pages 250–1.
79. Buhle, pages 259–61.
80. Buhle, pages 270–2.

★Chapter Five: The Socialist Women's Movement in Germany

1. How bureaucratic the SPD was becomes clear from the delegates to its 1911 conference in Jena. Out of 393 delegates only 52 were workers. There were 157 party officials, 45 trade union officials and 15 co-operative officials among others. Workers made up only one-eighth of the conference (D Fricke, **Die deutsche Arbeiterbewegung** (Berlin 1976) pages 281–2). In the same year workers made up 90 per cent of the party's membership (Fricke, **Zur Organisation und Tätigkeit der deutschen Arbeiterbewegung 1890–1914** (Leipzig 1962) page 90).

2. C E Schorske, **German Social Democracy 1905–1917** (New York 1965) page 6.
3. W Albrecht and others, 'Frauenfrage und deutsche Sozialdemokratie vom ende des 19 Jahrhunderts bis zum Beginnen der zwanziger Jahre' in **Archiv für Sozialgeschichte** 1979, pages 471 and 464.
4. G Hanna, 'Women in the German Trade Union Movement' in **International Labour Review**, July 1923.
5. Albrecht, page 471.
6. **Correspondenzblatt**, 28 November 1914.
7. On *Kartels*, see Fricke, **Die deutsche Arbeiterbewegung**, pages 693–5.
8. H Lion, **Zur Soziologie der Frauenbewegung** (Berlin 1925) page 158.
9. **Protokoll Parteitag 1906** (Berlin 1906) page 408.
10. Albrecht, page 471. The statistics for women membership of the SPD before 1908, when such membership ceased to be illegal, give a distorted picture. Many thousands of women were to all intents and purposes in the party without being *formal* members.
11. R J Evans, **Sozialdemokratie und Frauenemanzipation im deutschen Kaiserreich** (Berlin-Bonn 1979) pages 166–7.
12. Quoted in H Draper and A G Lipow, 'Marxist women and Bourgeois feminism' in **The Socialist Register 1976**, pages 192–201.
13. Draper and Lipow.
14. Quoted in Draper and Lipow.
15. R J Evans, **The Feminist Movement in Germany 1894–1933** (London 1976) pages 131–2.
16. Evans, **The Feminist Movement**, pages 137–8.
17. J Strain, **Feminism and Political Radicalism in the German Social Democratic Movement 1890–1914** (PhD thesis, University of California 1964) pages 145–8.
18. **Gleichheit**, 23 January 1895.
19. Letter of Friedrich Engels to Victor Adler, 18 January 1895, in Marx-Engels, **Works**, vol 39, page 400.
20. Evans, **Sozialdemokratie und Frauenemanzipation**, page 265.
21. **Gleichheit**, 5 January 1898.
22. Cited in Lion, page 93.
23. See Lion, page 155, and Fricke, **Die deutsche Arbeiterbewegung**, page 433. In trying to assess the real significance of the wide circulation of **Gleichheit** — especially when one sees how isolated Zetkin was a few years later — one has to look at the paper in the context of the general publishing effort of the SPD and the working of this mass movement. The journalistic output of the party was enormous. In 1914 it had 90 daily papers (of which 78 were different from one another only in the masthead), two twice-weeklies, and two weeklies. The total circulation of these averaged 1,488,346. (Fricke, **Zur Organisation**, page 133.)

    In addition, the SPD had a variety of other journals:

    Gleichheit (Equality), circulation 125,000 (1914)

    Die Wahre Jacob (The True Jacob), a satirical magazine, circulation 366,000 (1914)

    Die Neue Welt (The New World), an illustrated weekly, circulation

nearly 650,000 (1914)
Die Freie Turnerin (Free Woman Gymnast), circulation 18,000 (1913)
Moderne Külperkulture (Modern Physical Culture), circulation 18,000 (1913)
Arbeiter-Turnzeitung (Workers' Gymnastic Paper), circulation 119,000 (1913)
Jugend und Sport (Youth and Sport), circulation 15,000 (1913)
Athletik (Athletics), circulation 10,000 (1913)
Der Arbeiter Radfahrer (The Worker Cyclist), circulation 168,000 (1913)
Volksgesundheit (People's Health), circulation 16,000 (1913)
(All the sports papers together had an average circulation of 364,000)
Arbeiterjugend (Young Worker), circulation 103,000 (1914)
Der Abstinente Arbeiter (Teetotal Worker), circulation 5,100 (1913)
Freie Gästwirt (Free Hotelier), circulation 11,000 (1913)
Arbeiter Stenograph (Shorthand Worker), circulation 3,000 (1913). (Fricke, pages 160–2.)

24. Evans, **Sozialdemokratie und Frauenemanzipation**, page 168.
25. J H Quataert, **Reluctant Feminists in German Social Democracy 1885–1917** (New Jersey 1979) page 196.
26. Quataert, page 197.
27. **Internationaler Sozialisten Kongress 1907**, Anhang, pages 40–8.
28. Quoted in W Thönessen, **The Emancipation of Women: The Rise and Decline of the Women's Movement in German Social Democracy 1863–1933** (London 1976) page 98.
29. On the incorporation of the women's movement into the SPD, see Fricke, **Zur Organisation**, pages 81–2, and **Die deutsche Arbeiterbewegung**, page 325.
30. See A Hall, 'Youth in Rebellion: The Beginnings of the Socialist Youth Movement 1904–14' in R J Evans (editor), **Society and Politics in Wilhelmine Germany** (London 1978).
31. Albrecht, pages 471–2.
32. K Honeycutt, **Clara Zetkin: A Left-wing Socialist and Feminist in Wilhelmine Germany** (PhD thesis, Columbia University 1975) pages 293–8.

    One factor which facilitated the victory of the right on the woman question, and which exposed the conservative nature of SPD 'Marxism', was the party leaders' stand on sexual morality. A historian of the subject remarked of the SPD leaders that 'in spite of their attacks on traditional sexual morality and marriage they in fact shared many of the most widespread and repressive sexual misconceptions of their time.' (R P Newman, 'The Sexual Question and Social Democracy in Imperial Germany' in **Journal of Social History**, Spring 1974.)

    August Bebel, the foremost leader of the German socialist movement, took, for his time, a very radical stand. 'Of all the natural impulses human beings are instinct with, along with that of eating and drinking, the sexual impulse is the strongest . . . Upon maturity, its satisfaction is an actual necessity for man's physical and mental health.' (A Bebel, **Woman Under Socialism** (New York 1975) page 79.) On abstinence from sexual intercourse he proclaimed: 'What the consequences thereof are, our physicians, hospitals, insane asylums and prisons can tell — to say nothing of the thousands of tortured family lives' (page 82). Abstinent women often channelled their unfulfilled sexual desires into 'religious enthusiasm'. Bebel concluded that 'Mankind will have to return to Nature and to the natural intercourse of the sexes; it must cast off the now-ruling and unhealthy spiritual notions concerning man; it must do that by setting up methods of education that fit in with our own state of culture, and that may bring on the physical and mental regeneration of the race' (page 119).

This stand, very progressive for the age, and accepted by the great majority of SPD spokesmen, was, however, combined with a whole number of conventional attitudes. Thus an SPD pamphlet published in the **Workers' Health Library** said that normal men should refrain from sexual intercourse till the age of 24, since full sexual maturity was not reached till then. Even after marriage people should indulge in sex only in moderation. Bebel warned his readers of the harm of excessive sexual indulgence: 'Impotence, barrenness, spinal infections, insanity, at least intellectual weakness, and many other diseases, are the usual consequences' (Bebel, page 164). Eduard Bernstein recommended an interval of 'several weeks' between intercourse (quoted in Newman).

On contraception the SPD leaders differed. Kautsky supported it. Bebel supported abortion — but thought prior contraception 'unnatural'. Wilhelm Liebknecht opposed all contraception as 'immoral and offensive'. In the years before 1914 the SPD came round to supporting birth control as it was spreading among the German working class, but it failed to campaign for it, leaving this to individual socialists.

Masturbation was unquestionably the *bête noire* of almost every nineteenth-century writer on human sexuality. According to a writer in **Neue Zeit**, the party's theoretical journal, masturbation was 'a vice . . . Certainly it is unnatural. For every sexual activity is unnatural which does not lead to the preservation of the species.' There 'finally remains', declared the pamphlet from the **Workers' Health Library**, 'only abstinence . . .'; sexual energy should be sublimated through sports, gymnastics, an interest in politics, trade union activities and 'a moderate, bland, largely vegetarian diet' for young people during the years of abstinence.

Yet the SPD was the first political party to campaign openly for the legalisation of male homosexuality, with a speech by Bebel in the Reichstag in 1898. As early as 1887 a petition was launched by an early gay rights group called the Scientific Humanitarian Committee against that part of the German penal code which dealt with homosexual acts. The SPD supported the petition, and it was signed by Hilferding, Kautsky, Bernstein and Käthe Kollwitz, among others.

Yet Bernstein, himself gay, could write that masturbation could lead to 'homosexuality, sodomy, pederasty and sado-masochism'. As with most subjects, the SPD had a whole range of confused views on sex.

33. Lion, page 155, and Fricke, **Die deutsche Arbeiterbewegung**, page 433.
34. C Zetkin, **Augewählte Reden und Schriften** (Berlin 1957) vol 1.
35. Zetkin, page 622.

36. Zetkin, page 625.
37. P Nettl, **Rosa Luxemburg** (London 1969) page 371–2.
38. Thönessen, page 119.
39. Quataert, pages 212–3 and 227.
40. Albrecht, page 488.
41. For a detailed account of the revolution which followed the First World War in Germany, and the failure of the revolutionary socialist movement, see Chris Harman, **The Lost Revolution: Germany 1918–23** (London 1982).
42. R Wheeler, 'Zur sozialen Struktur der Arbeiterbewegung am Anfang der Weimarer Republik' in H Mommsen and others (editors), **Industrielles System und politische Entwicklung in der Weimarer Republik** (Dusseldorf 1974) page 182.
43. Thönessen, page 84.
44. Thönessen, pages 90–1.
45. Thönessen, page 91–2.
46. Quataert, page 223.
47. Quataert, page 122.
48. Evans, **The Feminist Movement**, pages 147–9 and 151.
49. Evans, pages 154–5.
50. Evans, page 157.
51. Evans, page 208.
52. Evans, page 244.
53. Evans, page 145.
54. Evans, page 259.

★Chapter Six: Russian Marxists and Women Workers

1. Rothchild-Goldberg, **The Russian Women's Movement 1859–1917** (PhD thesis, University of Rochester 1976) pages 29–30.
2. L L Filippova, 'On the History of Women's Education in Russia' in **Voprosy istorii** (February 1963) page 209.
3. G W Lapidus, **Women in Soviet Society** (Berkeley 1979) page 31.
4. Rothchild-Goldberg, pages 45–6.
5. R Stites, **The Women's Liberation Movement in Russia: Feminism, Nihilism and Bolshevism 1860–1930** (New Jersey 1978) page 69.
6. Rothchild-Goldberg, page 75.
7. Rothchild-Goldberg, pages 77–8.
8. Stites, page 192.
9. Stites, page 65.
10. A M Kollontai, **Sotsialnie osnovy zhenskogo voprosa** (St Petersburg 1909) page 21.
11. Rothchild-Goldberg, page 89.
12. Stites, page 199.
13. Rothchild-Goldberg, page 96.
14. V Bilshai, **The Status of Women in the Soviet Union** (Moscow 1957) pages 16–17.
15. Rothchild-Goldberg, pages 110–11.

16. Rothchild-Goldberg, pages 134–5.
17. Rothchild-Goldberg, page 103.
18. Quoted in Rothchild-Goldberg, pages 144–5.
19. Rothchild-Goldberg, page 129.
20. Quoted in Stites, page 202.
21. Rothchild-Goldberg, page 145.
22. Stites, pages 214–5.
23. Rothchild-Goldberg, pages 130–1.
24. Stites, page 116.
25. Stites, pages 148–9.
26. R H McNeal, 'Women in the Russian Radical Movement' in **Journal of Social History** (Winter 1971–2) page 144; M Perrie, 'The Social Composition and Structure of the Socialist Revolutionary Party before 1917' in **Soviet Studies** (October 1972) page 237.
27. McNeal, page 155.
28. M Fainsod, **How Russia is ruled** (Cambridge, Massachusetts) page 254.
29. **Selected Writings of Alexandra Kollontai**, edited by Alix Holt (London 1977) pages 39–42.
30. R L Glickman, 'The Russian Factory Woman 1890–1914' in D Atkinson and others, **Women in Russia** (Stamford 1978) pages 80–1.
31. V Bilshai, **Reshenie zhenskogo voprosa v SSSR** (Moscow 1956) page 58.
32. Glickman, page 82.
33. V Grinevich, **Professionalnoe dvizhenie rabochikh v Rossii** (St Petersburg 1908) page 278.
34. Glickman, page 81.
35. L Trotsky, **1905** (New York 1971) page 250.
36. Kollontai, **Sotsialnie osnovy**, pages 23–4.
37. A M Kollontai, 'Avtobiograficheskii ocherk' in **Proletarskaia revoliutsiia** no 3 (1921) pages 268–70.
38. Rothchild-Goldberg, page 108.
39. Kollontai, **Sotsialnie osnovy**, pages 102–6.
40. Rothchild-Goldberg, page 107.
41. Kollontai, 'Avtobiograficheskii ocherk', pages 261–70.
42. After the Bolshevik-Menshevik split in 1903, Kollontai (1872–1952) wavered between the two groups, though admitting that 'by temperament' she was a Bolshevik. In 1906 she became a Menshevik, but joined the Bolsheviks in June 1915. In March 1917 she returned to Russia. On 4 April she spoke in support of Lenin's April Theses. At the Sixth Congress (26 July – 3 August) she was elected a member of the Central Committee of the Bolshevik Party in absentia (being in one of Kerensky's prisons). After the October Revolution she became Commissar of Social Welfare. In protest against the Brest-Litovsk Treaty she resigned. At the end of 1920 she was a founder of the Workers' Opposition and continued to belong to it until early 1922. From October 1922 until 1945 she acted as Soviet Ambassador in Norway, Mexico, then again Norway. Throughout the years of Stalin's suppression of opposition, including the arrest and disappearance of her former lover, Alexander Shliapnikov, and the shooting of her subsequent husband, Pavel Dybenko, Kollontai kept quiet. She

received top awards from Stalin for her services. She died of a heart attack on 9 March 1952.

43. Rothchild-Goldberg, page 99.
44. Kollontai, **Sotsialnie osnovy**, page 45.
45. Kollontai, 'Avtobiograficheskii ocherk', pages 267–8.
46. Kollontai, 'Avtobiograficheskii ocherk', page 272.
47. I D Levin, 'Workers' Clubs in Petersburg 1907–14' in **Materialy po istorii professionalnogo dvizhenie v Rossii** vol 3 (Moscow 1924) pages 88–111.
48. Quoted in Rothchild-Goldberg, page 173.
49. Rothchild-Goldberg, page 181.
50. Rothchild-Goldberg, page 198.
51. Kollontai, **Iz moei zhizni i raboty** (Moscow 1974) page 114.
52. **Vsegda s Vami** (Moscow 1964) pages 15–16.
53. Rothchild-Goldberg, pages 183–5.
54. **Trudy pervogo vserossiiskogo zhenskogo sezda pri Russkom zhenskom obshchestvo Sankt-Petersburge 10–16 Dekabria 1908** (St Petersburg 1909) pages 456–8.
55. **Trudy pervogo**, page 318.
56. **Trudy pervogo**, page 340.
57. **Trudy pervogo**, pages 792–4 and 800–1.
58. Stites, page 231.
59. **Trudy pervogo**, page 496.
60. Stites, page 252. Kollontai was not present at the time of the walk-out. The police had got wind of her presence at the congress during the first four days and surrounded the meeting hall on the fifth. Kollontai, forewarned, was able to flee.
61. A Bobroff, 'The Bolsheviks and Working Women 1905–20' in **Soviet Studies** (October 1974) page 545.
62. Rothchild-Goldberg, pages 254–6.
63. Bobroff, pages 551–3.
64. Bobroff, pages 554–5.
65. A V Artiukhina and others, **Zhenshchiny v revoliutsii** (Moscow 1959) page 97.
66. Rothchild-Goldberg, pages 341–2.
67. R Dale, **The Role of the Women of Petrograd in War, Revolution and Counter-revolution 1914–21** (PhD thesis, New Brunswick University 1973) page 104.
68. Dale, pages 94–5.
69. V Drizdo, **Nadezhda Konstantinova** (Moscow 1966) pages 31–4, quoted in Dale, page 102.
70. Dale, pages 104–5.
71. A F Bessonova (editor), 'On the History of the Publication of the Journal **Rabotnitsa**' in **Istoricheskiii arkhiv** (Moscow 1955) pages 37–9.
72. A Balabanoff, **My Life as a Rebel** (Bloomington 1973) pages 132–3. When the same situation was repeated several weeks later at the International Youth Congress, Balabanoff again found Lenin sitting in the very place from which he had directed his followers a few weeks before. She asked, ironically, 'Vladimir Il'ich, did you come here for tea or for the

resolution?' He answered with an annoyed glance.

73. Bobroff, pages 564–5.
74. Rothchild-Goldberg, page 346.
75. Stites, page 282.
76. Stites, page 287.
77. Stites, pages 288–9.
78. Bilshai, **Reshenie zhenskogo**, page 96.
79. V Kaiurov, 'Six Days in the February Revolution' in **Proletarskaia revoliutsiia** no 1:13 (1923).
80. F W Halle, **Women in Soviet Russia** (London 1933) page 91.
81. L Trotsky, **History of the Russian Revolution** (London 1934) page 122.
82. Trotsky, page 109.
83. Rothchild-Goldberg, page 354.
84. Glickman, page 81.
85. S M Kingsbury and M Fairchild, **Factory, Family and Women in the Soviet Union** (New York 1935) page 80.
86. A L Sidorov and others, **Velikaia oktiabrskaia sotsialisticheskaia revoliutsiia: Dokumenty i materialy** vol 1 (Moscow 1957) pages 470–1 and 490–1; vol 3, pages 208–9.
87. Kollontai, **Selected Writings**, page 125.
88. Sidorov, vol 1, pages 316, 321, 323, 325, 327 and 331.
89. V I Lenin, 'The Revolution of 1917' in **Collected Works** vol 20, book 1 (1929) page 142, quoted in Kingsbury and Fairchild, page xxii.
90. Sidorov, vol 1, pages 55, 67, 74–5 and 80.

★Chapter Seven: Women's Movements in England

1. D Thompson, 'Women and Nineteenth Century Radical Politics: A Lost Dimension' in J Mitchell and A Oakley (editors), **The Rights and Wrongs of Women** (London 1976) page 116.
2. Thompson, page 124.
3. Thompson, page 138.
4. S Boston, **Women Workers and the Trade Unions** (London 1980) page 23.
5. B Drake, **Women in Trade Unions** (London 1920) page 11. In some cases bourgeois feminists had a *direct* interest in keeping women unorganised and weak. Mrs Millicent Garret Fawcett, wife of Herbert Fawcett, a minister in Gladstone's government, was the most prominent leader of the bourgeois feminists during the last quarter of the nineteenth century, and continued to be active up to the First World War. She was a share-owner in the Bryant and May Match Company. No wonder she opposed the match girls' strike of 1888! (M Ramelson, **The Petticoat Rebellion** (London 1976) page 107.) It was the same Mrs Fawcett who argued against family allowances. She wrote: 'I am one of those who regard the responsibility of parents for the maintenance of their children as an invaluable part of the education of the average man or woman. To take it away would dangerously weaken the inducements for steady industry and self-control . . . and would at the same time involve the country, already

overburdened by enormously high taxation, with an annual charge running into hundreds of milions.' (D Mitchell, **Women on the Warpath** (London 1966) page 165.)
6. Drake, page 22.
7. B L Hutchins and A Harrison, **A History of Factory Legislation** (London 1966) page 110.
8. Hutchins and Harrison, page 186.
9. Drake, page 21.
10. H A Clegg, A Fox and A F Thompson, **A History of British Trade Unions since 1889** vol 1 (Oxford 1964) pages 1–2.
11. Y Kapp, **Eleanor Marx** vol 2 (London 1979) pages 270.
12. Kapp, page 382.
13. S Rowbotham, **Hidden from History** (London 1974) page 61.
14. Drake, page 27.
15. Clegg, Fox and Thompson, pages 70–1.
16. Clegg, Fox and Thompson, page 83.
17. Drake, page 30.
18. Drake, page 30.
19. Drake, page 45.
20. Boston, page 149.
21. Boston, pages 60–2.
22. Boston, page 68.
23. Drake, Appendix Table 1.
24. M A Hamilton, **Mary Macarthur** (London 1925) page 96.
25. Drake, page 50 and Appendix Table 1.
26. H Pelling, **A History of British Trade Unionism** (London 1963) page 262; Albrecht, page 47.
27. J Hinton, **The First Shop Stewards' Movement** (London 1973) page 72. It took 91 years from the foundation of the union to take women in! In mid-1942 women made up 31.9 per cent of all employed in the British engineering industry. (R Croucher, **Engineers at War 1939–1945** (London 1982) page 145.) The 'exclusivencss' of the engineering union — one of the most craftist of all — crumbled because of its fear of being beaten by the general unions which had started recruiting women much earlier.
28. ASE, **Monthly Journal** (December 1915).
29. **Der DMV in Zahlen** (Berlin 1932) page 122.
30. **Der DMV in Zahlen**, page 122.
31. Clegg, Fox and Thompson, page 292.
32. R Milliband, **Parliamentary Socialism** (London 1961) pages 19–20.
33. D Butler and J Freeman, **British Political Facts 1900–1967** (London 1968) page 155.
34. H Pelling, **Social Geography of British Elections, 1885–1900** (New York 1967) page 8.
35. S Pankhurst, **The Life of Emmeline Pankhurst** (London 1935) page 49.
36. Proceedings, National Women's Trade Union League, USA (1919) page 29.
37. E Belfort Bax, **Essays in Socialism** (London 1907) page 109.
38. Bax, page 121.
39. Bax, pages 124–5.

40. J Liddington and J Norris, **One Hand Tied Behind Us** (London 1978).
41. Liddington and Norris, page 149.
42. Liddington and Norris, pages 25 and 29.
43. Liddington and Norris, page 26.
44. A Rosen, **Rise up Women! The Militant Campaign of the Women's Social and Political Union 1903–1914** (London 1974) pages 35–6.
45. Rosen, page 30.
46. S Pankhurst, **The Suffragette Movement** (London 1978) page 168.
47. Pankhurst, page 244.
48. Liddington and Norris, page 177.
49. Rosen, page 59.
50. Rosen, page 61.
51. Pankhurst, page 517.
52. Mitchell, page 35.
53. Rosen, pages 100–1.
54. W L O'Neill, **The Woman Movement: Feminism in the United States and England** (London 1969) page 82.
55. Rosen, pages 104–5.
56. Pankhurst, page 366.
57. Pankhurst, pages 336–7.
58. Rosen, page 207.
59. Mitchell, page 52.
60. M Mackenzie, **Shoulder to Shoulder** (London 1975) page 314.
61. Emmeline and Christabel Pankhurst ended their lives pathetically. They gave up speaking on feminist platforms. Mrs Pankhurst travelled across Canada denouncing the twin evils of venereal disease and unchastity. She returned to England to join the Conservative Party, and died in 1928. The later part of Christabel's career was even more bizarre. She took up the cause of the Second Coming of Christ, which the deteriorating situation in the 1920s and 1930s led her to believe was imminent, and died in California in 1958, a Dame Commander of the British Empire. (Liddington and Norris, page 258.) Adela, the youngest child of the Pankhurst family, emigrated to Australia. There she passed through the Communist Party, but ended her life as a member of the Fascist movement. (Mitchell, pages 267–8.)
62. Pankhurst, pages 401–2.
63. Pankhurst, page 339.
64. Pankhurst, **The Life of Emmeline Pankhurst**, page 141.
65. **Women's Dreadnought**, 18 March 1916.
66. S Pankhurst, **The Home Front** (London 1932) page 43.
67. **Women's Dreadnought**, 19 August 1914.
68. Mitchell, pages 280–1.
69. **Women's Dreadnought**, 2 January 1915.
70. Pankhurst, **The Home Front**, page 143.
71. Pankhurst, **The Suffragette Movement**, page 598.
72. A Shliapnikov, **On the Eve of 1917** (London 1982) pages 206–8.
73. Pankhurst, **The Suffragette Movement**, page 505.
74. **Daily Herald**, 29 October 1913.
75. **Women's Dreadnought**, 31 March 1917.

76. **Workers' Dreadnought**, 17 November 1917.
77. **Workers' Dreadnought**, 19 March 1921.
78. **Workers' Dreadnought**, 1 June 1918.
79. J Macfarlane, **The British Communist Party: Its Origins and Development until 1929** (London 1966) pages 31 and 46.
80. Lenin, **Works** vol 29, page 564.
81. Lenin, **Works** vol 31, page 202.

★Chapter Eight: France's sad story

1. J H Clapham, **The Economic Development of France and Germany, 1815–1914** (Cambridge 1928) page 258.
2. T Zeldin, **France 1848–1945** vol 2 (Oxford 1979) page 379.
3. M Guilbert, **Les femmes et l'organisation syndicale avant 1914** (Paris 1966) page 28.
4. As late as 1935 only 6 per cent of workers in private industry were organised in trade unions (Zeldin, page xi).
5. Zeldin, vol 1, page 222.
6. Zeldin, page 229.
7. Ridley, page 17.
8. Ridley, pages 234 and 239.
9. Guilbert, page 14.
10. Guilbert, page 29.
11. Guilbert, page 38.
12. Guilbert, page 206.
13. Guilbert, page 207.
14. Zeldin, vol 2, page 399.
15. Zeldin, vol 2, page 383.
16. R Wohl, **French Communism in the Making, 1914–1924** (Stanford 1966) page 290.
17. C Sowerwine, **Women and Socialism in France 1871–1921** (PhD thesis, University of Wisconsin 1973) page 46. This is by far the most useful work used in the present chapter.
18. See chapter 3.
19. Sowerwine, page 5.
20. Sowerwine, page 7.
21. Sowerwine, page 113.
22. R J Evans, **The Feminists** (London 1977) pages 129–30.
23. Sowerwine, page 28.
24. Evans, pages 133–4.
25. C Willard, **Les Guesdistes: Le mouvement socialiste en France, 1893–1905** (Paris 1965) page 367.
26. J M Boxer, **Socialism Faces Feminism in France 1879–1913** (PhD thesis, University of California 1975) page 190.
27. Sowerwine, pages 197–8.

★Chapter Nine: Revolution and Counter-revolution in Russia

1. V I Lenin, **On the Emancipation of Women** (Moscow 1977) page 65.
2. V I Lenin, 'Soviet Power and the Status of Women' in **Works** vol 30, page 40.
3. L Trotsky, **Women and the Family** (New York 1974) page 61.
4. R Schlesinger, **Changing Attitudes in Soviet Russia: The Family in the USSR** (London 1949) page 35.
5. Schlesinger, page 37.
6. Quoted in Schlesinger, page 310.
7. Schlesinger, page 44.
8. Schlesinger, page 44.
9. Lenin, **On the Emancipation of Women**, pages 65–6.
10. Quoted in Schlesinger, pages 48–53.
11. Lenin, **On the Emancipation of Women**, page 72.
12. Quoted in B E Clements, **Bolshevik Feminist: The Life of Aleksandra Kollontai** (Bloomington 1979) page 155.
13. Lenin, **On the Emancipation of Women**, pages 111 and 110.
14. Quoted in C E Hayden, 'The *Zhenotdel* and the Bolshevik Party' in **Russian History/Histoire Russe** III: 2 (1976) page 156.
15. Hayden, page 157.
16. T H Rigny, **Communist Party Membership in the USSR 1917–67** (Princeton 1968) page 36.
17. Hayden, page 168.
18. Hayden, page 159.
19. Lenin, **Works** vol 33, page 78.
20. Stites, page 335.
21. Stites, pages 321–2.
22. K Marx, **Die Moralisierende Kritik und die Kritische Moral. Beitrag zur deutschen Kulturgeschichte, Gegen Karl Heinzen, Aus dem literarischen Nachlass von Marx, Engels und Lassalle** (Stuttgart 1902) Bd 2, page 456.
23. Cliff, **Lenin** vol 4, page 121.
24. J Smith, **Women in Soviet Russia** (New York 1928) pages 15–17.
25. Cliff, **Lenin** vol 4, page 146.
26. Hayden, page 169.
27. K H Geiger, **The Family in Soviet Russia** (Cambridge, Massachusetts 1968) page 73.
28. Geiger, pages 61–2.
29. Stites, page 371.
30. Schlesigner, page 99.
31. Schlesigner, page 140.
32. See the development of this argument in T Cliff, **State Capitalism in Russia** (London 1974) especially chapter 4.
33. G W Lapidus, **Women in Soviet Society** (Berkeley 1978) page 166.
34. Quoted in Schlesinger, page 287.
35. Quoted in Schlesinger, page 254.
36. Schlesinger, page 278.

37. Quoted in D and V Mace, **The Soviet Family** (London 1964) page 86.
38. Mace, page 87.
39. **Sotsialisticheskaya Zakonnost** (1939) no 2 quoted in N Timasheff, 'The Attempt to Abolish the Family in Russia' in **The Family** (New York 1960) page 59.
40. Geiger, page 104.
41. Quoted in Schlesinger, pages 364 and 393–4.
42. Schlesinger, pages 373–4.
43. Schlesinger, pages 367–73.
44. R H McNeal, **Guide to the Decisions of the Communist Party in the Soviet Union 1917–67** (Toronto 1972).
45. For a documented analysis see Cliff, **State Capitalism in Russia**.
46. S Firestone, **The Dialectic of Sex** (New York 1970) page 198.

★Chapter Ten: The failure of success — the American Women's Liberation Movement

1. S Evans, **Personal Politics: The Roots of Women's Liberation in the Civil Rights Movement and the New Left** (New York 1980).
2. Evans, page 41.
3. Evans, page 35.
4. Evans, page 81.
5. Evans, page 82.
6. Evans, page 97.
7. Evans, page 106.
8. Evans, page 105.
9. Evans, page 132.
10. Evans, page 132.
11. Evans, page 141.
12. Evans, page 141.
13. S Brownmiller, **Against our Will: Men, Women and Rape** (New York 1975) pages 80–1.
14. E Cleaver, **Soul on Ice** (New York 1968) pages 11–14.
15. J Freeman, **The Politics of Women's Liberation** (New York 1975) page 60.
16. Evans, page 170.
17. Evans, page 179.
18. Evans, page 175.
19. Evans, page 198.
20. S Firestone, **The Dialectic of Sex** (New York 1970).
21. Freeman, pages 59–60.
22. Freeman, pages 60–1.
23. At present (1983) there are over two hundred black mayors in United States cities, including 18 major ones (Chicago, Detroit, Los Angeles, New Orleans, Atlanta, Washington DC). At the same time 45.7 per cent of the black youth and 19 per cent of black adults are unemployed (more than twice the rate of unemployment among whites). **The Economist** remarks: '. . . the militants became respectable as they grew older, feted

on the lecture circuits, endowed by foundations to conduct research. Literally thousands of projects for black advancement were evolved by federal, state and local governments, more again by charitable and private institutions.' (**The Economist**, 15 May 1982.)

24. J Mitchell, **Woman's Estate** (London 1971) pages 51, 63–4, 73–4 and 182.
25. Firestone, pages 15–17, 20–1 and 105.
26. Firestone, pages 91–2.
27. M L Carden, **The New Feminist Movement** (New York 1974) page 19.
28. Domitila Barrio, **Let Me Speak!** (London 1978) pages 198–9 and 202–3.
29. Barrio, pages 203 and 234.
30. B Hooks, **Ain't I a Woman? Black Women and Feminism** (London 1981) pages 124 and 188.
31. A Davis, **Women, Race and Class** (London 1982) page 179.
32. See F Venturi, **Roots of Revolution** (London 1960) page 327.
33. Freeman, page 117–8.
34. Freeman, pages 103–4.
35. Carden, pages 71–2.
36. Carden, page 73.
37. **Spare Rib** (October 1978).
38. Freeman, pages 121–2.
39. M Dixon, 'On Women's Liberation' in **Radical America** (February 1970).
40. **Spare Rib** no 17.
41. Freeman, pages 136–7.
42. M Evans (editor), **The Woman Question** (London 1982) pages 50–1.
43. Freeman, pages 141–2.
44. Freeman, page 139.
45. Freeman, page 92.
46. B Friedan, **The Second Stage** (London 1982) page 238.
47. B Dockard, **The Women's Movement** (New York 1979) pages 364–74 and 395–407.
48. Dockard, pages 383–5.
49. Diane St Claire, 'The New Right: Wrong Turn USA' in **Spare Rib** (September 1981).
50. B Winslow, 'Why the ERA Lost' in American **Socialist Worker** (July 1982).
51. Friedan, page 338.
52. Friedan, page 204.
53. Dockard, pages 388–90.
54. Dockard, page 385.
55. **Spare Rib** (February 1979).
56. Venturi, page 253.

★Chapter Eleven: The Women's Movement in Britain

1. R Price and G S Bain, 'Union Growth Revisited: 1948–1974, in Perspective' in **British Journal of Industrial Relations** (November 1976).
2. A Coote and B Campbell, **Sweet Freedom. The Struggle for Women's Liberation** (London 1982) page 18.

3. J Hunt and S Adams, **Women, Work and Trade Union Organisation** (London 1980) page 15.
4. **Spare Rib** (April 1978).
5. Coote and Campbell, pages 20–21.
6. **Spare Rib** (April 1978).
7. S Rowbotham, L Segal and H Wainwright, **Beyond the Fragments** (London 1980) page 45.
8. Rowbotham and others, page 41.
9. **No Turning Back: Writings from the Women's Liberation Movement 1975–1980** (London 1981). Compare this with the statement: 'Marriage is an oppressive institution for both the married and the unmarried, and provides the major legal support for the current family form. We believe that socialists and feminists should not get married themselves and should not attend or support the marriages of any who can be convinced of our critique of the family . . . Nobody should have a housewife. Nobody, man, child, invalid, or woman, needs a long-term "housewife" or has the right to have one. Unpaid domestic service is in principle inferior to social provision. For those who can afford it, paying someone to clean the house or cook meals is preferable to making it the duty of one household member.' (M Barrett and M McIntosh, **The Anti-Social Family** (London 1982) pages 143–4.)
10. **No Turning Back**, pages 123–5.
11. **Spare Rib** (September 1981).
12. **Spare Rib** (April 1978).
13. Rowbotham and others, page 197.
14. Rowbotham and others, page 164.
15. Rowbotham and others, page 176.
16. Rowbotham and others, page 180.
17. Rowbotham and others, page 205.
18. Rowbotham and others, page 76.
19. K Marx and F Engels, **Selected Correspondence** (London 1941) pages 150–1.
20. Marx and Engels, **Selected Correspondence**, page 315.
21. Coote and Campbell, page 35.
22. **No Turning Back**, page 170.
23. **Love your Enemy?** (London 1981) pages 5–6 and 8.
24. **Love your Enemy?** page 56.
25. Coote and Campbell, page 225.
26. Many journals died. To list but a few: **Shrew**, **Socialist Woman**, **Red Rag**, **Women's Report**, **Women's Struggles Notes**, **Red Shift**, **Enough!**, **Women Now**, **Body Politic**, **Leviathan**, **Woman Liberation Review**, **Women's Newspaper**, **Power of Women Journal**, **Women's Voice**.
27. **Spare Rib** (December 1980).
28. A symptom of the extreme man-hating position of the lesbian feminists is their idiosyncracies in spelling. 'Woman', 'women', they spell as womyn, wimmin. Again, instead of using the word 'history', they write herstory. (By the way, they overlook the fact that the origin of the word in Greek — 'historia' — means 'finding out' or 'knowing'; 'historia' is actually a

feminine noun.)
29. E Malos (editor), **The Politics of Housework** (London 1980) page 22.
30. Malos, page 161.
31. Selma James, in an interview with Angela Singer of **The Guardian**, said: 'We should be paid for all the housework we do . . . sex included.' (**The Guardian**, 24 February 1982.)
32. Coote and Campbell, page 41.
33. Coote and Campbell, page 43.
34. Coote and Campbell, page 147.
35. **Spare Rib** (December 1979).
36. **Daily Mirror** (21 January 1983).
37. S Atkins in **The Guardian** (28 March 1983).
38. T Cliff, 'The Balance of Class Forces in Recent Years' in **International Socialism** 2:6 (1979) page 47.
39. **Time Out** (21–27 November 1980) quoted in **No Turning Back**, page 140.
40. **Gay Left** issue 10 (1980) quoted in **No Turning Back**, page 100.
41. A Oakley, **Subject Women** (Oxford 1981) pages 318–9.
42. J Weeks, **Coming Out: Homosexual Politics in Britain from the Nineteenth Century to the Present** (London 1977) pages 191 and 196.
43. A Walter, **Come Together: The Years of Gay Liberation 1970–73** (London 1980) page 28.
44. Weeks, page 206.
45. Walter, pages 31–2.
46. Weeks, page 202.
47. A Karlen, **Sexuality and Homosexuality** (London 1971) pages 517 and 530.
48. L Starling, 'Glad to be Gay: The Gay Movement and the Left' in **Socialist Review** (May/June 1978).
49. Weeks, pages 210, 213 and 267.
50. J Lindsay, **A Culture for Containment** (London 1978) page 5.
51. L Jones (editor), **Keeping the Peace: Women's Peace Handbook** (London 1983) pages ix, 3, 21, 24, 27, 29 and 56.
52. P Hain (editor), **The Debate of the Decade: The Crisis and the Future of the Left** (London 1980) pages 23, 45, 49 and 52.
53. **Spare Rib** (November 1980).
54. Coote and Campbell, page 247.
55. Coote and Campbell, pages 136–7.

★Chapter Twelve: Class Roots of the Women's Movement

1. Marx and Engels, **Works** vol 6, page 485.
2. E V Wright, **Class, Crisis and the State** (London 1978) pages 61–3. To be precise one should not refer to this collection of strata as a class: a class is defined above all through *conflict* with other classes. As Marx and Engels put it: 'The separate individuals form a class only insofar as they have to carry a common battle against another class.' (Marx and Engels, **The German Ideology** in Marx and Engels, **Works** vol 5, page 77.) With this

rider we shall continue to write about the 'new middle class', as we have not found a better term. See also A Callinicos, 'The "New Middle Class" and Socialist Politics' in **International Socialism** 2:20 (1983).

3. Nicos Poulantzas argues, incorrectly, that all white-collar workers, plus technicians and supervisors, belong to the 'new petty bourgeoisie'. (N Poulantzas, **Classes in Contemporary Capitalism** (London 1975).)
4. See, for instance, Marx's analysis of commercial employees in **Capital** vols 2 and 3.
5. B and J Ehrenreich, 'The Professional-Managerial Class' in P Walker (editor), **Between Labour and Capital** (London 1979) page 14. The Ehrenreichs' estimate of the new middle class is too high, even by their own definition. See M Albert and R Hahnel, 'A Ticket to Ride: More Locations on the Class Map' in Walker, page 155.
6. R Sennet and J Cobb, **The Hidden Injuries of Class** (Cambridge 1972) page 229.
7. Ehrenreichs, in Walker, page 29.
8. **Financial Times** (22 November 1982).
9. A Szymanski, 'A Critique and Extension of the Professional-Managerial Class', in Walker, page 57.
10. Freeman, page 33.
11. J Cassell, **A Group Called Women** (New York 1977) page 104.
12. Cassell, pages 98 and 184.
13. C Epstein, **Woman's Place** (London 1971) page 138. Carl Friedan, the ex-husband of Betty Friedan, author of **The Feminine Mystique**, the pioneering book of modern feminism, once exclaimed in exasperation: 'I supported **The Feminine Mystique**. She had time to write it because she lived in a mansion on the Hudson River, had a full-time maid and was completely supported by me . . . Betty never washed 100 dishes in 10 years of marriage.' She herself describes stopping writing 'to make a martini when my husband got home, fix dinner, argue, go to the movies, make love, join an expedition to the supermarket or a country auction on Saturday, organise a clambake on the beach . . .' (**The Leveller**, 9–22 July 1982.)
14. Cassell, pages 175–6.
15. A Hackett, 'Feminism and Liberalism in Wilhelmine Germany, 1890–1918' in B A Carroll (editor), **Liberating Women's History** (Chicago 1976) page 128.
16. Marx and Engels, **Works** vol 5, page 4.
17. K Marx, **Grundrisse** (London 1973) page 84.
18. Marx and Engels, **Works** vol 6, pages 509–10.
19. Marx and Engels, **Works** vol 11, page 187.
20. Cassell, page 17.

★ Chapter Thirteen: The Survival of the Family

1. Marx and Engels, **Works** vol 5, pages 180–1.
2. Marx and Engels, **Works** vol 6, pages 501–2.
3. Engels, **The Origin of the Family, Private Property and the State** (New York 1979) page 80.

4. I Pinchbeck, **Women Workers and the Industrial Revolution** (London 1981) pages 187–8.
5. Hutchins and Harrison, page 110.
6. J B Jefferys, **The Story of the Engineers** (London 1945) page 207.
7. L A Tilly and J W Scott, **Women, Work and Family** (New York 1978) page 196.
8. See, for instance, H Hartmann, 'The Unhappy Marriage of Marxism and Feminism' in L Sargent (editor), **The Unhappy Marriage of Marxism and Feminism** (London 1981).
9. Jane Humphries has documented this well in 'The Working Class Family, Women's Liberation and Class Struggle: Nineteenth Century British History' in **Review of Radical Political Economy** (February 1977).
10. Pinchbeck, pages 248–9.
11. J Foster, **Class Struggle and the Industrial Revolution** (London 1974) pages 91–2.
12. R Davies, **Women and Work** (London 1975) page 126.
13. M Anderson, **Family Structure in Nineteenth Century Lancashire** (Cambridge 1971) pages 137–8.
14. P Hollis (editor), **Class and Conflict in Nineteenth Century England, 1815–1850** (London 1973) page 210.
15. B Taylor, **Eve and the New Jerusalem** (London 1983) pages 205 and 273.
16. Sargent, pages 95 and 99.
17. A Davis, **Women, Race and Class** (London 1982) pages 7–8.
18. J A Ladner, 'Racism and Tradition: Black Womanhood in Historical Perspective', in Carroll, page 188.
19. Ladner, page 187.
20. Davis, pages 4 and 14–15. One crucial role of the pass laws in South Africa today is the deliberate destruction of the family life of black workers.
21. Foster, page 87.
22. Quoted in Hollis, pages 193–4.
23. Tilly and Scott, page 199.
24. Sargent, page 21.
25. Humphries.
26. L Gordon, **Woman's Body, Woman's Right** (London 1977) page 110.
27. M Poster, **Critical Theory of the Family** (London 1978) pages 192–3.
28. J Donzelot, **The Policing of Families** (London 1980) pages 39–40.

★Chapter Fourteen: The Family — haven in a heartless world?

1. E Shorter, **The Making of the Modern Family** (London 1975) pages 230–1.
2. Marx and Engels, **Works** vol 3, pages 274–5.
3. M Komarovsky, **Blue-Collar Marriage** (New York 1967) and L Rubin, **World of Pain: Life in the Working-Class Family** (New York 1976).
4. S Sharpe, **Just like a Girl: How Girls learn to be Women** (London 1976) page 71.
5. Sharpe, page 305.
6. Komarovsky, page 25.

7. Sharpe, pages 210–1.
8. Rubin, pages 80–1 and 90–1.
9. Komarovsky, page 93.
10. Rubin, pages 99, 113, 160–1 and 179.
11. Glenton is a name given by Komarovsky to two contiguous, closely interwoven industrial townships forming a county.
12. Komarovsky, pages 311–2.
13. Rubin, page 188.
14. Rubin, page 189.
15. Komarovsky, page 51.
16. Komarovsky, pages 151–2.
17. Rubin, page 178.
18. Rubin, page 190.
19. Komarovsky, pages 49, 55 and 57.
20. Komarovsky, pages 56 and 60.
21. Rubin, pages 36–7 and 55.
22. Komarovsky, pages 76 and 78.
23. Rubin, pages 30, 38, 40–1 and 46.
24. S Steinmetz and M Straus (editors), **Violence in the Family** (New York 1975) page 4.
25. J Renvoize, **Web of Violence: A Study of Family Violence** (London 1978) pages 133–4.
26. R J Gelles, **The Violent Home** (London 1972) pages 125, 130 and 192.
27. Komarovsky, page 366.
28. D C Gil, 'Violence against Children' in **Journal of Marriage and Family** (November 1971).
29. J E Oliver and others, **Severely Ill-treated Young Children in North-East Wiltshire** (Oxford 1974).
30. Gelles, pages 55 and 77.
31. Steinmetz and Straus, page 196.
32. Renvoize, page 182. The power of males over females, especially young females, combined with sexual exploitation, leads many of the victims of incest to use their oppression as a weapon of power. As Jean Renvoize reports: 'Many girls unquestionably enjoy such a relationship with their father once they have accepted it, even if at the same time they feel guilty about it. It gives them a sense of power, and some even indulge in petty blackmail, demanding gifts as the price of their silence. If their parents' relationship is poor they may get great satisfaction out of playing the role of "little mother", so that as father and daughter act out their private fantasies the real mother is pushed into the background. Inevitably the girl will have mixed feelings about her mother. She will feel both anger that her mother is not protecting her from her father, for she will know the relationship is wrong even if she is actually enjoying it, and guilt that she is depriving her mother of her rightful place.' (Renvoize, pages 184–5.)
33. Gelles, pages 164–5.
34. Study Commission on the Family, **Families of the Future** (London 1983) page 19.
35. J W Brown and T Harris, **Social Origin of Depression: A Study of**

Psychotic Disorder in Women (London 1978) pages 154, 178–9 and 291.
36. W R Gove, 'The Relationship between Sex Roles, Marital Status, and Mental Illness' in **Social Forces** (University of North Carolina, September 1972).
37. C Lasch, **Haven in a Heartless World** (New York 1978) pages xvii–xviii.
38. H Benyon, **Working for Ford** (London 1977) page 75.
39. P E Mott and others, **Shift Work: The Social, Psychological and Physical Consequences** (Ann Arbor 1966) page 18, quoted in T Cliff, **The Employers' Offensive** (London 1970) page 71.
40. G Frankl, **The Failure of the Sexual Revolution** (London 1974) pages 116–7.
41. Kollontai, **Selected Writings**, page 231.
42. A C Kinsey and others, **Sexual Behaviour in the Human Male** (Philadelphia 1948) and **Sexual Behaviour in the Human Female** (Philadelphia 1953).
43. G P Murdock, 'World Ethnographic Sample' in **American Anthropologist** no 59 (1957).
44. C S Ford and F Beach, **Patterns of Sexual Behaviour** (New York 1951) page 130.
45. Walter, page 86.
46. S Abbott and B Love, **Sappho was a Right-on Woman: A Liberated View of Lesbianism** (New York 1972) pages 92 and 97.
47. A Karlen, **Sexuality and Homosexuality** (London 1971) page 198.
48. Karlen, page 527.
49. Abbott and Love, pages 80–1.
50. **Gay Left** (Spring 1976) quoted in Weeks, page 223.

★ Chapter Fifteen: The Struggle for Socialism and Women's Liberation

1. F Engels, **The Origin of the Family**, pages 25–6.
2. Engels, **The Origin of the Family**, page 68.
3. Engels, **The Origin of the Family**, page 74.
4. R Briffault, **The Mothers** (1927).
5. E Reed, **Women's Evolution** (1975).
6. M Poster, **Critical Theory of the Family** (London 1978) page 185.
7. See F Mount, **The Subversive Family** (London 1982).
8. Marx, **Capital** vol 1, pages 536–7.
9. **Social Trends 1972**.
10. M Barrett, **Women's Oppression Today** (London 1980) page 147.
11. Compare the facts given here with feminist ideas, as in Jill Tweedie's words: 'Any rich woman who is a wife and mother has had a great deal more in common with any poor woman who is also married and a mother than any rich man with poor men, since men are defined by their incomes.' (**The Guardian**, 19 January 1981.)
12. L German, 'Theories of Patriarchy' in **International Socialism** 2:12 (Spring 1981).
13. M S Rice, **Working-class wives** (London 1981) pages 105–6.
14. Sharpe, page 54.

15. Gordon, page 406. Only a woman highly successful in the professions, like Simone de Beauvoir, the eminent feminist, could say the following: 'I think a woman must not fall into the trap of children and marriage. Even if a woman wants to have children, she must think very hard about the conditions in which she will have to bring them up, because child-bearing, at the moment, is real slavery. Fathers and society leave to women, and to women alone, the responsibility of bringing up children. It is women who must stop working to bring up children. It is women who must stay at home when children are ill, and it is women who are blamed when children fail.

    'And if a woman is still determined to have children, it would be better to have them without being married, because marriage is the biggest trap.' ('Talking to Simone de Beauvoir, **Spare Rib**, March 1977.) By the way, Simone de Beauvoir had no children. For her, child care could not have appeared less alienating or more creative than her work as a successful author.
16. L Gordon, 'The Struggle for Reproductive Freedom: Three States of Feminism' in S R Eisenstein (editor), **Capitalist Patriarchy and the Case for Socialist Feminism** (New York 1979) page 125.
17. A Oakley, **The Sociology of Housework** (London 1974) page 94.
18. Study Commission on the Family, **Families of the Future**, page 19.
19. US Department of Labour, **Perspectives on Working Women** (1980) pages 30 and 53.
20. J Hunt and S Adams, **Women, Work and Trade Union Organisation** (London 1980) page 8.
21. US Bureau of Labor Statistics, **Special Labor Force Reports** 13, 130 and 183; also US Department of Labor, **Perspectives on Working Women**, page 3.
22. H Halter, **Sex Roles and Social Structure** (Oslo 1970) pages 73–4.
23. Marx, **Capital** vol 1, page 460.
24. Department of Employment, **Women and Work: A Review** (London 1975) page 46.
25. Clegg, Fox and Thompson, page 489; Hunt and Adams, page 14; and B C Roberts, **The Trade Union Congresses 1868–1921** (London 1958) page 379.
26. R Price and C S Bain, 'Union Growth Revisited: 1948–1974 in Perspective' in **British Journal of Industrial Relations** (November 1976).
27. Marx and Engels, **The Communist Manifesto** in **Works** vol 6, pages 490, 492 and 494.
28. A Gramsci, **Selections from the Prison Notebooks** (London 1971) pages 324 and 333.
29. Lenin, **Works** vol 5, pages 412 and 414.
30. Marx and Engels, **The German Ideology** in **Works** vol 5, page 47.
31. Marx and Engels, **The Communist Manifesto** in **Works** vol 6, page 506.
32. Engels, **Principles of Communism** in Marx and Engels, **Works** vol 6, page 354.
33. Engels, **The Origin of the Family**, pages 83 and 88.
34. L Trotsky, **Women and the Family** (New York 1974) page 53.
35. Quoted in Boxer, pages 68–9.

Index

Other books published by Bookmarks

Rosa Luxemburg
by Tony Cliff
'In Rosa Luxemburg the socialist idea was a dominating and powerful passion of both heart and brain, a truly creative passion which burned ceaselessly . . She was the sharp sword, the living flame of revolution.' So wrote her friend Clara Zetkin. Sixty years after Rosa Luxemburg was murdered, her ideas are still central to socialist struggle. This book, first published in 1959, remains the best short introduction. *£2.50/US$4.75*

Bailing out the System
Reformist socialism in Western Europe 1944-1985
by Ian Birchall
In 1945 an astute Tory politician told the House of Commons: 'If you do not give the people reform, they are going to give you revolution.' In the years since, reformism has again and again saved the capitalist system from disaster, defusing working-class struggle whenever it threatened to bring radical change. This book shows how. *£5.95/US$12.00*

The revolutionary ideas of Karl Marx
by Alex Callinicos
Marx is one of a handful of people who fundamentally changed the way we look at the world. This book is a clear and straightforward introduction to his life and ideas. *£3.95/US$7.85*

Festival of the Oppressed
Solidarity, reform and revolution in Poland 1980-81
by Colin Barker
The trade union Solidarity was the most impressive working-class movement the world has seen for half a century. This book not only recaptures its achievements, but gives new insight into the class forces that gave it birth and the weaknesses that led to its suppression. *£4.25/US$8.50*

BOOKMARKS

These and many other books are available from good bookshops, or by post from the publishers (please add 15 per cent to cover postage). For our current catalogue, write to:
Bookmarks, 265 Seven Sisters Road, London N4 2DE, England.
Bookmarks, PO Box 16085, Chicago, Illinois 60616, USA.
Bookmarks, GPO Box 1473N, Melbourne 3001, Australia.